Enjoying
VIRGINIA OUTDOORS

A Guide to Wildlife Management Areas

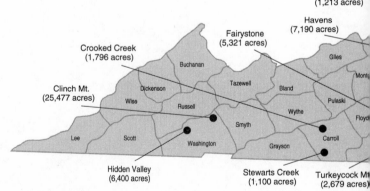

Goshen–Little North
(33,697 acres)

Gathright
(13,428 acres

James River
(1,213 acres)

Havens
(7,190 acres)

Fairystone
(5,321 acres)

Giles

Crooked Creek
(1,796 acres)

Buchanan

Mont

Tazewell

Clinch Mt.
(25,477 acres)

Dickenson

Bland

Wise

Pulaski

Russell

Wythe

Floyd

Lee

Smyth

Scott

Carroll

Washington

Grayson

Hidden Valley
(6,400 acres)

Stewarts Creek
(1,100 acres)

Turkeycock Mt
(2,679 acres)

Enjoying
VIRGINIA OUTDOORS
A Guide to Wildlife Management Areas

BOB GOOCH

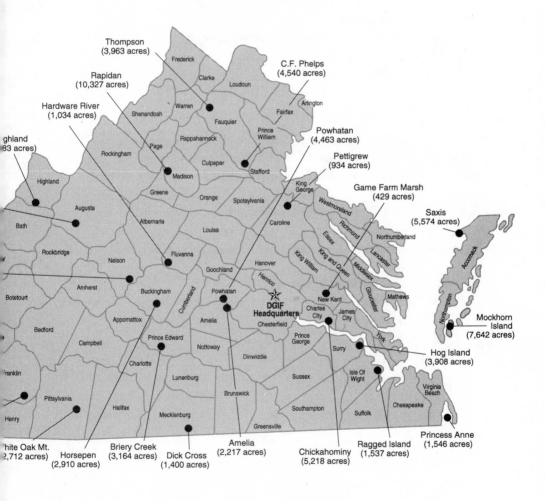

Thompson
(3,963 acres)

Frederick

C.F. Phelps
(4,540 acres)

Rapidan
(10,327 acres)

Clarke

Loudoun

Hardware River
(1,034 acres)

Warren

Arlington

Shenandoah

Fauquier

Fairfax

ghland
83 acres)

Page

Rappahannock

Prince
William

Powhatan
(4,463 acres)

Rockingham

Culpeper

Stafford

Pettigrew
(934 acres)

Highland

Madison

King
George

Game Farm Marsh
(429 acres)

Greene

Orange

Spotsylvania

Westmoreland

Saxis
(5,574 acres)

Augusta

Albemarle

Caroline

Richmond

Northumberland

Bath

Louisa

Essex

Lancaster

Accomack

Rockbridge

Nelson

Fluvanna

Hanover

King William

King and Queen

Middlesex

Amherst

Goochland

Henrico

Northampton

Botetourt

Buckingham

Powhatan

Gloucester

Mathews

Mockhorn
Island
(7,642 acres)

Appomattox

Amelia

DGIF
Headquarters

New Kent

Charles
City

James
City

Bedford

Prince Edward

Chesterfield

Prince
George

Surry

York

Hog Island
(3,908 acres)

Campbell

Nottoway

Dinwiddie

Charlotte

Lunenburg

Sussex

Isle Of
Wight

Virginia
Beach

ranklin

Brunswick

Southampton

Chesapeake

Pittsylvania

Halifax

Mecklenburg

Suffolk

Henry

Greensville

Princess Anne
(1,546 acres)

hite Oak Mt.
2,712 acres)

Horsepen
(2,910 acres)

Briery Creek
(3,164 acres)

Dick Cross
(1,400 acres)

Amelia
(2,217 acres)

Chickahominy
(5,218 acres)

Ragged Island
(1,537 acres)

University Press of Virginia

Charlottesville and London

The University Press of Virginia
Printed in the United States of America

First published in 2000

Library of Congress Cataloging-in-Publication Data
Gooch, Bob, 1919-
    Enjoying Virginia outdoors : a guide to wildlife management areas / Bob Gooch.
        p.   cm.
    ISBN 0-8139-1961-4 (pbk. : alk. paper)
        1. Wildlife management areas—Virginia—Guidebooks. 2. Virginia—Guidebooks.
    I.   Title.

SK457 .G66 2000
917.55'0442—dc21   00-028988

Contents

Introduction   1

Northwest Mountains and Valley   7
   Gathright Wildlife Management Area   9
   Goshen–Little North Mountain Wildlife Management Area   15
   Highland Wildlife Management Area   23

Upper Piedmont and Coastal Plains   31
   C. F. Phelps Wildlife Management Area   33
   Chickahominy Wildlife Management Area   41
   Game Farm Marsh Wildlife Management Area   49
   G. Richard Thompson Wildlife Management Area   53
   Hardware River Wildlife Management Area   61
   James River Wildlife Management Area   67
   Pettigrew Wildlife Management Area   75
   Rapidan Wildlife Management Area   81

Lower Tidewater and Eastern Shore   89
   Mockhorn Island Wildlife Management Area   91
   Princess Anne Wildlife Management Area   97
   Saxis Wildlife Management Area   103

Southside   109
   Amelia Wildlife Management Area   111
   Briery Creek Wildlife Management Area   119
   Dick Cross Wildlife Management Area   127

Contents

Fairystone Farms Wildlife Management Area   135
Hog Island Wildlife Management Area   143
Horsepen Lake Wildlife Management Area   151
Powhatan Wildlife Management Area   157
Ragged Island Wildlife Management Area   165
Stewarts Creek Wildlife Management Area   173
Turkeycock Mountain Wildlife Management Area   181
White Oak Mountain Wildlife Management Area   187

Southwest   195

Clinch Mountain Wildlife Management Area   197
Crooked Creek Wildlife Management Area   207
Havens Wildlife Management Area   215
Hidden Valley Wildlife Management Area   223

Index   231

Enjoying
VIRGINIA OUTDOORS

A Guide to Wildlife Management Areas

Virginia
Department of Game and Inland Fisheries
Wildlife Management Areas

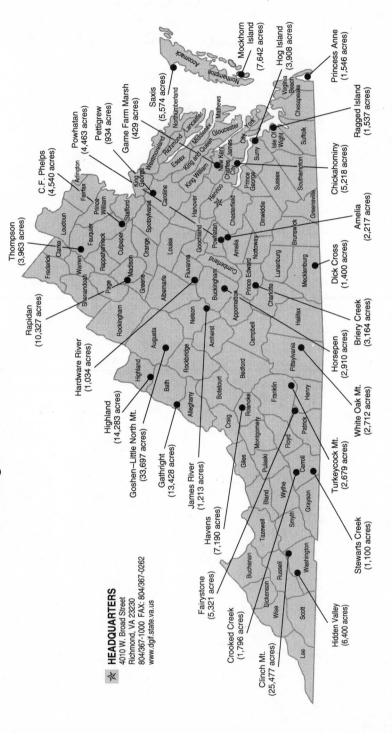

HEADQUARTERS
4010 W. Broad Street
Richmond, VA 23230
804/367-1000 FAX: 804/367-0262
www.dgif.state.va.us

Mockhorn Island (7,642 acres)

Hog Island (3,908 acres)

Princess Anne (1,546 acres)

Ragged Island (1,537 acres)

Saxis (5,574 acres)

Powhatan (4,463 acres)

Pettigrew (934 acres)

Game Farm Marsh (429 acres)

C.F. Phelps (4,540 acres)

Chickahominy (5,218 acres)

Amelia (2,217 acres)

Thompson (3,963 acres)

Dick Cross (1,400 acres)

Rapidan (10,327 acres)

Briery Creek (3,164 acres)

Hardware River (1,034 acres)

Horsepen (2,910 acres)

White Oak Mt. (2,712 acres)

Highland (14,283 acres)

Goshen–Little North Mt. (33,697 acres)

Gathright (13,428 acres)

Turkeycock Mt. (2,679 acres)

James River (1,213 acres)

Havens (7,190 acres)

Stewarts Creek (1,100 acres)

Fairystone (5,321 acres)

Crooked Creek (1,796 acres)

Hidden Valley (6,400 acres)

Clinch Mt. (25,477 acres)

Introduction

The growing human population, increasingly turning to the outdoors for recreation, will find an abundance of open spaces in Virginia. Land and water are available for relaxation and unwinding where the pressures of the working-day world quickly evaporate. Whether you live in the Old Dominion or merely visit it for a day or several weeks, a great variety of outdoor space awaits you. It is administered at all levels of government and often by the private sector.

The major federal lands include the George Washington and Jefferson National Forests, the Blue Ridge Parkway, and the Shenandoah National Park. These public lands are mostly to the western part of the state, far from the northern and eastern population centers. Virginia's sprawling system of state parks, however, touches all parts of the state. The state forests are more limited in their range.

There is still another system of public lands available for outdoor recreation, one that is not as well known as the national forests and parks and the state parks. These are the wildlife management areas, the only public lands in Virginia managed specifically for wildlife. Although good wildlife management programs are in effect in the national forests, wildlife is only one of several land management programs on such lands. Multiple use is the usual term used to describe the national forest land use. This is also true of the state forests. Both the national and state parks, however, follow the philosophy of allowing nature to produce wildlife native to the area.

The wildlife management areas are owned and administered by the state's Department of Game and Inland Fisheries with the goal of providing good public hunting for those who pay for it. These lands were purchased by the hunters, anglers, and trappers of Virginia with their hunting, fishing, and trapping license dollars and the tax they pay on hunting, fishing, and trapping equipment. The tax money is collected at the federal level under the Fish and Wildlife Restoration Programs and distributed proportionally to the various states.

Most of these wildlife management areas were acquired years ago when land was relatively inexpensive. Some land was even donated. The high cost of land today has slowed the acquisition of additional wildlife management areas, particularly in the eastern part of the state where land is most expensive, but ironically where it is most in demand for outdoor recreation.

Because anglers and hunters pay for the purchase of the lands and their management, the programs are directed primarily toward hunting and fishing, hunting particularly and to a lesser extent fishing and trapping. This, however, does not exclude others who share the hunter's and angler's love of the outdoors. There is room for backpackers, bicyclists, bird-watchers, boaters, campers, canoeists, hikers, nature lovers, picnickers, and horseback riders—and also those who simply like to loaf and relax in an outdoor setting. Many of the areas have nature-viewing platforms or towers for use by the public. Hunting related are ranges for sighting-in rifles and target shooting and facilities for field trials.

There are twenty-nine wildlife management areas, varying in size from the 429-acre Game Farm Marsh to the 33,697-acre Goshen–Little North Mountain area. Together the twenty-nine areas contain a total of 180,000 acres. Like the state parks, they are scattered throughout Virginia. No one should have to travel far to enjoy one. Thanks to its system of wildlife management areas, the Department of Game and Inland Fisheries owns more land than any other state agency including the Department of Forestry and the Division of State Parks and Recreation.

Introduction

Conflicts of interest can be avoided by bearing in mind that hunting is the primary use of these areas, but hunting seasons are short. Much of the year there are no hunting seasons open, and even during the open hunting seasons there is no hunting on Sundays. To avoid conflict, pick up a copy of the current hunting regulations from just about any gun and tackle shop and schedule your visits around the seasons, particularly the big-game seasons for bears, deer, and turkeys (see also www.dgif.state.va.us).

Generally the big-game hunting seasons open in late October and end early in January, making November and December the major months for big-game hunting. There is also the spring turkey season, which opens in April and ends in May, extending roughly a month. But hunting during this brief spring season ends at noon each day. Small-game hunting and trapping generally do not conflict as seriously with other uses of the lands. The hunting year usually gets under way in early September with the opening of the dove season and the early squirrel season in some parts of Virginia. Of the twenty-nine wildlife management areas, however, less than half offer dove hunting, and the early squirrel season is limited to some Southside and Southwest counties. September dove hunting does not begin until noon. In many of the wildlife management areas, there is no hunting until October. For exact dates, however, refer to the current hunting regulations.

For safety purposes it is a good idea to wear some item of blaze orange if visiting the areas during a hunting season. A cap or vest will suffice. Even licensed hunters cannot have a bow or gun in their possession on the wildlife management areas outside of the regular hunting seasons—that is, between the end of the spring turkey hunting season in the middle of May to the opening of the dove season in early September. There is no hunting activity in June, July, or August, popular vacation months.

Primitive camping is permitted up to fourteen days per trip, but it is prohibited within 100 yards of a boat ramp or fishing lake.

Swimming is prohibited in many wildlife management area lakes, but some offer access to streams or other lakes where swimming is allowed. Boats or canoes are allowed on the lakes, but they cannot be propelled by a gasoline motor or sail.

Complete regulations are posted at the primary entrances to the wildlife management areas and should be reviewed before entering. Common to all of the wildlife management areas is the prohibition of the use of ATVs, all-terrain vehicles. These regulations should not hamper one's enjoyment of the area and are there only to protect the resource and make it a viable wildlife haven.

Although the wildlife management programs are directed toward game animals, all wildlife benefits. This practice makes the wildlife management areas attractive to bird-watchers and those who simply enjoy viewing nature. Within the boundaries of the wildlife management areas across Virginia are 674 species of wild critters. Most are not considered game animals.

Bearing in mind the regulations that are needed to protect the resources, the Department of Game and Inland Fisheries welcomes the public to the various wildlife management areas. There is no fee for using these areas, nor is a permit needed. Just go and enjoy them, but show respect for the land and the wild creatures that live there. They enhance the attractiveness of these unique wild places.

Virginia's excellent system of Interstate Highways, U.S. Highways, and Virginia Primary Highways provides fast access to all parts of the state. To reach most of the wildlife management areas, one eventually also will have to travel the Virginia Secondary Highways, mostly numbered in the 600s, 700s, and 800s. For the sake of brevity these highways are identified as routes here. Both interstate and primary highways carry double digit numbers such as Interstate 81 and Primary Highway 53. The interstate roads are so labeled, but the primary highways, like the secondary ones, are called simply routes. Because U.S. Highways may be designated with single digits such as U.S. Highway 1, double digits such as U.S. Highway 15, or triple digits such as U.S. Highway 522, they are also specially labeled.

The maps in this volume have been adapted from Department of Game and Inland Fisheries maps with the permission of the department. The light gray areas are the wildlife management areas, and the dark gray areas are national forests or land of other agencies.

If communication with the outside is considered necessary, it might be best to carry a cellular telephone. Although there may be telephones at the wildlife management area headquarters, that telephone could be miles away across the area. The headquarters could also be on another wildlife management area because often one headquarters serves several areas.

Remember the code of the wilderness. Pack it in and pack it out. Leave nothing to indicate your presence. Leave the wilderness area as you found it so others will have an equal opportunity to enjoy it.

Northwest Mountains and Valley

Counties: Alleghany, Augusta, Bath, Highland, and Rockbridge

This region runs from Roanoke north to the West Virginia border and from the Skyline Drive and the Blue Ridge Parkway west to the West Virginia border. It is a region of rich farmlands, fascinating mountains, and fast rivers. The western slopes of the Blue Ridge Mountains, the rugged Allegheny Mountains, the picturesque Shenandoah Mountains, and the rugged Massanutten Mountains dominate the region. The North and South Forks of the Shenandoah River and its main stem are the best-known rivers, but the Maury River to the south gets lots of attention from anglers and canoeists. To the west are the Cowpasture and Jackson Rivers, which form the headwaters of the James River. There are also hundreds of miles of delightful mountain streams, many of which hold trout. The only large lake is the 2,500-acre Lake Moomaw, a U.S. Corps of Engineers impoundment on the Jackson River.

The George Washington National Forest claims much of the region to the west, and to the east is the western slope of the Shenandoah National Park and the Blue Ridge Parkway. A small section of the Jefferson National Forest juts north into Botetourt County. While the mountains here don't challenge high Mount Rogers in Southwest Virginia, Elliott Knob in Augusta County stretches to 4,458 feet, and Jack Mountain in Highland County reaches 4,378 feet.

This is the home of the Gathright, Goshen–North Mountain, and Highland Wildlife Management Areas.

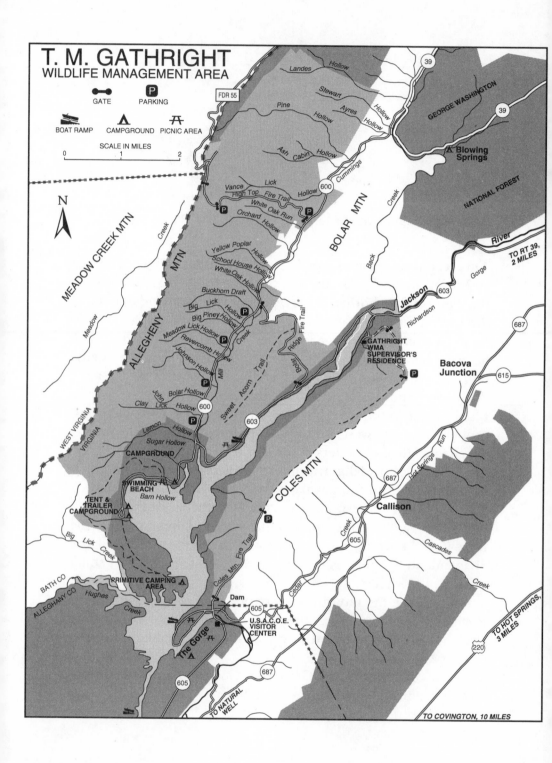

Gathright Wildlife Management Area

Supervising Office: Department of Game and Inland Fisheries
P.O. Box 996
Verona, VA 24482
Telephone 540-248-9360
Location: Alleghany and Bath Counties
Elevation: 1,400 to 3,600 feet

Rugged and all but inaccessible mountains, singing mountain streams, and a sparkling mountain lake might best describe the Gathright Wildlife Management Area. It holds particular appeal to those who love the mountains where they can shoulder a pack and strike off into a rich wilderness area. Trails may lead part of the way, but for the most part the backpacker hiker is on his or her own, challenging a remote region where outdoor skills will receive a true test. Such land is becoming increasingly hard to locate as a rapidly growing population places an ever-growing demand on land for homes, factories, highways, and other facets of modern civilization.

Purchased in 1958, Gathright was one of the first areas to come on board. It was named for the late T. M. Gathright who for many years maintained a hunting lodge here. During the early years wild turkeys were captured here for restocking all over Virginia. The area still holds good populations of wild turkeys. The original tract was 18,500 acres, much of it fertile bottomland along the Jackson River, but after the Department of Game and Inland Fisheries acquired it, the U.S. Army Corps of Engineers claimed approximately 5,000 acres to build the Gathright Dam on the Jackson River and create the 2,500-acre Lake Moomaw. Much of that 5,000 acres was the rich bottomlands that made the area so popular among hunters. Currently 13,428 acres of mostly mountain land make up this wildlife management area located mainly in Bath County. A small part of Lake Moomaw and the wildlife management area is located across the county line in Alleghany County. There is, however, some flat bottomland left between Mill Creek and the western shores of the lake and a little near the supervisor's residence at the upper end of the lake. Three mountains, Allegheny, Bolar, and Coles, are the dominant terrain features, with elevations ranging from 1,400 to 3,600 feet. Lake Moomaw divides the property, with Coles Mountain on the east side and Allegheny and Bolar on the west. The Virginia–West Virginia line forms the western border of the area. Numerous small mountain streams race down the eastern slope of Allegheny Mountain to flow into Mill Creek, which runs south between Allegheny and Bolar Mountains to enter Lake Moomaw. Most of the area is covered by hickory and oak forests that are dotted with small clearings maintained for use by wildlife.

The wildlife management area is best reached off Route 39. Route 603 leads south off the primary highway and follows the Jackson River to the lake. It then crosses the headwaters of the lake and runs south along the lake to join Route 600, which follows Mill Creek north back to Route 39. Or you can reverse that route, taking Route 600 south to intersect with Route 603, then following that road north back to Route 39. Another possibility is to take the various roads following the Jackson River north from Interstate 64 near Covington, pick up Route 605 near Natural Well, and cross the Gathright Dam. This leads only to the Coles Mountain section of the wildlife management area. To reach the western section, it is necessary to travel Routes 605 and 687 north to Route 39 and then follow Route 603 or 600. The pair of access points off Route 39 are the better choice.

The wildlife management area offers backpackers a number of interesting possibilities. One is to shoulder a pack and strike out in the untracked wilderness, of which there are several choices — all of which call for plenty of climbing. A number of parking places along Secondary Route 600 can serve as a trailhead from which to follow a singing mountain stream toward the crest of the

Allegheny Mountains. Coles Mountain also offers an untracked wilderness which can be approached from Coles Mountain Fire Trail or from a trail that leads from the upper reaches of Lake Moomaw off Route 603 and then a dirt road near the area supervisor's residence. Other backpacking possibilities include High Top Fire Trail, Bolar Ridge Fire Trail, and Sweet Acorn Trail. High Top Fire Trail leads to the western boundary of the wildlife management area. One approach to wilderness traveling is to go by boat or canoe to the Lake Moomaw shoreline, beach it safely ashore, and strike out. A good compass and the ability to read it are of utmost importance.

Although motorized vehicles are not allowed on the trails, these trails can be traveled by trail bicycles. Bicyclists, however, should be prepared to climb some steep grades. This is mountain country, some of the most rugged mountains in Virginia. Flat country is rare.

Bird-watching opportunities are varied. High hardwood forests, a multitude of streams of varied sizes, beaver flowages, and the shoreline of Lake Moomaw attract a good variety of birds, depending upon their migration patterns.

Bird-watchers need binoculars for the best results. With a little climbing, the bird-watcher should be able to locate a high vantage point from which he or she can work most of the area with binoculars. Get up there, make yourself comfortable, and enjoy scanning the area for birds. A great variety of birds use the area. Many of them such as the bald eagle, northern goshawk, and Appalachian wren, as well as the Virginia big-eared bat, are on the federal endangered or threatened list but are here to be viewed and enjoyed. Others such as the purple finch, moorhen, nuthatch, barn owl, hermit thrush, golden-winged warbler, and winter wren are on the state special concern list but usually are more numerous. Some birds such as the red-winged blackbird, cardinal, crow, grackle, Cooper's and red-tailed hawks, great blue heron, blue jay, barred owl, raven, various sparrows, and the starling are here just about all year. Others such as the goldfinch, junco, and robin are here only during spring and fall migrations. The little junco, commonly called the snowbird, is a winter dweller.

Unlike many of the wildlife management areas where boating or canoeing opportunities are limited, Lake Moomaw offers boating and canoeing on a beautiful mountain lake. The shoreline of the lake is owned and managed by the National Forest Service, but like the wildlife management areas, it is open to the public. There are a number of boat-launching ramps around the lake. One is off Route 605 at Coles Point; another is across the lake at Bolar Flats Marina. Coles Point is near the dam, but Bolar Flats Marina is on the western side of the lake and reached off Route 603. A third launching ramp is at Fortney Branch near the dam.

Both Back Creek and the Jackson River offer good trout fishing, though they flow mostly through private land where "No Fishing" signs abound. Both flow southwest into the headwaters of the lake. Fortunately, stretches of these good trout streams flow through the George Washington National Forest and are open to the public. Several small mountain streams nearby also offer fishing for native brook trout. Among the best is Mill Creek, accessed from Route 600. Many of these streams all but dry up during the warmer months. But check out some of the larger ones; they may hold trout. The stretches of Back Creek and the Jackson River in the national forest are stocked regularly with hatchery trout. Lake Moomaw is noted for its rainbow trout and big brown trout. The lake also holds largemouth bass, smallmouth bass, catfish, crappie, chain pickerel, and sunfish, and it has produced two state record yellow perch, somewhat of a rarity in this part of the state. Lake Moomaw can be fished from the shore, but a boat provides better access to the fishing.

Once a prime hunting land, much of the best hunting country was lost when Lake Moomaw claimed the rich bottomlands. There is still a small amount of flatland left, mostly between Mill Creek and the lake, but most of the wildlife management area is steep and well forested with hardwoods. The turkey populations are still good, and there is some deer hunting, but it is for the most part tough hunting. Other forest game includes grouse and squirrels. Lake Moomaw offers some waterfowl hunting, and there are bobcats and raccoon for night hunters who are willing to do some climbing.

Only primitive camping is permitted, but a camper can set up for a two-week period wherever a suitable campsite can be located. The only flat land is that along Mill Creek, and a campsite can likely be found there. Take Route 600 south from the mouth of Mill Creek. There is also a limited amount of flat land near the manager's residence. Camping within 100 yards of a lake or stream is prohibited, but plenty of the land along Mill Creek meets that requirement. There are several developed campgrounds along the western shores of Lake Moomaw. All are on national forest lands, but they are, of course, open to the public.

Bolar Ridge, Coles Mountain, and High Top Fire Trails and Routes 600 and 603 offer the easiest hiking, but day hikers should be prepared to do a little climbing on the fire trails. Several designated trails on the western side of the lake traverse both wildlife management land and the national forest lands. Another designated trail leaves Route 603 near the residence of the wildlife management area manager. Finally, there is Sweet Acorn Trail off Bolar Ridge Fire Trail. It leads the hiker along the ridge of Bolar Mountain and offers good views to both the east and the west. Otherwise hiking is limited to striking out through the wilderness, a possibility that has more appeal to the experienced backpacker than to the day hiker.

Probably the best way to enjoy and observe nature is to walk slowly and quietly along one of the trails, pausing frequently to look and listen. Pack some lunch in a day pack and make a day of it. Another possibility is to put a canoe on the lake and paddle slowly and quietly along the shore. A good canoeist can dip a paddle in and out of the water without making a sound. Binoculars are almost a necessity for close-up viewing. Another possibility is to find a high point overlooking the lake. Binoculars are particularly handy here for studying the far side of the lake. Wildlife is generally most active early and late in the day. It is a good time to view nature and the spectacular sunrises and sunsets. Nature, of course, includes flowers and plants as well as wildlife. Over two dozen butterflies use the area. "They're here from snow to snow," said the area manager. Poisonous snakes include both the copperhead and the timber rattler, but there are also at least a dozen non-poisonous snakes such several blacksnakes, the garter snake, and the water snake. A great variety of salamanders use the small streams and the larger ones such as Mill Creek. There are also at least a half-dozen species of crayfish and several turtles, mostly in Lake Moomaw although the forests have some box turtles. The spring months, particularly April and May, bring forth a splash of color with first the dogwoods and redbuds and then the mountain laurel and rhododendron in full bloom and many flowers such as iris, orchids, and trilliums.

Picnickers will find picnic tables at the Bolar Flats Marina and near the visitors' center at the dam in the George Washington National Forest. But possibly a better approach is to drive slowly along Routes 600 and 603 and look for a pleasing location. Route 603 offers sites overlooking the lake. There are a number of parking areas along Route 600 that might serve as a picnic site.

Individual horseback riders are allowed on the roads and trails, but not organized groups of riders.

A glance at the accompanying map of the wildlife management area will show that many of the roads and trails are gated. This means that motorized vehicles are prohibited except during regular hunting seasons when the gates are opened to allow hunters on the trails and roads. Even the seasonally opened gates may be closed during inclement weather to prevent damage to the roads or trails. The gates, however, do not prohibit hikers, trail bikes, or riders on horses from passing.

Despite the loss of its rich bottomlands to the lake, Gathright Wildlife Management Area remains a gem for those who love the outdoors.

Goshen–Little North Mountain Wildlife Management Area

Supervising Office: Department of Game and Inland Fisheries
P.O. Box 996
Verona, VA 24482
Telephone 540-248-9360
Location: Augusta, Bath, and Rockbridge Counties
Elevation: 1,326 to 3,400 feet

At 33,697 acres Goshen–Little North Mountain Wildlife Management Area is big, the largest of the twenty-nine wildlife management areas in Virginia. With elevations ranging from 1,326 to 3,400 feet, it is mostly high country by Virginia standards. A rugged forest-covered mountain area, it is clothed for the most part with mixed hardwoods and pines. This is the dominant cover. Along the spine of Little North Mountain, immature hardwoods in the early stages of development are numerous, the consequence of managed timber harvesting to improve wildlife cover. There are actually two separate wildlife management areas here, but they are managed as one. The Little North Mountain tract is long and narrow with steep terrain. It lies in parts of both Augusta and Rockbridge Counties and follows the spine of Little North Mountain. The Goshen section, wider and almost circular in shape, is totally within Rockbridge County. This is unforgiving mountain country. The Goshen tract's topography is steeper than Little North Mountain and harder to climb. Three major mountains, Bratton, Forge, and Hogback, dominate the Goshen section. Also unique to this section of the wildlife management area is the Meadow Ground, providing a valuable, native herbaceous habitat. Goshen is to the south of Little North Mountain across the racing and tumbling Maury River. A footbridge over the Maury River accommodates

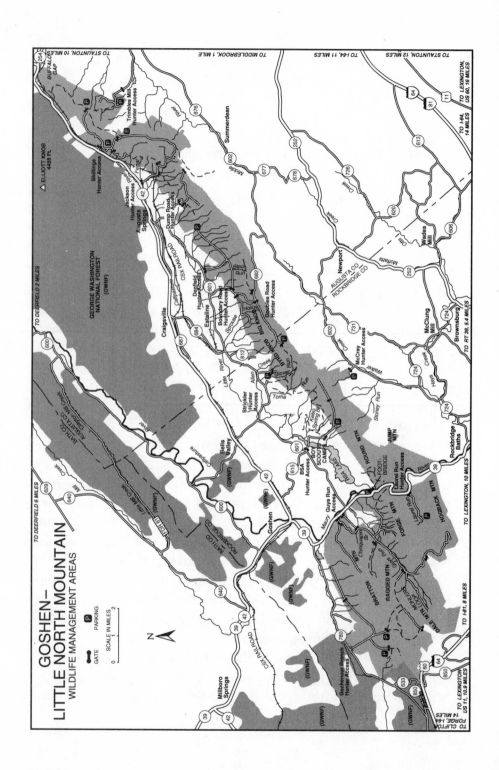

GOSHEN–
LITTLE NORTH MOUNTAIN
WILDLIFE MANAGEMENT AREAS

P   PARKING

🚧   GATE

SCALE IN MILES
0   1   2

N

hikers passing from one section of the wildlife management area to the other.

Virginia Primary Highway 39 off Interstate 64 at Lexington provides access to the southern section of the area. Routes 633 and 780 off Interstate 64 provide access from the west. Route 601 north off Route 39 provides access to the western portion of Little North Mountain. For the eastern portion Route 602 provides access at the McCray Hunter Access, Doubles Road Hunter Access, and Trimbles Mill Hunter Access. From the north Route 42 provides access at the Shillings Hunter Access, Jackson Hunter Access, and Dump Road Hunter Access on the western side. For Goshen there is access off Route 780 to the west and off Route 39 to the north.

The wildlife management area offers backpackers plenty of room to roam. One good hike leaves Route 601 at the Denfield Hunter Access and follows the spine of Little North Mountain north to exit at the Dump Road Hunter Access on Route 42 near Augusta Springs. This is a good six- or seven-mile hike, but mostly along a level road once you climb the mountain. Several road or trail loops or combinations of the two lead off Route 601 along the western side of the wildlife management area. Several also cross the mountain going over its spine to the valley on the other side. They could be worth arranging a shuttle for a party of backpackers, leaving a vehicle on the opposite side of the mountain, taking another to the other side, and backpacking across. This is much like running a shuttle when canoeing a stream. A hike along the spine of Little North Mountain where the mountain is narrow offers interesting views of the countryside that stretches away from the foothills on either side of the mountain. There is also a loop combining a trail and road on the Goshen tract. A backpacker can leave Route 780 on the west side of the tract at the Gouchenour Branch Hunter Access and hike through to Route 39 at the Guys Run Access—or do the reverse of that. A ride is needed at the other end, unless you want to retrace the route. The wildlife management area along Little North Mountain is seldom as much as a mile wide, often much less than that. For that reason a true wilderness backpacking trip is difficult. At a distance, civilization is always in sight, particularly at night when lights from the countryside dance in the darkness. The Goshen section offers a better opportunity for wilderness backpacking. The Guys Run Road leads along Guys Run to the top of Ragged Mountain, and from there a hiking trail heads down the western side of the mountain to exit eventually on Route 780. Many jeep roads lead deep into the area. These are gated, some seasonally and open during the hunting season, but the gates do not bar hikers, who do not have to share the roads with motor vehicles when the gates are closed. The seasonal gates may also be closed during very wet weather to prevent damage to the roads or trails.

Bicyclists will find an abundance of roads and trails they can travel, but the going can be strenuous at times, particularly on steep climbs up the mountains. Although many of the roads and trails are gated, they can be legally bypassed by bicyclists and hikers. The jeep trails can be rough—deeply rutted and marked with water-filled mudholes, particularly during and after the hunting season when they experience heavy jeep and truck traffic. In fact, venturing onto them with low-clearance sedans is risky, a chance of getting stuck far from help. A pickup truck will handle the roads, but a 4×4 jeep-type vehicle is ideal.

There are almost unlimited bird-watching opportunities, though there are no lakes or ponds to help attract them. A number of small accessible streams run down the western flank of Little North Mountain, and a few down the western flank of Goshen. Guys Run and Laurel Run, which flow north on Goshen to enter the Maury River, might offer the best opportunity to locate a variety of birds. Maury River itself should provide some bird-watching opportunities. Stand on the footbridge and watch for birds following the river or watering near its banks. Ducks also use the Maury River, particularly the colorful little wood duck. The Little River flows south on private land just outside of the wildlife management area, but it gathers its headwaters in the northern reaches of Little North Mountain. It flows into the Boy Scouts of

America Lake, and it should attract birds that can be viewed from a distance with binoculars. Well over 150 different kinds of birds live on the wildlife management area, pass through on migrations, and simply visit there. So the bird-watching opportunities are all but unlimited. Some such as the eagle, egret, falcon, purple finch, goshawk, barn owl, hermit thrush, some warblers, and winter wren are on the federal or state endangered species list, but that doesn't mean they can't be enjoyed. When entering the area, a bird-watcher might first look to the skies. Up there, circling on the air currents, could be predator birds such as the bald eagle or the red-tailed or some of the other hawks. Soaring lazily above them might be a black or turkey vulture, scavengers with eyes alert for an easy meal. Listen carefully, and there may be the hoarse cronking of a raven or the noisy chatter of a disturbed crow. All of these large birds are found on the wildlife management area. But there are many more, those that stay all year such as the cardinal, grackle, red-winged blackbird, and the colorful and noisy pileated woodpecker. Others are more evident during the fall and spring migrations, birds such as the robin, junco, some of the sparrows, and wrens. A songbird field guide is a must here for the serious bird-watcher.

Except for a long stretch of the Maury River, there are no boating or canoeing opportunities on the Goshen–Little North Mountain Wildlife Management Area. But probably close to three miles of the Maury flow through or skirt the wildlife management area. When it is flowing full, it provides some fast water that will test the skills of the best canoeist or kayaker. The river can get very low, however, during dry spells, primarily during the summer months. The wildlife management area offers public access to the Maury River at the footbridge for those who want to launch canoes or kayaks and travel downstream. The Maury flows through the city of Lexington and beneath Interstate 64 and U.S. Highway 11 and skirts the city of Buena Vista, eventually entering the James River at Glasgow. The Maury River is characterized by numerous Class I, II, and III rapids.

The Maury River is a put-and-take trout stream, or designated trout-fishing waters. For that reason it is probably the most popular fishing water in the wildlife management area. It is stocked regularly throughout the year. The river also provides good fishing for rock bass and smallmouth bass. But the angler shouldn't overlook the dozens of small mountain streams that tumble down both flanks of Little North Mountain as well as numerous tributaries of Guys Run in the Goshen section south of the Maury River. Wading is probably the best approach to fishing these streams, though the Maury River is canoeable. Many of these little mountain streams, particularly the larger ones such as Guys Run, hold native brook trout, colorful little fish that hit dry flies with abandon—provided the angler presents his fly without exposing his figure to the little fish.

Bears, deer, and turkeys are the game sought by big-game hunters. Most hunters concentrate on the areas close to the road, but deer tend to move to the backcountry and high mountains when the pressure gets heavy. Hunters take 200 to 250 deer per season here. The southern reaches of the Little North Mountain unit offer good turkey hunting, and the best bear hunting is in the rugged terrain of the Goshen unit. Although these are the top hunting areas, bears, deer, and turkeys are found throughout the wildlife management area. Many hunters camp in the area, and their fire rings and crude game poles remain as symbols of their successful hunts. Many of the roads or jeep trails are open to jeep-type vehicles or trucks during the hunting seasons, primarily November, December, and early January. Many hunters, however, prefer to walk into likely hunting cover. Both units hold grouse and squirrels and attract small-game and bird hunters. There are also a few cottontail rabbits, usually at the lower elevations, and wood ducks use the Maury River. Wildlife management consists of controlled timber harvesting, the seeding of clearings, and planting soft mast to supplement acorns and other native food.

As is true of most of the wildlife management areas, camping is permitted, but there are no designated campsites. Only primitive camping is allowed. Most camping probably is done by backpackers or hunters, but for those who like to escape the crowds and camp under primitive conditions, there are plenty of opportunities. Find a secluded spot beside a singing mountain stream, in a high mountain meadow, or along the rambunctious Maury River where the kids in the family can find a quiet pool to play in and skip flat rocks.

Those same trails and roads used by backpackers and bicyclists will appeal to day hikers, those who like to shoulder a day pack and strike out for a day outdoors.

The high elevations, countless small streams, and occasional beaver flowages offer opportunities simply to enjoy viewing nature, be it a doe and her young, a flock of turkeys, or birds and squirrels cavorting in the forest. In the spring laurel and other high-elevation plants and shrubs bloom. Would you believe that there are over seventy different kinds of butterflies on this big wildlife management area? Or eight kinds of frogs including the popular bullfrog and the spring peeper? And fifteen kinds of salamanders and the red-spotted newt are found mostly in the small streams but also in the Maury River. The timber rattlesnake and the copperhead are the poisonous snakes, but there are also fifteen nonpoisonous snakes. This, of course, is mountain country with both mountain laurel and rhododendron in bloom in May and June. Earlier, dogwoods and redbuds add their brilliant colors to the spring countryside. Spring is a good time to visit for the great variety of wildflowers such as jonquils, orchids, and trilliums and to gather mushrooms at the proper season. The edible ones are morels, of course, and it behooves the picker to be able to identify them.

You won't find picnic tables in most wildlife management areas, but there is no scarcity of picnic sites. Something should appeal to all picnickers regardless of their tastes. Many hikers pack a picnic lunch and look for the ideal spot. But long hikes are not necessary to picnic. Drive the ungated jeep trails or roads and look for a spot. It may be a flat boulder high on Little North Mountain or

Ragged Mountain or a spot beside a delightful little stream. Or maybe it is a high mountain meadow with an imposing view of the surrounding country. The possibilities are all but unlimited.

Those responsible for managing Gathright, Goshen–Little North Mountain, and Highland Wildlife Management Areas do not like organized rides where a large number of horses are involved, but the jeep trails and roads offer interesting bridle trails for lone riders, couples, or small groups. Check with the area manager before riding to avoid conflicts with other users.

Goshen–Little North Mountain Wildlife Management Area probably most appeals to those who love the mountains.

Highland Wildlife Management Area

Supervising Office: Department of Game and Inland Fisheries
P.O. Box 996
Verona, VA 24482
Telephone 540-248-9360
Location: Bath and Highland Counties
Elevations: 1,800 to 4,390 feet

The Highland Wildlife Management Area is located in pictur-esque and mountainous Highland County, often called the "Little Switzerland of Virginia." Syrup-producing sugar maples and a struggling population of snowshoe hares set this county on the West Virginia border aside from more typical Virginia. Tiny tips of the Bullpasture Mountain section of this wildlife management area dip into Bath County near Williamsville, but for the most part this is a Highland County wildlife management area. High-land is generally regarded as having the highest average elevation of any county east of the Mississippi River. High mountains that pitch down to a rich river valley might best describe this interest-ing wildlife management area. There is a small plot of private land in the middle of the area near Sounding Knob.

Combined, three separate tracts of land, Bullpasture Mountain, Jack Mountain, and Little Doe Hill, offer a total of 14,283 acres of choice outdoor country. As Donald McCaig says in his best-selling book *An American Homeplace*, "Most of Bullpasture Mountain is State Game Commission land." Elevations range from 1,800 feet along the Bullpasture River to 4,390 feet at Sounding Knob on Jack Mountain. Most of the mountain ridges, however, are in the 2,500- to 3,200-foot range. Unique features include a long section of the rapidly flowing Bullpasture River, acres of forested moun-tains, and an eighty-acre plot of bluegrass sod that once served as

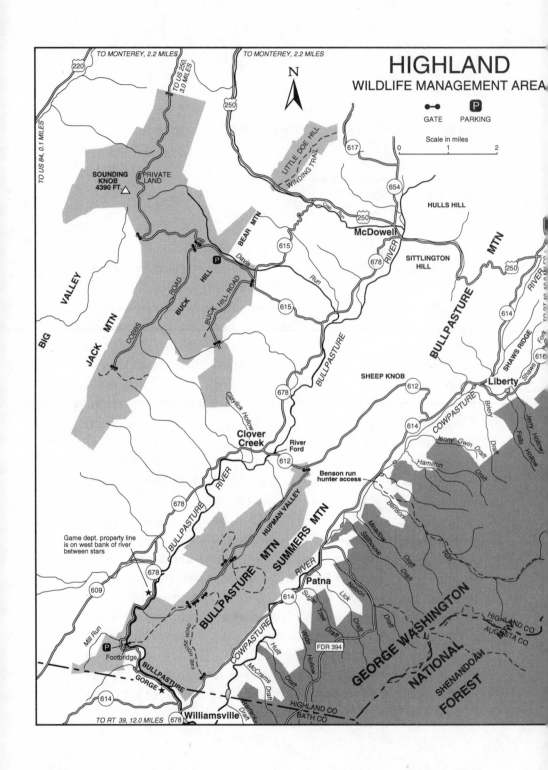

a summer pasture. Most of the wildlife management area is forested with hardwood stands of oak and hickory and mixed oak stands. Small wildlife clearings and seeded logging roads provide herbaceous cover and food in addition to native soft mast and hard mast such as acorns. A part of the wildlife management plan includes limited harvesting of timber to create habitat and increase the production of hard mast. Trees and shrubs such as apple and cherry trees and dogwood produce soft mast for wildlife.

Various road and trails off U.S. Highway 250 between McDowell and Monterey provide access to all three tracts of the Highland Wildlife Management Area. Little Doe Hill is on the north side of U.S. Highway 250, and Winding Trail off the highway runs through this tract, providing access.

There are several approaches to the Bullpasture River tract, most of which is on the eastern side of the river. From McDowell, Route 678 off U.S. Highway 250 runs south along the Bullpasture River to Williamsville. At Clover Creek, Route 612 leads east off Route 678, fords the Bullpasture River, and brushes the northern end of the Bullpasture Mountain tract. At this northern tip a seasonally gated jeep road or trail runs south through Hupman Valley deep into the tract where several gated trails swing off the jeep road. One trail leads south over a footbridge across the Bullpasture to a parking area on the western side of the river. Route 678 continues south along the river, passing through the tract just upstream from the footbridge and skirting the tract through the Bullpasture Gorge just north of Williamsville. Another approach to this section of the wildlife management area is take Route 614 off U.S. Highway 250 east of McDowell. It follows the Cowpasture River south to connect with Route 612 south of Liberty. This leads to the Hupman Valley road from the east. Route 614 continues south along the Cowpasture River to Williamsville. The only access to the tract off this route is the gated firehouse road that crosses Bullpasture Mountain to connect with the Hupman Valley jeep road.

The Jack Mountain tract, the largest of the three tracts, is reached by Route 615 off Route 678 south of McDowell. Route 615 loops back to U.S. Highway 250 west of McDowell but skirts the wildlife management area midway to provide access to the Buck Hill Road and another long jeep road leading north through the tract. Possibly a better approach to the Jack Mountain tract is to catch this long jeep road at U.S. Highway 250 on the top of Jack Mountain just east of Monterey. It is well marked. Heading south, this jeep road enters the wildlife management area approximately three miles from U.S. Highway 250, passes in the northern shadow of Sounding Knob, and connects with Cobbs Road and Buck Hill Road, both seasonally gated. This route provides access to the very heart of the Jack Mountain tract.

From the south the wildlife management area can be reached by Route 678 off Route 39. Route 678 follows the Cowpasture north from Millboro Springs to Williamsville. An interesting feature is a ford across the Bullpasture River near Clover Creek where Route 612 crosses the river. This is just outside of the wildlife management area, but to reach the Hupman Valley road from Route 678, you must cross the river by way of the ford. Creek and river fords are a rarity today, but in the not-too-distant past they were an important segment of our system of roads. Cross the Bullpasture at this ford, and let your imagination drift back to frontier times.

A good backpacking trip might be to cross the footbridge over the Bullpasture River and take the trail that leads high on Bullpasture Mountain. There a variety of trails lead to all parts of this tract. Some are looping trails that eventually connect with the Hupman Valley road. All are gated, but this does not interfere with backpacking. Higher up on Jack Mountain a number of jeep roads lead off the main road. Among them is Cobbs Road, which connects with a trail leading into the southern section of the tract, Buck Hill Road. Each of these roads has a seasonal gate off the main road and the usual closed gate at the other end. The road leading off U.S. Highway 250 to the north and ending at Route 615 to the south covers six to seven miles through the wildlife management area. The road, of course, is a public one. Winding Trail, going from one end of Little Doe Hill to the other, offers a short trip of approximately two miles one way—two in and two out. The eastern end of the trail is just a few hundred yards from Route 617, but across private land only. This wildlife management area has plenty of interesting country for a backpacker to explore.

Motorized vehicles, including ATVs and 4×4s, are not allowed on the gated trails. In fact, ATVs, all-terrain vehicles, are not allowed on any of the wildlife management areas. The only exception is those which are seasonally closed to protect them during wet weather. Motorized vehicles other than ATVs might be allowed at other times. All, however, are open to bicyclists, who can shoulder a pack and spend days exploring this country. A bicyclist who enters the main trail here three miles off U.S. Highway 250 and ends on Route 678 will travel downhill most of the way: relatively easy peddling. The Hupman Valley road offers bicycling along a mountain foothills stream, crossing it several times. There are twenty miles of roads plus many miles of seeded trails in this wildlife management area.

Bird-watchers have several interesting options. One is the open meadows on Jack Mountain, which offer the chance to watch ground-nesting birds that like the high open cover and the insects it provides for food. Another interesting option is the Bullpasture River and its valley. The footbridge across the river might be a good vantage point from which to watch birds using the river and its shoreline. Expect to see some wood ducks. Several somewhat rare and endangered or threatened birds such as the bald eagle, falcon, northern goshawk, and Appalachian wren, as well as Indiana and Virginia big-eared bats, might produce unexpected thrills here for those who love to watch birds. More prevalent, however, are birds that frequent hardwood forests and cutover areas. Expect the likes of the blackbird, bluebird, cardinal, flicker, several kinds of hawks, blue jay, junco, several kinds of owls, robin, a variety of sparrows, warbler, red-headed and pileated woodpeckers, and many others. Take along a bird book and enjoy trying to identify some of the many birds.

Boating opportunities are pretty much limited to approximately two miles of the Bullpasture River including the Bullpasture Gorge. Route 678, which passes through a section of the wildlife management area and skirts other parts of it, offers access to the river. The property boundary of the Department of Game and Inland Fisheries is on the west side of the stream and is marked by signs. This extension of the boundary across the river provides public access to that part of the river.

The Bullpasture River is the very heart of the fishing in this wildlife management area. The Department of Game and Inland Fisheries keeps the river stocked with trout—except for the hot summer months or during periods of drought when the river is too low. The Bullpasture also has smallmouth bass and rock bass. The George Washington National Forest to the east of the wildlife management area offers limited access to the Cowpasture River and fishing for smallmouth bass and rock bass. That river joins the Bullpasture downstream from Williamsville. The stream then becomes the Cowpasture all the way to its junction with the Jackson River to form the James River. There are several small mountain streams in both the Jack Mountain tract and the Bullpasture tract that offer limited fishing for native brook trout. The main road running through the Jack Mountain tract provides easy access to Davis Run, a good native trout stream.

Bears, deer, and turkeys are the choice of most hunters who travel to the Highland Wildlife Management Area. The Bullpasture Mountain tract is best known for its deer and turkeys. These two big-game animals plus black bears also are found in the more rugged Jack Mountain tract. Grouse, rabbits, and squirrels are also reasonably abundant. For the squirrel hunter who has never bagged a fox squirrel, the Bullpasture Mountain tract probably offers the best opportunity as these big squirrels are found near streams and in meadows bordered by woodlands. Another possibility is to launch a canoe on the Bullpasture River and jump shoot for ducks, but hunting is limited to the section of the river that runs through the wildlife management area or that skirts it. That portion of the river would make a good duck-hunting trip of several hours.

Only primitive camping is allowed on the wildlife management area. The high meadows of the Jack Mountain tract or along the Bullpasture River have some good spots. Camping is limited to a period of two weeks. Driving or hiking the main road through the Jack Mountain section reveals numerous fire rings built of native stone, and these can be used. Some may have been made by campers, but probably most were built by camping hunters. Another camping possibility is to pack a light outfit and follow Winding Trail into the Little Doe Hill tract.

Hiking opportunities are abundant whether it is taking the main road through the Jack Mountain tract or hiking through Hupman Valley. There is no better wildlife management area in Virginia in which to shoulder a day pack with a light lunch and take off on a wilderness trail, be it along the spine of a high mountain or beside a lowland stream.

Good spots for viewing nature include the footbridge across the Bullpasture River in the Bullpasture Mountain tract or a vantage point high in the Jack Mountain tract. Or dress in camouflage and move slowly along Davis Run, which runs down the southern slope of Jack Mountain. A great variety of wild critters live here, in addition to the game animals already mentioned. Unique to this wildlife management area are snowshoe hares. There are also Appalachian cottontail rabbits. Both the hare and the cottontail are currently protected. Don't surprised to see an occasional coyote, though the sly critters are pretty evasive. Highland County is sheep country, and nothing pleases a coyote more than a young lamb. The great variety of snakes includes two poisonous ones, the copperhead and the timber rattler. Try to avoid them. They are not aggressive, but they will strike quickly if threatened. Look for salamanders in Davis Creek and in the shallows of the Bullpasture River. The spring months bring forth a profusion of wildflowers including lady slippers, wild violets, buttercups, and jonquils. Late April and May are the season to enjoy blooming dogwood, redbud, mountain laurel, and rhododendron. Butterflies? There are between 50 and 100 varieties.

Picnickers will find an abundance of likely spots. Park your automobile in the parking area near the footbridge in the Bullpasture Mountain section, cross the bridge, and find a spot to stretch out a blanket and enjoy a hearty meal outdoors. It would be difficult to find a better spot. The footbridge was once destroyed in a raging flood, but the basic structure held, and the bridge has since been rebuilt. For more of a wilderness setting, load up in a comfortable 4×4 and drive any of the jeep trails until you find something you like.

Those same trails that appeal to backpackers or hikers will also appeal to horseback riders. Let them serve as bridle trails for a day in the outdoors on your favorite mount.

Mountains, rivers, and green valleys make this wildlife management area a pleasure to spend some time in.

Upper Piedmont and Coastal Plains

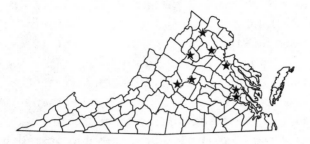

Counties: Caroline, Charles City, Clarke, Culpeper, Fauquier, Fluvanna, Greene, Madison, Nelson, New Kent, and Warren

A land of sharp contrasts, this region claims the piedmont and coastal plains lying north of the James River, east of the Blue Ridge Parkway and Skyline Drive, and west of the counties that border on the Chesapeake Bay. Most of the land is gently rolling hill country, but there is some rugged mountain terrain along the eastern slopes of the Blue Ridge Mountains. To the east in the coastal plains, it becomes mostly flatlands. The elevation ranges from sea level in the flat eastern marshes to 4,050 feet where Mount Pleasant reaches toward the heavens in Amherst County.

Singing mountain streams race down the eastern slopes of the Blue Ridge Mountains, pouring clean water into big rivers such as the James, Potomac, Rapidan, and Rappahannock. Rivers such as the Rapidan and Rappahannock originate here as fast foothills streams and become tidal rivers before they reach the Chesapeake Bay. All of the rivers flow east here to enter the bay. Much of the Potomac River belongs to Maryland, but thanks to a reciprocal agreement between Virginia and Maryland, properly licensed anglers and hunters enjoy access to it.

Big lakes are rare. Lake Anna, a 10,000-acre Virginia Power Company impoundment, is by far the largest. It spreads into Louisa, Orange, and Spotsylvania Counties.

Several of Virginia's major population centers are located in this region, primarily Richmond, the state capital, and Northern Virginia, the Washington, D.C., suburb that is rapidly spreading south and west into the state. An increasing demand for outdoor recreation puts a lot of pressure on wildlife management areas and other public lands, requiring careful management on the part of the Department of Game and Fisheries and other government agencies that hold their lands in trust for public use.

Fortunately the Department of Game and Inland Fisheries owns and manages an even half-dozen wildlife management areas in this crowded region. They vary in terrain from rugged mountain country to flat marshes. Collectively they offer almost 25,000 acres of prime outdoor country.

C. F. Phelps Wildlife Management Area

Supervising Office: Department of Game and Inland Fisheries
1320 Belman Road
Fredericksburg, VA 22401
Telephone 540-899-4169
Location: Culpeper and Fauquier Counties
Elevation: 100 to 400 feet

Named for Chester F. Phelps, for many years the executive director of the Department of Game and Inland Fisheries, the C. F. Phelps Wildlife Management Area is an oasis in a region where large open space for public use is at a premium. That plus six to seven miles of frontage along the bass-rich Rappahannock River; the Kellys Ford rapids that have challenged generations of white-water canoeists; the Hogue tract, split by the Rappahannock River, that is set aside for handicapped hunters; and a small impoundment that is managed for waterfowl are the major features of this wildlife management area. Handicapped hunters' prospective game includes deer and turkeys as well as small game. The main tract is separated from the Hogue tract with a short stretch of the Rappahannock River between. There is something here for every outdoor person, regardless of his or her preference.

The wildlife management area's 4,539 acres claim a big chunk of Fauquier County and a lesser amount of Culpeper County. That portion of the Hogue tract west of the Rappahannock River is in Culpeper County. Generally this is gently rolling hill country that does not challenge its visitors as do the mountain wildlife management areas. The only steep land is along the Rappahannock River where cliffs either drop off to the river or bottom out in a sandy, level bottomland. This was farming land supporting crops and livestock before it was acquired by the Department of Game and Inland Fisheries, and approximately 1,000 acres of the area

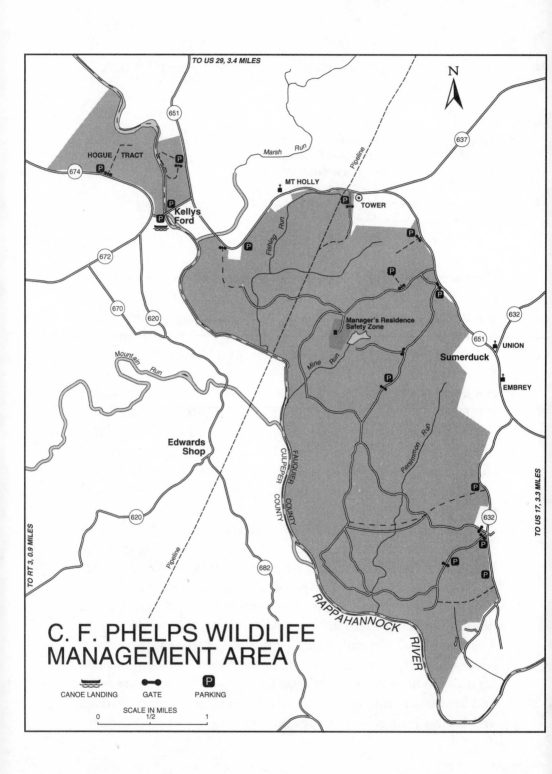

C. F. PHELPS WILDLIFE
MANAGEMENT AREA

TO US 29, 3.4 MILES

651

Marsh Run

Pipeline

N

637

HOGUE TRACT

674

P

Kellys Ford

P

672

MT HOLLY

TOWER

Fishing Run

P

P

P

P

Manager's Residence
Safety Zone

670

620

Mine Run

Sumerduck

651

632

UNION

EMBREY

Mountain Run

Edwards
Shop

FAUQUIER
CULPEPER
COUNTY

Persimmon Run

P

P

632

P

P

620

Pipeline

682

TO RT 3, 0.9 MILES

TO US 17, 3.3 MILES

RAPPAHANNOCK RIVER

CANOE LANDING   GATE   PARKING

SCALE IN MILES
0   1/2   1

remain open. There are also a number of wildlife clearings in the acres of forest that cover the area, made to let in the sun and encourage new growth. The forest cover includes both hardwood and pine timber ranging in age from seedlings to mature trees. Wildlife food plots dot much of the open area, and hedgerows have been developed by the planting of pine seedlings and shrubs. There are several small dove fields and a larger twenty-acre one.

A number of small streams including Fishing Run, Mine Run, and Persimmon Run ramble through the wildlife management area and eventually flow into the Rappahannock River. A three-acre pond impounds the headwaters of Mine Run. It is near the manager's residence and is reached off Route 651. Marsh Run, a larger stream, flows beneath Route 651, skirts the northern edge of the main tract, and enters the Rappahannock River just downstream from Kellys Ford.

The wildlife management area is located near the village of Sumerduck just south of the little riverside town of Remington. Routes 651 and 632 off Route 651 skirt the northern and eastern sides of the area. A number of roads and trails off these two public roads lead deep into the wildlife management area. Routes 651 and 632 are reached off U.S. Highway 29 through Remington from the north or off U.S. Highway 17 a mile north of Goldvein Post Office from the east and south.

The absence of steep inclines makes backpacking in this wildlife management area a joy. Winding service roads and trails lead deep into the area, some within a mile of the banks of the Rappahannock River. Reaching the river, however, means descending a steep cliff and then scaling it when you return to the service road. At the extreme southwestern edge of the area, a service road will take you reasonably close to the river, but it is still a good hike. The Hogue tract has a pair of short trails, one of which leads along the Rappahannock River and makes a circle back to the trailhead. The main tract has several fairly short trails, but the service roads provide better access to the interior of the area. Backpacking and camping along the river in the main tract mean leaving the service roads or trails and striking out through the forests. Most of the roads and trails are gated. Although the gates prohibit motorized vehicular travel, they do not block travel on foot, bicycle, or horseback.

Well-maintained roads that feature gentle slopes make this wildlife management area a pleasure for bicyclists. The system of roads and trails leads to just about all parts of the wildlife management area.

The C. F. Phelps Wildlife Management Area was one of the first to be included in a wildlife survey made by the Department of Game and Inland Fisheries. This survey, conducted primarily by nongame wildlife biologists, has as its goal the determination of all wildlife species in the area. The available game species have been pretty well established, but no prior effort to gather data on the nongame species had been made. This information is now available from the Department of Game and Inland Fisheries, P.O. Box 11104, Richmond, VA 23230, telephone 804-367-1000 (see also www.dgif.state.va.us).

Likely spots to observe birds and other wildlife include the wildlife clearings in the forests, the edges of open land, the small streams, the three-acre pond, and the shoreline of the Rappahannock River. At various times of the year, hundreds of birds visit or spend time on the wildlife management area. Some live here all year, while others come through on migration patterns. The combination of river bottom, hardwood forests, and large open fields attracts a variety of birds. Among the endangered or threatened are the bald eagle, great egret, purple finch, upland sandpiper, and several warblers. The area offers bird-watchers an opportunity to view birds that they might not otherwise see in a long time. In the open fields look for doves, meadowlarks, robins, a great variety of sparrows, and other field birds. In the hardwood forests and edges there are the cardinal, junco, several woodpeckers, and other forest-dwelling birds. The variety is rich and the list too long to include here. Also look for several hawks and owls.

Boating and canoeing are pretty much limited to the three-acre pond and the Rappahannock River. The pond is really too small for such activities, and because it was built for fishing, other uses might create a conflict. The Rappahannock River offers the best canoeing. White-water enthusiasts launch their canoes at the U.S. Highway 29 bridge near Remington, run the Kellys Ford rapids, and take out at the department's launching area on the west side of the river just below the rapids. This is, however, not a trip for inexperienced canoeists. Depending upon the season, the Kellys Ford rapids are Class II or III water. The Kellys Ford access point is a popular spot for launching canoes for an overnight trip on the river, taking out at Motts Landing near Fredericksburg. For six or seven miles below Kellys Ford, the wildlife management area offers public access to the river but no improved access points. Leaving the river here means hauling a canoe up the riverbank and carrying it for at least a mile. Persimmon Run, which flows through the area and into the Rappahannock River, might be the best place to exit the river, but it could be tough going. At the best it means carrying a canoe approximately a mile.

The small three-acre pond near the manager's residence holds largemouth bass, bluegill, channel catfish, and redear sunfish. The best fishing opportunity is offered by the Rappahannock River, which forms the area's western boundary. It is noted for its small-mouth bass fishing, and many anglers float the stream just to do battle with the scrappy bass. Redbreast sunfish are even more abundant—and delicious on the table. There are a few chain pickerel, the occasional largemouth bass, and an abundance of fallfish, fun to catch but too bony to eat. The river can be fished from a canoe or light boat or by wading. If wading, watch out for sudden drop-offs. Probably the best approach to fishing the river is to launch a boat or canoe powered by a small outboard motor, float down the river for approximately a mile, and then motor back to the launching area. Just keep an eye on the depth of the water as you float downstream. When it becomes too shallow to run your motor, it's time to head back upstream. In periods of dry weather the river may be too low for even a small outboard motor. Check this before launching. And don't overlook the angling possibilities in Marsh Run where it skirts the wildlife management area property. Fishing in tributaries of this size can often be productive. Route 651 crosses Marsh Run, providing access, but stay on the wildlife management area side of the stream. The other side is private property. At most a quarter of a mile of stream here can be fished.

Like all of the wildlife management areas, C. F. Phelps was purchased primarily with hunters' license money, and its management is directed mainly toward hunting. Deer and turkeys are the big game hunted here, while doves, quail, rabbits, and squirrels make up the small-game populations. The squirrel populations have been down because of gypsy moth damage to the oak trees that squirrels look to for acorns. Upland hunters might also flush an occasional ruffed grouse or woodcock. The fall dove populations can be high, but hunters tend to shoot at birds out of range, turning them from the fields. Dove-hunting plots are planted annually. Several species of ducks, including the colorful little wood duck, use the river. Also expect good numbers of mallard. The handicapped hunter access area in the Hogue tract features gravel-covered trails to accommodate wheelchairs and stands that include covers for protection from rain or snow. The Hogue tract handicapped hunter access area was planned with the help of Tom Reese Jr., a handicapped hunter himself. Management practices that favor hunting include disking, timber harvesting to create new growth, and wildlife food plantings on woodland roads and clearings. Located as it is so close to a major metropolitan center, the area gets a lot of hunting pressure.

As is true of most of the wildlife management areas, camping is permitted for periods of up to two weeks, but there are no designated or developed campgrounds. Campfires are prohibited, and camping must not be within 100 yards of a lake or pond. Campers n set up on a site that appeals to them and enjoy the outdoor opportunities that the area offers. Camping along the river might appeal to many, but access to it is not good for packing a lot of camping gear, though backpackers can handle it. One approach might be to load a canoe at the Kellys Ford access point and locate a suitable area for approaching from the river. Just remember there is no easy access once you leave the launching site. Breaking camp will mean loading your canoe and rowing against the current back to the Kellys Ford access point.

Thanks to a good system of roads and trails, day hikes are popular. With limited hill country, the walking is relatively easy. Combine it with enjoying the nature of the area. Sighting of deer and turkeys is possible. A day pack and binoculars can add to the success of such hikes. Also take along a camera for photographic opportunities. One possibility is to follow one of the several small streams to the Rappahannock River. Wildlife loves small waterways. The stream can also keep you oriented. All of the little streams are crossed by the service roads. Pick up one at the road and follow it to the river, and when returning follow the stream back to the road. Persimmon Run at the extreme southern end of the wildlife management area offers the shortest hike to the river. The wildflowers can be spectacular during the spring, with buttercups, dogwoods, redbuds, and mountain laurel in bloom. May is a good month to view wildflowers. Expect to see some lady slippers and other woodland flowers. By late summer and early fall, the goldenrod will sparkle in the open fields. In addition to the more popular game species, the nature watcher might get glimpses of the river otter, several snakes, of which the copperhead and timber rattler are the only poisonous ones, several turtles, beaver, foxes, raccoon, opossum, and even an occasional bobcat. Exploring any of the small streams might turn up a variety of salamanders, crayfish, and frogs. Butterflies are everywhere, with several dozen different species.

All of the trails and service roads make fine bridle trails for those who want to transport their favorite mounts to the wildlife management area and spend some time riding. If the road or trail is gated, simply ride around the gate. The gates are there to discourage entrance by motorized vehicles, which are allowed only when the gates are open—usually during the hunting seasons.

This is one of several wildlife management areas that have archery and rifle ranges.

The C. F. Phelps Wildlife Management Area is truly an oasis in an area fast being claimed by housing developments and industrial progress.

Chickahominy Wildlife Management Area

Supervising Office: Department of Game and Inland Fisheries
5806 Mooretown Road
Williamsburg, VA 23188
Telephone 757-253-4180
Location: Charles City County
Elevation: 25 to 50 feet

This 5,217-acre flatlands wildlife management area is located in the James River plantation country where large blocks of public land are at a premium. It is entirely within Charles City County. It offers public access to the Chickahominy River, a major tributary of the James River, and to Morris Creek, a winding tributary of the Chickahominy River. Morris Creek serves as the boundary along much of the southern portion of the wildlife management area. The larger Chickahominy River serves as its eastern boundary. Virginia Secondary Route 623 serves as its western border, though small patches of private land indent this border of the public land. Near Rustic one small tract south of Morris Creek is separated from the major part of the wildlife management area. A pair of trails in this small tract lead to the upper reaches of Morris Creek. One of the trails is gated, but the other is not. Only motorized vehicles are prohibited from passing around the gates. Cyclists, hikers, and horseback riders can bypass the closed gates. Several parking areas along Route 623 serve as trailheads for trails that lead deep into the area.

This is the only wildlife management area in the coastal plains that, despite its many acres of marshes, is made up mostly of woodlands. Mixed hardwood and pine forests cover most of the area. Even so, it is lowlands country with elevations ranging from 25 to 50 feet. It is managed primarily for upland game instead of wetland species. Located midway between Richmond, the state

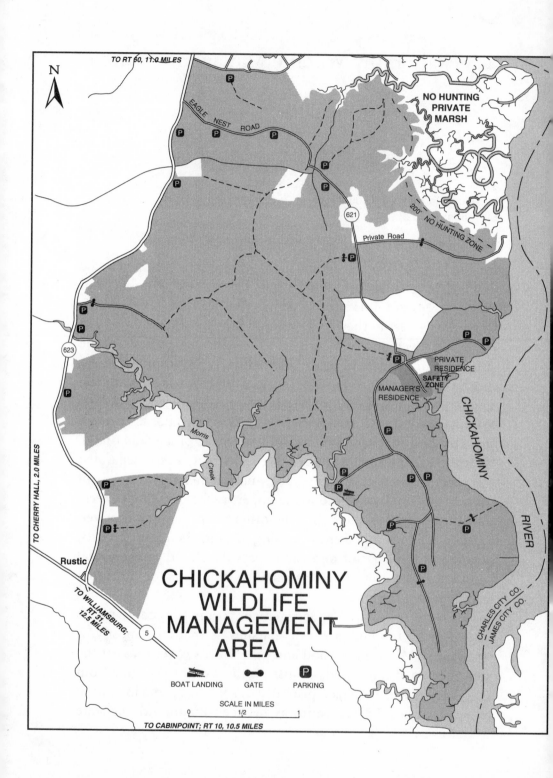

N

TO RT 60, 11.0 MILES

EAGLE NEST ROAD

621

Private Road

200' NO HUNTING ZONE

NO HUNTING
PRIVATE
MARSH

623

Morris
Creek

PRIVATE
RESIDENCE

SAFETY
ZONE

MANAGER'S
RESIDENCE

CHICKAHOMINY

RIVER

TO CHERRY HALL, 2.0 MILES

Rustic

TO WILLIAMSBURG;
RT 31
12.5 MILES

5

CHARLES CITY CO.
JAMES CITY CO.

CHICKAHOMINY
WILDLIFE
MANAGEMENT
AREA

BOAT LANDING   GATE   PARKING

SCALE IN MILES

0   1/2   1

TO CABINPOINT; RT 10, 10.5 MILES

capital, and the densely populated Hampton Roads area, it is convenient to two major population centers. The area is heavily forested, but a number of old fields that carry over from when the area was farmed dot the area. There are also several wildlife clearings in the vast lowlands forest. The eastern shoreline along the Chickahominy River is indented with small tidal creeks and marshy guts. Even though the area is managed primarily for upland game, the extensive wetlands attract ducks and other marsh and wetlands wildlife.

Although the marshes within the boundaries of the wildlife management area and on its side of the Chickahominy River and Morris Creek are public, those on the far sides of these unique streams are privately owned. There are also some tracts of private land deep within in the wildlife management area. Eagle Nest Road, Route 621, passes through several of them. Trails also lead through a number of private tracts in the northern part of the area. They are well marked. The area can be reached by boat from both the Chickahominy River and Morris Creek, but the major access is off Route 623. Several trails lead off this secondary road, two south of Morris Creek, one just north of it, and another just south of Eagle Nest Road, which leads deep into the wildlife management area.

Route 5, a Virginia By-Way south off Interstate 295, leads to the southern boundary of the wildlife management area at Rustic. At Rustic turn left on Route 623 to Eagle Nest Road. Or take the Providence Forge exit off Interstate 64 and follow Route 155 south. You will cross U.S. Highway 60 at Providence Forge, but continue to Route 614 where you turn left, continue to Route 615 and turn left again, continuing to Route 623 where you turn right. Watch for Route 621 or Eagle Nest Road and turn left. Eagle Nest Road, Route 621, leads deep into the area with side roads leading both left and right off it. One road in the vicinity of the manager's residence leads to the shore of the Chickahominy River. Here is a small beach where fishermen fish from the bank. This is not a formal boat-launching ramp, but canoes and johnboats can be launched here. Several hundred yards beyond this turnoff, another road leads to the shores of Morris Creek and a boat-launching ramp. Follow the "Boat Ramp" signs. From the Williamsburg area, take Route 5 north to Rustic.

The combination of roads and trails leads to just about every corner of the wildlife management area. They are an open invitation to backpackers. Several lead to the water's edge on the Chickahominy River and Morris Creek and others to the headwaters of tidal creeks. With elevations just a few feet above sea level, hiking is easy, and the forests are relatively open for anyone who wants to backpack under wilderness conditions. A number of parking areas along Route 623 can serve as trailheads. Some mark the beginning of trails, but others are for the convenience of those who want to take off in the untracked wilderness. Some of the trails and roads are gated, but this does not block backpackers. They can simply go around the barriers. Another possibility is to go by boat to a secluded shoreline or tidal creek, secure the boat safely ashore, and hike from there. A compass should be in every backpacker's possession — and in warm weather don't forget insect repellent. The trails are mowed periodically for the benefit of wildlife.

Although motorized vehicles are not allowed off the main roads, bicycles are permitted. Like the hikers, bicyclists can go around barriers and ride as long as they desire. This is reasonably level country, and biking along the roads and trails can be relaxing and fun. Bicycles are nearly noiseless, and they provide an opportunity to view a variety of wildlife.

A great variety of birds can be seen in this area, depending upon the season. Inland are the usual forest inhabitants, and the wildlife clearings attract birds that nest and feed on the ground. Endangered or threatened species include the bald eagle, peregrine falcon, redbreast nuthatch, barn owl, and several wrens. More common are birds such as the American bittern, bluebird, bunting, cardinal, catbird, Carolina chickadee, American goldfinch, grackle, several hawks including the Cooper's and red-tailed, blue jay, purple martin, robin, several sparrows, several thrushes, a number of warblers, and several woodpeckers including the pileated and red-headed. The marshes and tidal creeks are an entirely different attraction. Here you can expect to see a variety of shorebirds as well as ducks and other migrating wetlands critters. Among them are the coot, egret, several gulls, kingfisher, osprey, several rails and sandpipers, and tern. A chance to sight bald eagles and ospreys is always a possibility. Take a canoe and move quietly up some of the tidal creeks or through cuts in the marshlands to enjoy the marsh wildlife.

Together the Chickahominy River and Morris Creek offer almost unlimited boating and canoeing opportunities. The concrete launching ramp on Morris Creek will accommodate sizable boats, and it's an area reasonably protected from the wind. Getting on and off the water should not be a problem. Exploring the tidal creeks and marshes in a canoe can be a real joy. For those who enjoy sailing, both Morris Creek and the larger Chickahominy River offer plenty of open water. Check the launching ramp thoroughly before launching anything other than a canoe or small boat—including small sailboats. You will want to satisfy yourself that it will handle a larger boat. There is plenty of room for parking automobiles at the Morris Creek launching area.

The fishing opportunities are almost unlimited with the Chickahominy River and Morris Creek bordering the wildlife management area and the big James River not too far away by boat. Morris Creek offers excellent largemouth bass and crappie fishing. Fishing for blue, channel, and white catfish can be good. Bank fishermen take them from the small beach at the end of the road beyond the manager's residence. The many small tributaries of Morris Creek and those that enter the Chickahominy River also produce bass, crappie, and the various catfish. Also expect to catch some bluegills and other members of the panfish family. The boat-launching ramp on Morris Creek offers the possibility of bank fishing. There is also a railed pier here that can be used for fishing but remember that those using the ramp for launching their boats get first choice. In addition to the species already mentioned, the Chickahominy River offers both white and yellow perch and striped bass. A boat powered by a small outboard motor is extremely handy for moving about the creeks and river. We are talking about reasonably big water, and the motor will save fishing time. The small creeks that either originate or run through the area offer fishing possibilities for chain pickerel, always an interesting fish to go after. A number of beaver ponds on the small creeks attract and hold chain pickerel and other creek fish.

Like all wildlife management areas, Chickahominy is managed primarily for hunting. Deer hunters work it hard, but even so there is a healthy population of white-tailed deer. Charles City is a shotgun-only county, a regulation that diminishes its attractiveness to some hunters, but muzzle-loading rifles are legal. Although deer are the primary game hunted, there is also good hunting for turkeys. Squirrels are abundant in most years, and other upland game includes doves, rabbits, and a few quail. Deer hunting is limited to bucks only. Agricultural crops beneficial to wildlife are planted on an annual basis. Timber is sold periodically to create wildlife clearings and provide edge cover for quail and rabbits. Waterfowl hunting can be good in the vast marshes along the Chickahominy River and Morris Creek. Although stationary blinds are prohibited, floating blinds, a well-camouflaged boat for example, are allowed. Waterfowl hunting from the shore is also allowed, but hunters must maintain a distance of 500 yards between each other. Those ponds far up the small creeks created by the always busy beaver also offer a unique kind of duck hunting, particularly for the colorful little wood duck. And don't overlook the possibility of hunting for the little sora rail in the marshes. The little freshwater rail is abundant in some years and less so in others, but some are always there. The usual hunting method is to pole a boat through the marshes with the gunner in the bow ready to take the birds when they flush ahead of the boat.

Camping possibilities are somewhat limited in the area unless you can locate a wildlife clearing—which should not be difficult. One good possibility is to roam the shoreline in a boat and find a suitable waterfront site. Locating a wooded campsite is a possibility, but mosquitoes can be a problem during the warmer months that appeal to most campers. A favorite camping area is a stand of open pines on the shores of the Chickahominy River. It is reached by turning left off Route 621 just before you reach the manager's residence. Camping tastes vary, but a trip after the first frost when the mosquitoes and ticks are gone might well be the best choice. The fall and winter weather is more favorable in this part of the state than in the high country to the west. Given over 5,000 acres of public land where camping is allowed up to two weeks, the experienced camper should be able to find some appealing place. This is primitive camping, of course: no running water, electricity, or other frills.

For those who like to shoulder a day pack and head out for a few hours, the Chickahominy Wildlife Management Area offers a good choice of possibilities. If you would like to hike to the river's edge, several trails and roads offer this option. Or maybe you would like to take a hike through the woods. For such outings many roads and lead to the very heart of the wildlife management area. For comfort take along some insect repellent, particularly during the warmer months. It is unnecessary after the first killing frost in the fall. Take along a good compass to help you stay oriented.

No motorized vehicles are allowed on the trails, but bicycles are a possibility for those who prefer biking to hiking. Gated trails, while off-limits to motorized vehicles, are not barred to cyclists.

There are a number of ways to enjoy the rich variety of wildlife on this wildlife management area. One is to walk the trails slowly and quietly or ride a bike the same way. Use the deer hunter's technique of moving as quietly as possible, then stopping to listen and look. It is during the stops between the moves that you are most likely to spot wildlife. That wildlife could take the form of any of the game animals and birds mentioned above or the likes of ospreys, eagles, hawks, or even an owl that happens to venture forth in the daytime. Visit those beaver ponds. Approach them slowly, and you might get a chance to view the busy critters at work. The railed dock at the boat-launching area is a good point from which to study the marshes across the river with binoculars. Be patient and watch the marsh life at work. Another good approach is to slip a canoe in the water and paddle slowly up one of the several tidal creeks. Forests, marshes, and wetlands are a winning combination when it comes to enjoying nature. Possible sightings include several frogs such as the green and pickerel, red-spotted newt, a great variety of salamanders, several snakes, of which only the copperhead is poisonous, a variety of turtles, and a great variety of butterflies. Interesting flowers and shrubs include buttercups, dogwood, mountain laurel, and redbud, all of which bloom in April and May, and holly, which produces beautiful red berries in the winter. Foxtail and ragweed also add a touch of color, and goldenrod sparkles beneath the late summer and autumn sun.

Trails that lead to forest clearings might be the best place to plan a picnic, or you can take one of the roads to the river's edge. Insects including mosquitoes and ticks can be a problem in the warmer months. Wait until the first killing frost, choose an Indian summer autumn day, and picnicking can be a joy. You might even want to launch a boat or canoe and move slowly along the shoreline until you find a spot that delights you.

Those same trails and roads that appeal to backpackers, bikers, or hikers also provide good bridle trails for those who like to climb into the saddle for a ride through a wilderness area. Keep your party small. Organized rides involving a large number of riders are discouraged.

Popular in this area are archery and rifle ranges. Signs on the entrance road lead to them.

Game Farm Marsh
Wildlife Management Area

Supervising Office: Department of Game and Inland Fisheries
5806 Mooretown Road
Williamsburg, VA 23188
Telephone 757-253-4180
Location: New Kent County
Elevation: Lake level. All under water.

Marshes and more marshes might best describe the Game Farm Marsh Wildlife Management Area in New Kent County. At only 429 acres it is by far the smallest wildlife management area in Virginia, but every acre is valuable as a parcel of wetland. Its value to wildlife is immeasurable. Lands belonging to the Virginia Division of Forestry form its northern border, and to the south the headwaters of Chickahominy Lake serve as its border. Two creeks in the eastern section of the wildlife management area provide limited boat access to the interior. Otherwise the area is generally inaccessible. Cypress forests and water stained by tannic acid add to the area's charm. Chickahominy Lake is part of the water supply system for the city of Newport News.

To reach this wildlife management area, take U.S. 60 east from Richmond or west from Williamsburg. It is located midway between Providence Forge and Walkers Dam and approximately two miles up Chickahominy Lake from the dam. Access to the area is by boat only. No roads lead to the area or into it. Private boats can be launched at several commercial boat ramps along the northern shores of Chickahominy Lake. Rental boats and motors are also available at these launching areas. Another possibility is to launch a canoe or light boat on the Chickahominy River approximately three-quarters of a mile west of the area, where Route 155 crosses the river. There is an informal launching area north of the river on

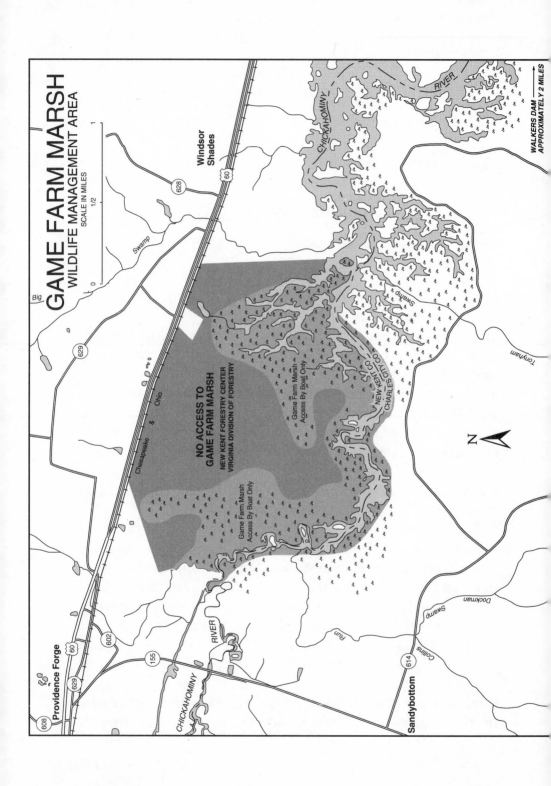

GAME FARM MARSH
WILDLIFE MANAGEMENT AREA

SCALE IN MILES

0   1/2   1

Big

Swamp

Windsor
Shades

628

60

629

Chesapeake   &   Ohio

NO ACCESS TO
GAME FARM MARSH

NEW KENT FORESTRY CENTER
VIRGINIA DIVISION OF FORESTRY

Game Farm Marsh
Access By Boat Only

Game Farm Marsh
Access By Boat Only

CHICKAHOMINY

RIVER

Swamp

NEW KENT CO.
CHARLES CITY CO.

Tonyham

N

Providence Forge

608   629   60   155   602

CHICKAHOMINY   RIVER

Run

Collins

614   Sandybottom

Dockman   Swamp

WALKERS DAM
APPROXIMATELY 2 MILES

the downriver side of the highway, but it is on private land so the permission of the landowner is needed. Route 155 can be reached off Interstate 64 or U.S. Highway 60 at Providence Forge.

This wildlife management area is not one for backpacking, bicycling, camping, hiking, horseback riding, or picnicking—unless you want to picnic from your boat. It can, however, be a real joy for bird-watching. At the proper season it is one of the best areas in eastern Virginia to watch a great variety of birds. This is best done by boat or canoe. Dress in camouflage, conceal your boat as much as possible, and wait or paddle softly hugging the shores of the many guts and small coves along the southern side of the wildlife management area. Expect to see herons, ospreys, and wood ducks. Endangered or threatened species include the bald eagle, black rail, Henslow's sparrow, several terns, hermit thrush, and winter wren. More common are the red-winged blackbird, bluebird, bunting, cardinal, egrets, flicker, several gulls and hawks, blue jay, junco, oriole, rail, robin, sandpiper, and a number of sparrows, warblers, and woodpeckers.

The water is generally very shallow in this area, clogged with submerged vegetation and covered by duckweed during the warmer months. This makes the use of an outboard motor difficult. Once you reach the area, the best approach is to tilt your motor and move by oars, paddle, or a long pole. Even Chickahominy Lake is tough on outboard motors during the warm months. Travel by canoe might be the best approach. Launch at an up-lake ramp or at the Route 155 bridge, and the distance to the wildlife management area is not great.

Chickahominy Lake is one of eastern Virginia's richest fishing holes. The lake forms the southern border of the wildlife management area. It is noted for its largemouth bass and chain pickerel fishing. Some real trophies come out of the 1,500-acre lake every fishing season. It also holds some big rough fish such as bowfin and gar as well as the likes of striped bass, catfish, crappie, white and yellow perch, northern pike, and sunfish. Bait and other fishing needs are available at the commercial boat-launching ramps along the northern shores of the lake.

Waterfowl hunting is excellent on this wetlands wildlife management area. The variety of ducks and geese using this area is rich, but the colorful little wood duck is by far the most abundant. The construction of permanent blinds is illegal, so most hunters resort to floating blinds. A roomy marsh-green johnboat rigged with camouflage netting to conceal the hunter makes an effective and comfortable blind. Some of the water is shallow enough to wade. That offers the possibility of concealing the boat, pulling on waders, and then concealing yourself among the cypress trees. This technique is not unlike the duck hunting in the flooded oaks of Arkansas, a hunting style that has won national acclaim.

As is true of most marshes and wetlands, the variety of wildlife is great—and interesting. In the cypress forests and tannic-stained water there are beavers, herons, ospreys, and wood ducks for the nature lover to enjoy. Other possible sightings include otters, a wide variety of frogs and turtles, snakes including the poisonous copperhead, and many butterflies. Viewing has to be done by boat or canoe, of course, and camouflage and quiet paddling will produce the best results. The area is covered with water lilies that bloom during the warm months, and the submerged cypress forests are interesting.

This is one of the few wildlife management areas on which trapping is not allowed.

At only 429 acres, the Game Farm Marsh Wildlife Management Area is small, a drop in the bucket in a system that includes 180,000 acres of wild lands, but its uniqueness makes it one of the most interesting in the statewide system.

G. Richard Thompson
Wildlife Management Area

Supervising Office: Department of Game and Inland Fisheries
1320 Belman Road
Fredericksburg, VA 22401
Telephone 540-899-4169
Location: Clarke, Fauquier, and Warren Counties
Elevation: 700 to 2,200 feet

The G. Richard Thompson Wildlife Management Area offers a near-wilderness experience convenient to the densely populated Washington, D.C., area better known as Northern Virginia. Its 4,160 acres along the rugged eastern slopes of the Blue Ridge Mountains can be a haven for those who want to escape for a day or a week or so from the hustle and bustle of life in the shadow of the nation's capital. Reaching its interior is possible mostly by foot, although bicycles and horses can be used to provide transportation along the miles of trails. The Appalachian Trail runs the length of the wildlife management area, entering near its southwestern corner and exiting from the Davenport tract at its northeastern corner.

The wildlife management area is almost totally in Fauquier County, but it backs up against sections of Clarke and Warren Counties, and small portions of the area dip into those counties. Virginia Secondary Route 638 running northeast serves as the northwestern border of the area, and the general boundary between the counties—except where small parcels cross the border. Beginning at a lower elevation along Route 688, the wildlife management area rises in a series of steep inclines and benches to the crest of the Blue Ridge Mountains. Elevations range from 700 feet to 2,200. "Some of it is straight up," said Bob Henson, area manager. Predominantly covered by hardwood forests, it has some

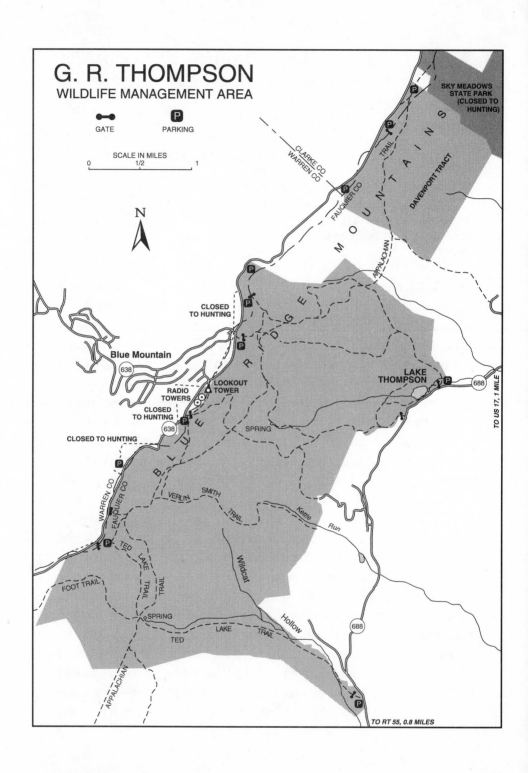

G. R. THOMPSON
WILDLIFE MANAGEMENT AREA

GATE

PARKING

SCALE IN MILES
0   1/2   1

N

SKY MEADOWS
STATE PARK
(CLOSED TO
HUNTING)

CLARKE CO
WARREN CO

FAUQUIER CO

DAVENPORT TRACT

M O U N T A I N S

APPALACHIAN

CLOSED
TO HUNTING

Blue Mountain
638

LAKE
THOMPSON
688

B L U E   R I D G E

LOOKOUT
TOWER

RADIO
TOWERS

CLOSED
TO HUNTING
638

SPRING

TO US 17, 1 MILE

CLOSED TO HUNTING

WARREN CO
FAUQUIER CO

VERLIN

SMITH   TRAIL

Kettle   Run

TED

LAKE

TRAIL

Wildcat

FOOT TRAIL

SPRING

Hollow

688

TED   LAKE   TRAIL

APPALACHIAN

TO RT 55, 0.8 MILES

open land at the lower elevations and at the top of the Davenport tract. Terraced slopes at the lower elevations remain as symbols of long-ago fruit orchards. Other terrain features include rock out-croppings, spring seeps, and several small streams including Kettle Run and the major feeder stream for Lake Thompson, a ten-acre trout lake located just off Route 688. The Davenport tract, sepa-rate from the main tract, backs up against Sky Meadows State Park.

The upper reaches of the wildlife management area can be reached from Route 55 at the hamlet of Linden. From Route 55 fol-low Route 638. Several parking areas along this route provide ac-cess to trails leading deep into the wildlife management area. For the lower portion, exit Interstate Highway 66 at Markham and take Route 688 north to various parking areas. Or exit Route 17 at Paris and take Route 688 south.

With approximately seven miles of the Appalachian Trail run-ning through this wildlife management area, it holds a lot of ap-peal to backpackers. The trail also links the main section of the wildlife management area with the Davenport tract by crossing a block of private land between the two. In addition to the Ap-palachian Trail, a number of other trails lead to just about all parts of the wildlife management area. Many cross the area. Ted Lake Trail, for example, connects with the Foot Trail to provide a con-tinuous trail leading from a parking area off Route 688 in the far southeastern corner to a parking area off Route 638 on the far side of the wildlife management area. Another trail forms near Lake Thompson and crosses the area to Route 638. It also has several loops that can be used to reach other parts of the area. Verlin Smith Trail follows Kettle Run for awhile to connect with the Ap-palachian Trail. The system of trails allow backpackers to plan a variety of trips. Because several trails traverse the area from one side to another, a pair of hikers with two automobiles can park one at a parking area on one edge of the area, drive to the other edge, and hike through. This way they can choose to hike down the mountain if they desire, an easier hike, or up the mountain.

Several of the trails lead to spring seeps. One is at the headwaters of the stream feeding into Lake Thompson, and the other is just off the Appalachian Trail, at the intersection of Ted Lake Trail and the Appalachian Trail. Ted Lake Trail, which runs from Route 688 to top out on Route 638, leads through a 500-acre wildflower refuge. Of course there is nothing to prohibit a backpacker from shouldering a pack and striking out across the untracked wilderness—with a good compass to keep him oriented.

Although motorized vehicles are not allowed on the trails, most of the trails can be traveled by bicycles. Some of these trails are steep in places, however, and most cyclists probably will want to dismount and walk their bikes up the steeper grades. This is mountain country, the eastern slopes of the Blue Ridge Mountains, and flat country is limited.

The same trails used by backpackers will serve bird-watchers as well. There are a total of eleven parking areas along the two secondary routes. Trails from these parking areas lead to all parts of the wildlife management area. Likely birding locations include the two springs, one feeding the stream to Lake Thompson and the other at the intersection of the Appalachian and Ted Lake Trails. The little stream originating at the latter spring follows Ted Lake Trail to a parking area off Secondary Route 688. Part of Verlin Smith Trail follows Kettle Run. All of these little stream valleys should offer opportunities to watch birds of various kinds. Birds are also attracted to the shores of Lake Thompson. Depending upon the migration patterns, the area is rich in a variety of birds. Many such as the bald eagle, peregrine falcon, night heron, barn owl, upland sandpiper, magnolia warbler, and Appalachian and winter wrens, as well as the Indiana bat, are either endangered or threatened, offering the possibility of sighting some of these somewhat rare creatures. Much more common are the bittern, blackbird, bluebird, bobolink, bunting, cardinal, chickadee, finch, flicker, goldfinch, grackle, grosbeak, a half-dozen hawks, heron, blue jay, junco, killdeer, lark, meadowlark, oriole, a trio of owls, robin, a dozen different sparrows, starling, swallow, thrasher, thrush, several vireos, over a dozen warblers, whippoorwill, a half-dozen woodpeckers, and both the Carolina and house wrens, as well as a half-dozen bats.

There are limited boating and canoeing opportunities in this wildlife management area. Lake Thompson is a possibility, but getting a canoe or boat into the water first means carrying it from the parking area up the trail to the lake. There is no formal launching ramp on the lake.

Lake Thompson is designated trout water, meaning that it is stocked with hatchery-reared trout. The lake is Category B trout water, meaning it is stocked once in November–December, again in the January–February period, once in March, and twice during the April–May period. Anglers fishing the lake need a trout license in addition to the basic state fishing license. There is also fishing for smallmouth bass, channel catfish, and redear sunfish, better known as shellcrackers. None of the small streams supports a native trout population, because they all tend to dry up during the warmer months of the year.

Although this wildlife management area receives heavy hunting pressure because of its proximity to the densely populated Washington, D.C., metropolitan area, it offers good hunting for both big game and small. The deer populations have increased significantly in surrounding counties, and the wildlife management area serves as a refuge for the animals when the hunting pressure in the counties gets heavy. There are many remote parts of the area that are difficult to hunt, and this is likely where the critters hole up during the deer hunting season. In addition to deer, a good population of turkeys provides hunting during the fall and spring seasons. Squirrels and grouse are the most abundant small game, but there is also hunting for woodcocks along the brushy streams. There is also a fair population of rabbits. The development and maintenance of wildlife clearings foster game populations, and old homesites, particularly old apple orchards, provide a diversity of habitat. The gypsy moth infestation has been a problem also a blessing. It killed oaks that provided acorns for deer, rels, and turkeys, but their demise encouraged low-growing vegetation that provides dense ground cover and browse for deer. Fortunately there are still stands of hickory, oak, ash, and other hardwoods that provide good mast as well as den trees. Selective logging and the daylighting of several miles of trails have tended to open up the forest canopy. The wildlife management offers hunting in a part of the state where public hunting land is scarce. Hunters might sight black bears occasionally, but there is no open season on bears in Fauquier County or in Clarke. Although there is a bear season in Warren, very little of the wildlife management area is in that county.

Only primitive camping is available, and finding an ideal site might take a little time. Camping is not permitted in the parking areas or within 100 yards of the lake. Camping stays are limited to two weeks. Hikers can shoulder a day pack and enjoy miles of hiking trails. Of course there is the Appalachian Trail, accessible from Route 638 at several locations. It's easy to get on the Appalachian Trail, hike awhile, and then get off at another access point. Ted Lake Trail and Verlin Smith Trail both follow mountain streams for some of their length. There are through trails and looping trails that you can follow back to a parking area for short hikes.

The G. Richard Thompson Wildlife Management Area is particularly attractive for those who enjoy viewing nature. In addition to the deer, turkeys, and other game species plus a rich variety of songbirds, there are rich displays of wildflowers at the appropriate seasons. A 500-acre area has been designated as a wildflower refuge. This was prompted by the finding of nodding trilliums and other rare plants. Additionally the likes of bellwort, Dutchman's-breeches, jonquils, lady slippers, and wild orchids grace the forest floor with an unbelievable display of color. Ted Lake Trail winds through the area, reaching from Route 688 to Route 638. The flowering dogwoods, redbuds, mountain laurel, rhododendron, stands of mature hardwoods, and evergreens are also pleasing to the eye. Check out the little streams for salamanders and a variety of crayfish, frogs, mussels, newts, and peepers. In addition to poisonous copperheads and timber rattlers, there are another dozen nonpoisonous snakes, some very colorful. Box and snapping turtles are fairly common, but there are also painted and several other kinds of turtles. In season, butterflies are everywhere—over 80 different species.

It's hard to imagine a more pleasing place to enjoy a picnic lunch than in the 500-acre wildflower refuge. Another possibility is on the shores of sparkling Lake Thompson. Just don't interfere with the fishermen, if any happen to be there. Fishermen are most abundant during the trout-stocking periods. Or put your picnic in a day pack and hike to one of the mountain springs or seepages.

Horseback riding is permitted on the various trails, but large organized groups of riders are discouraged. A lone rider, a pair, a family, or several friends riding the trails on their favorite mounts do not present a problem.

Because of its proximity to a heavily populated metropolitan region, users of the G. Richard Thompson area can expect to come in contact with other outdoor lovers. Respect their right to be there. But ATVs (all-terrain vehicles) and shooting outside of the regular hunting seasons are both prohibited.

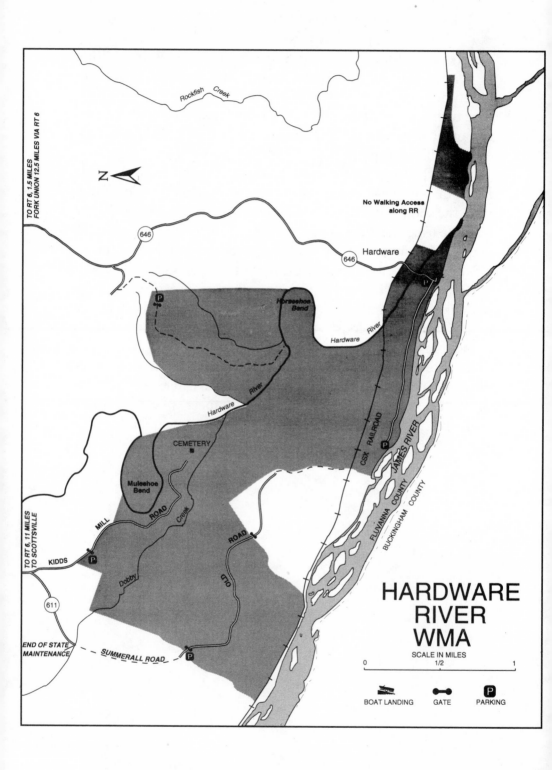

TO RT 6, 1.5 MILES
FORK UNION 12.5 MILES VIA RT 6

Rockfish Creek

N

No Walking Access
along RR

646

646   Hardware

Horseshoe
Bend

Hardware   River

Hardware   River

CEMETERY

Muleshoe
Bend

MILL   ROAD

CSX RAILROAD

JAMES RIVER

FLUVANNA COUNTY

BUCKINGHAM COUNTY

Creek

ROAD

OLD

KIDDS

Dobby

TO RT 6, 11 MILES
TO SCOTTSVILLE

611

END OF STATE
MAINTENANCE

SUMMERALL ROAD

HARDWARE RIVER WMA

SCALE IN MILES

0   1/2   1

BOAT LANDING   GATE   PARKING

Hardware River Wildlife Management Area

Supervising Office: Department of Game and Inland Fisheries
1320 Belman Road
Fredericksburg, VA 22401
Telephone 540-899-4169
Location: Fluvanna County
Elevation: 250 to 450 feet

Approximately three miles of river frontage with a concrete boat-launching ramp, a broad lowlands meadow, and beyond the meadow almost 1,000 acres of hardwood forests might best describe the Hardware River Wildlife Management Area in Fluvanna County. Across the island-studded James River is Buckingham County. The river serves as the boundary between the two counties. The islands are privately owned, and the landowner's permission is needed to explore them. The terrain of the area is gently rolling hill country typical of Fluvanna County. Elevations range from 250 feet at the James River's edge to 450 feet in the highlands. The lowland meadow is in the floodplain and completely inundated when the river runs at flood stage. Various oaks make up the hardwood forests, with a rich mixture of gum, hickory, and maple. At the higher elevations are some stands of pines that now occupy farmlands abandoned back in the 1930s. Giant sycamores and river birches are found in the lowlands and along the river.

The total acreage of the wildlife management area is 1,034 acres, most of which is in a single tract. A small outlying tract is found between the river and the CSX Railroad to the east. The river provides the only access to this small tract. The railroad, following the course of the river, serves as the southern boundary along the western portion of the main tract but runs between the uplands and the meadow lowlands in the central part. It then crosses the

Hardware River to form the northern boundary to a portion of this tract. The meandering Hardware River, for which the area is named, flows a southeast course through the area, forming a couple of horseshoe loops on its journey. It enters the James River at the eastern edge of the area. Before the area was purchased and a boat-launching ramp was built, anglers and hunters used the Hardware to enter the James River. Much smaller Dobby Creek flows into the northwest corner of the area and enters the Hardware River near the center of the wildlife management area. Two jeep roads enter the area at the northwestern corner, both off Route 611. One, known as Kidds Mill Road, leads to an old family cemetery. The other, known as Old Road, passes through the area and then through a tract of private land. At the far end of the road a trail skirts the area leading to the railroad. A trail also runs from Route 646 to the Hardware River. Another road, which is ungated, leads off Route 646 at the boat-launching ramp near the eastern edge of the area and runs west parallel to the James River. All of the trails are gated at the entrances to the area, and parking space is provided for those who want to hike or ride bicycles into the area. Motorized vehicles are not permitted on gated trails, but hikers, bicyclists, and those on horseback can skirt the gates and use the trails.

The wildlife management area is reached by Routes 611 and 646 off Route 6 between Fork Union and Scottsville. Department of Game and Inland Fisheries Highway signs mark the routes. Route 646 leads to the boat ramp and the river's edge.

Backpackers won't find long trails in this wildlife management area, but there are several possibilities for backpacking trips. One is to take the road near the boat-launching ramp and head west along the James River. This road dead-ends after approximately a mile, as is true of most of the trails. On them you return to the trailhead by the same route. Another possibility is to take the Kidds Mill road to the old family cemetery, take a compass reading, and go due east for several hundred yards until you hit the

Hardware River. You can then follow the river downstream to the launching ramp at the end of Route 646, a hike of approximately three miles. The trail off Route 646 at the northeast corner of the wildlife management area also leads to the Hardware River. The Summerall Road off Route 611 becomes the Old Road at the western edge of the wildlife management area and leads through a parcel of private land to reenter the area. It ends at the CSX railroad near the river, and a short hike from the railroad will take you to the wildlife management area road along the James River. Because this is rolling hill country, hiking is relatively easy. Experienced backpackers might prefer to take a compass reading at the gated entrance to the Kidds Mill Road and strike out across country to the boat ramp on the James River.

The same trails that serve backpackers also will appeal to bicyclists, but it's mostly a ride to the end of a road or trail and then heading back over the same route. There are no roads or trails that lead completely through the area or that make a loop returning you to the gated entrance.

Approximately 1,000 acres of hardwood and pine forests here have many birds. The hardwoods with a wider variety of food and habitat are likely to appeal to a greater number of species. The James River, of course, attracts various kinds of birds including waterfowl and shorebirds. An all-day canoe trip from the boat ramp downstream to the Department of Game and Inland Fisheries river access and launching ramp at Bremo Bluff on U.S. Route 15 offers a excellent opportunity to watch a variety of birds including the colorful little wood duck and other waterfowl. A canoe trip on the Hardware River also can present a view of many birds. Some canoeists put in at the Route 6 bridge and float through to the boat-launching ramp. The endangered or threatened species of birds using this area are considerably fewer than found on most wildlife management areas, but they include the brown creeper, purple finch, red-breasted nuthatch, barn owl, migrant shrike, hermit thrush, cerulean and magnolia warblers, and winter wren. The combination of the hardwood and pine forest and river bottomland offers good habitat for the more common cardinal, catbird, chickadee, crossbill, crow, finch, flicker, goldfinch, grackle, grosbeak, several hawks, heron, blue jay, junco, killdeer, lark, purple martin, meadowlark, mockingbird, nuthatch, oriole, osprey, several owls, rails, robin, sandpiper, a number of sparrows, barn swallow, tern, several vireos, a great number of warblers, whippoorwill, pileated, red-bellied, and red-headed woodpeckers, and wren, as well as a number of bats.

The boat-launching ramp probably draws more people to this wildlife management area than any other attraction. The James River is popular among canoeists. There is limited white water, but the major attraction is that it is a fast-flowing river that moves you along with a minimum of paddling. Navigating the many stretches of fast water appeals to many, though there are few rapids that challenge the experienced canoeist. The wildlife management area is a popular stopover for boaters traveling the James River. The Hardware River also appeals to canoeists. Some enter it far upstream, camp on a sandbar, and end their trip at the launching ramp.

The James River is noted for its excellent fishing for smallmouth bass, but its river mate, the yellowbreast sunfish, is even more abundant. There are also scattered muskies and walleyes. Native fish include catfish, fallfish, chain pickerel, and suckers. A few largemouth bass, bluegills, and crappies, escapees from farm ponds in the river basin, are usually present. The Hardware River offers much the same fishing, though you are more likely to catch pickerel in the Hardware than in the James. Some anglers launch their canoes at the Route 6 bridge where it crosses the Hardware and float downstream to the boat ramp area. The boat ramp is a popular launching area for a boat or canoe for an all-day fishing trip to Bremo downstream. It also serves as a take-out point for anglers entering the river upstream at the Scottsville public boat ramp. Many also fish from the banks of the two rivers.

Hunting is the major recreational pursuit here, as it is on most wildlife management areas, and good populations of white-tailed deer and turkeys provide exciting big-game hunting. The rich stands of oak and hickory trees are ideal for gray squirrels, and the hunting can be fair to excellent depending upon the abundance of acorns and other mast. When the mast crop is good, the squirrel hunting is excellent. Hunters also occasionally encounter grouse and woodcocks, possibly a covey of quail, and a few rabbits. Annual plantings in the lowlands along the river are designed to attract doves. The various roads and trails open up the interior of the area to hunting. Other wildlife includes the likes of beavers, foxes, mink, muskrat, opossums, and raccoon, game sought mostly by night hunters and trappers. Good populations of ducks and geese use the James River, and waterfowl hunting is popular.

As is true of most wildlife management areas, there are no formal campgrounds here, but primitive camping is permitted for up to two weeks at a time. Many set up along the river where the jeep road offers good access. The area is also popular as an overnight stay for campers traveling the river by boat or canoe. Campers are drawn to the river for a quick dip, but it should be noted that the river runs fast here, and ledges and drop-offs are common. Care should be exercised.

This wildlife management area is ideal for day hikes. Shoulder a day pack and make a day of it. Or if your time is limited, the short trails will consume only an hour or so. Hike along the river or through the hardwoods. Exercise your legs and breathe in some clean, fresh air.

In addition to game animals, there is a great variety of songbirds at different times of the year, and during the warm months such wildflowers as gentian, wild ginger, lady slipper, and squawroot are abundant. Wildlife plantings include sunflowers, which sparkle when in bloom. Late in the summer and in early autumn, goldenrod adds late-season color. The nature lover will find plenty of opportunities in this river wildlife management area. Walk slowly and quietly along the trails or find a high point from which to observe and sit quietly. Or canoe quietly near the banks of the Hardware or James River. Check out Dobby Creek for beavers and beaver flowages. The rare sighting of a river otter is a possibility. Check out the Hardware River and Dobby Creek for salamanders and various kinds of frogs. The copperhead is the only poisonous snake, but there are over a dozen species of nonpoisonous snakes. Turtles use both the Hardware River and the James. Some of the snappers are big. Butterflies are common in the river meadow, and coyotes are gradually moving into the wildlife management area. Bring along a good pair of binoculars. They are the secret to viewing nature close up.

The boat-launching area along the river is a good spot for a picnic. Bring along some folding chairs, spread a picnic, and enjoy all that the wildlife management area offers. If the area near the ramp is crowded, as it well could be on summer weekends, follow the jeep trail upstream along the river until you find a suitable site. Some may prefer to take one of the woodlands trails and find a spot in the acres of hardwood forest.

Those same jeep roads and trails described for bicyclists or hikers are also available to horseback riders. Unload your mount at a trailhead where there is ample parking space, skirt the gate, and enjoy a fine bridle trail.

Hunt, fish, canoe, camp on the river, swim, or enjoy nature and wildlife. There is a season for all on the Hardware River Wildlife Management Area.

James River Wildlife Management Area

Supervising Office: Department of Game and Inland Fisheries
910 Thomas Jefferson Road
Forest, VA 24551
Telephone 804-525-7522
Location: Nelson County
Elevation: 350 to 500 feet

Access to the James River and possibly the best dove hunting found on any of the twenty-nine wildlife management areas across Virginia might best describe the James River Wildlife Management Area in Nelson County. This is Blue Ridge Mountains foothills country, most of it hills that are clothed in hardwood forests of oak and hickory. Some once-open fields have since been claimed by stands of Virginia pine. But of its 1,213 acres, approximately 200 acres remain open, land that for many years before its purchase by the Department of Game and Inland Fisheries was crop and pasture land. These lands were once part of one of the many estates that flourished along the James River. A centuries-old cemetery near the entrance off Route 743 to the wildlife management area serves as a symbol of long-ago life along the James River. A concrete boat ramp and a parking space for automobiles and trailers get heavy use during the warmer months and also by duck hunters and winter anglers. Approximately a mile of the area fronts on the James River. A very narrow strip of wildlife management area land lies between the southern extreme of the area and the James River. There are several islands in this stretch of the river, but they are privately owned and accessible only with the permission of the owner. Across the river is Buckingham County. The James River serves as a boundary between Buckingham and Nelson Counties.

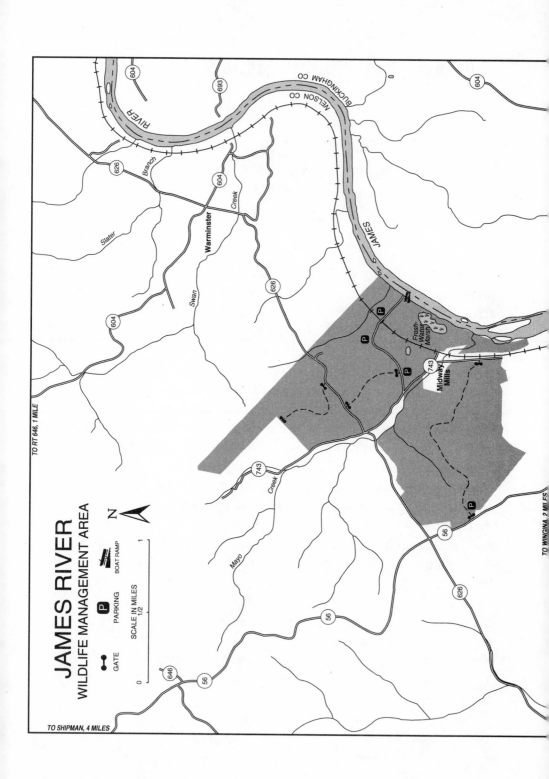

JAMES RIVER
WILDLIFE MANAGEMENT AREA

GATE

P PARKING

BOAT RAMP

SCALE IN MILES

0   1/2   1

N

TO RT 646, 1 MILE

TO SHIPMAN, 4 MILES

TO WINGINA, 2 MILES

NELSON CO
BUCKINGHAM CO

RIVER

JAMES

JAMES

Fresh-Water Marsh

Midway Mills

Slater

Branch

Warminster

Swan

Creek

Mayo

Creek

743

604

604

626

693

604

604

626

626

743

743

56

56

626

646

56

56

Though hilly country, this is not high country. Elevations range from 350 feet at the river to 500 feet in the hills. Gently rolling might best describe the hills back from the river bottomlands. The lowlands are managed for doves and other game, and there is a six-acre freshwater marsh just back from the river that is managed for waterfowl. Management consists primarily of drawing the water down during the growing season to encourage the growth of plant life. This provides food for waterfowl for the rest of the year. There is also a small one-acre freshwater pond near the entrance to the wildlife management area off Route 743. Management of the open fields includes prescribed burning, hedgerows, disking, and annual and perennial planting of wildlife food patches. There is limited vehicular access to the area. Route 56 skirts the western edge, Route 626 skirts the southwestern corner and passes through the area, and Route 743 runs through the area to the railroad track and then follows the railroad south for a short distance and dead-ends. A wildlife management area road from the entrance off Route 743 runs through the open fields to the boat-launching area.

The wildlife management area is probably best reached by Route 56 from Lovingston—approximately fifteen miles. Follow the wildlife management area signs once you get near the area. Take Route 626 left off Route 56, then right on Route 743, which will pass the entrance to the wildlife management area. From the south take Route 56 out of Buckingham Court House, cross the James River at Wingina, and turn right on Route 626.

Several trails could provide limited backpacking outings for those who enjoy this form of healthy outdoor recreation. None is long, so we are not talking about a real wilderness experience. One trail leads off Route 56 where it skirts the southwestern corner of the wildlife management area. It is gated there. A through trail, it exits onto Route 743 near the CSX railroad. It is not a long trip, a little over a mile at the most. Two other even shorter trails are approximately a half mile long each. Both lead off Route 626. One runs south to exit onto the wildlife management area road to the boat ramp, and the other goes northwest to exit at the edge of the wildlife management area. Both are gated at each end. This eliminates travel by motorized vehicles but not backpackers, who simply walk around the gates. Backpacking is not a strenuous undertaking on this wildlife management area, but the trails do lead through hardwood forests that offer opportunities to enjoy nature and wildlife. Backpackers have the option of hiking the length of these trails and then returning by the same route or arranging for a pickup at the end of the trail.

This wildlife management area, like all in the state, is open to bicyclists but not to motorized ATVs (all-terrain vehicles) or motorbikes. The slopes are gentle, and riding is not difficult. Even the gated trails are open to bicyclists. They simply go around the gates and proceed. The same trails used by backpackers are open to bicyclists. So is the wildlife management area road from the entrance to the boat-launching ramp on the James River.

Bird-watchers have a variety of options. They can hike the trails and pause frequently to watch the wildlife around them. They can also take a concealed spot near the six-acre freshwater marsh or the one-acre pond. Another possibility is to set up near the river and watch ducks and other birds that travel and use the river. Probably the most productive of the various bird-watching options is the freshwater marsh. Ideally the watcher should set up a simple blind. Camouflage netting that can be used to assemble a blind might be the best choice. Or simply using what natural concealment that is available might work. Dress in camouflage. Blinds or stands must be removed when leaving the area; no permanent structures are allowed.

Several birds classified as endangered or threatened use the area. Among them are the brown creeper, peregrine falcon, purple finch, red-breasted nuthatch, barn owl, hermit thrush, cerulean and magnolia warblers, and winter wren. The area offers birdwatchers the opportunity to glimpse these somewhat rare birds. More common are birds such as the red-winged blackbird, east-

ern bluebird, snow bunting, cardinal, catbird, Carolina chickadee, white-winged crossbill, flicker, several flycatchers, goldfinch, grebe, several grosbeaks, a half-dozen hawks including the
Cooper's, red-shouldered, red-tailed, and sharp-shinned hawks,
great blue and green herons, blue jay, junco, killdeer, kingfisher,
lark, meadowlark, mockingbird, oriole, osprey, great horned owl,
king and yellow rails, raven, robin, sandpiper, a number of sparrows, starling, a quartet of swallows, wood thrush, several vireos,
a number of warblers, whippoorwill, downy, pileated, and red-
headed woodpeckers, and Carolina and house wrens.

The boat-launching ramp could well be the most popular facility on the wildlife management area. Boaters or canoeists can
launch upstream at the Wingina Department of Game and Inland
Fisheries ramp and take out at the James River Wildlife Management Area, or they can launch at the James River area and take out
downstream at department access points at Howardsville, Scottsville, or others downstream, depending upon how long they want
to stay on the river.

The section of the James River that skirts the wildlife management area is one of the best in the river for smallmouth bass. It's a
favorite stretch for floating the river and fishing. In addition to
smallmouth bass, for which the James River is noted, there is
an abundant population of yellowbreast sunfish, a hard-hitting,
spunky little sunfish that is an excellent table fish. Some anglers
routinely release their bass and keep the sunfish for the table. The
river also offers good fishing for channel catfish and an occasional
musky or walleye. The one-acre pond holds a rich population of
bluegills and other sunfish. A path or trail off the road to the boat-
launching ramp leads to the pond. It's a short walk. A light boat or
canoe can be carried the short distance without a problem.

The wildlife management area with approximately 200 acres
of open land, much of which is planted in sunflowers or other
vegetation to attract the birds, is probably the best of the wildlife
management areas for dove hunting. As is true of most public

dove-hunting lands, the shooting is limited to Saturday and Wednesday afternoons for the September season. This gives the birds a rest; otherwise they might stop using the area. The area also offers limited deer and turkey hunting, and small-game possibilities include quail, rabbits, and squirrels. Night hunters will find a good raccoon population. The waterfowl hunting can be good at the freshwater marsh and on the James River proper. A jump-shooting trip from Wingina downstream to the wildlife management area could be productive for mallard, wood ducks, and other species that use the river. The small one-acre pond might also produce some ducks. There are also good populations of Canada geese in the general area. They too might use the open fields for feeding, particularly on winter wheat or other plantings.

Primitive camping is allowed throughout the area. One popular spot is the grassy area at the entrance to the wildlife management area. Hunters use this area during the hunting seasons. There are no facilities, however, and campers are on their own. Camping stays are limited to two weeks. Good campers, of course, wet down their campfires when striking camp. Camping is not allowed within 100 yards of the lake. Swimming in the James River appeals to many campers or picnickers, but care should be exercised. The James River is a beautiful stream, but it can also be dangerous because of ledges and drop-offs that mark its bottom. Experienced swimmers should have no problems, but inexperienced swimmers and small children should be kept under surveillance.

Nature lovers will find plenty to enjoy, be it birds, wildflowers, animals, or just the charm of a mature hardwood forest. In addition to bird-watching, the game animals can also be interesting, particularly in the spring and early summer when you might get a glimpse of a doe with her fawn, a hen turkey with her brood of young, or young rabbits playing near the edge of some of the wildlife plantings. Give a nature lover over a thousand acres of unspoiled wild country, and he or she can spend hours there enjoying all that nature has to offer. Those who want to enjoy young critters should adopt some of the hunter's lore. Wear camouflage, move quietly and slowly, and stop frequently to look and listen. If you see a deer and want to get closer to it, move only when it is unalarmed. If the deer raises its head and looks in your direction, freeze and move again only when it resumes whatever it was doing.

A sampling of the fauna and flora includes the somewhat rare Appalachian cottontail rabbit, river otter, a number of frogs, including the spring peeper, red-spotted newt, several salamanders, a trio of toads, over half a dozen snakes including the poisonous copperhead and timber rattler, several skinks or lizards, eastern box, painted, and snapping turtles, over half a dozen bats, beaver, bobcat, coyote, both the gray and red foxes, both fox and gray squirrels, a number of mussels and crayfish, and several dozen butterflies. Particularly during the spring and early summer expect a number of flowering plants and shrubs such as jonquils, buttercups, dogwood, redbud, mountain laurel, and rhododendron, and in late summer and autumn there is goldenrod.

Picnickers will have no problem finding a quiet place to spread a blanket and lay out a picnic meal. The grassy area at the entrance is a possible spot. Or go down to the river and find a desirable spot overlooking the water. Just don't set up in parking areas.

All of the trails for backpackers, bikers, and hikers are also available to those on horseback. They become fine bridle trails when the rider on horseback enters them.

Obviously the outdoor opportunities are numerous on this wildlife management area in the James River valley.

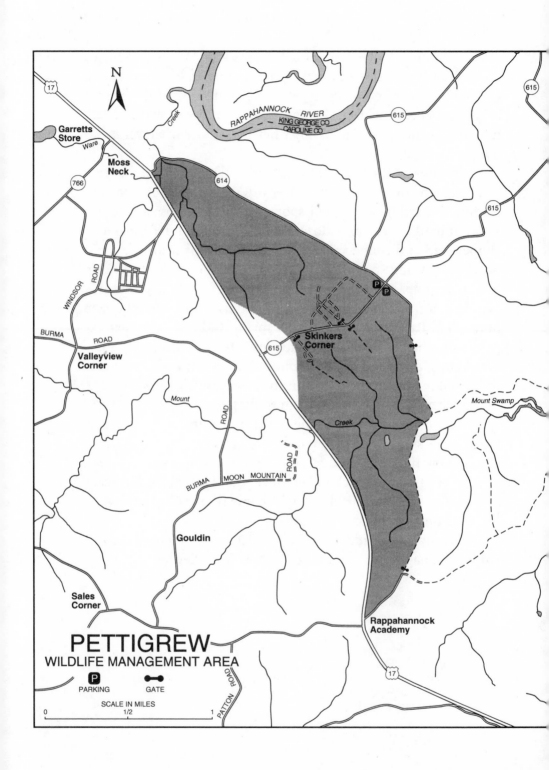

N

615

615

615

Garretts
Store

Ware

Creek

RAPPAHANNOCK   RIVER
KING GEORGE CO
CAROLINE CO

Moss
Neck

766

614

WINDSOR   ROAD

BURMA   ROAD

Valleyview
Corner

615

Skinkers
Corner

P
P

Mount

ROAD

Creek

Mount Swamp

BURMA   MOON   MOUNTAIN   ROAD

ROAD

Gouldin

Sales
Corner

Rappahannock
Academy

PETTIGREW
WILDLIFE MANAGEMENT AREA

P
PARKING

GATE

SCALE IN MILES

0   1/2   1

PATTON   ROAD

17

Pettigrew Wildlife Management Area

Supervising Office: Department of Game and Inland Fisheries
1320 Belman Road
Fredericksburg, VA 22401
Telephone 540-899-4169
Location: Caroline County
Elevation: 50 to 200 feet

Once a part of the Fort A. P. Hill military reservation, the Pettigrew Wildlife Management Area is long and narrow, bordering on U.S. Highway 17 from Rappahannock Academy northwest to Moss Neck, a distance of approximately three miles. Its width is less than a mile at its widest point. All of its 934 acres are in Caroline County in the Rappahannock River drainage system. Though relatively flat, it features several deep and wooded ravines. Rich stands of mature hardwoods are dominated by beech and oaks. Loblolly and Virginia pines are the major softwoods. Small holly trees are scattered throughout the hardwoods, and fields that were once open when used for military training are now being reclaimed by greenbrier, honeysuckle, and Virginia creeper. Although the area is relatively flat with the exception of the ravines, the elevation ranges from 50 to 200 feet as it climbs from the river valley toward rolling hills. Thanks to the work of beavers on the main stream as well as its tributaries, Mount Creek, which flows through the southern portion of the area, forms the area's primary wetlands. Ware Creek flows through the northern tip of the area and into the Rappahannock River, which at this point is less than half a mile from the wildlife management area. The tributaries of the two creeks ribbon the entire wildlife management area. There is also a small pond near the main stem of Mount Creek in the southern tip of the area.

Route 615 off U.S. Highway 17 runs a northeasterly route through the center of the area near Skinkers Corner. There are a pair of roomy parking areas where the secondary road exits the area. A power line runs through the area near its northeastern border. The power line's route is available for biking, hiking, and horseback riding but is not open to motorized vehicles. Route 614 runs from the northern tip of the area near Moss Neck to a point just south of the parking areas. There a gated trail picks up and runs south to where it connects with Route 719 near Rappahannock Academy. Together the gated trail and the secondary roads form the northern border of the area, with U.S. Highway 17 forming the southern boundary. Several short gated trails and dirt roads also lead from both sides of Route 615.

To reach the wildlife management area, take U.S. Highway 17 north from Tappahannock or south from Fredericksburg. It is located approximately fifteen miles south of Fredericksburg. Routes 614 and 615 off U.S. Highway 17 provide access to the area.

Because of its small size, this wildlife management area does not offer a true backpacking experience, but those who need a challenge might try crossing one of the deep ravines. Despite its small size, the wildlife management area offers 934 acres of wilderness. Shoulder a pack and take off on a compass reading that will take you from one end of the narrow land to the other. You will cross deep ravines and woodland creeks and pass through mature hardwood forests.

A bicyclist taking the gated trail from its beginning near Rappahannock Academy to the parking areas off Route 615 will enjoy a good ride. Among other challenges he or she will have to cross Mount Creek as it leaves the area and flows through private land and Mount Swamp. Or for a smoother ride, take Route 614 near Moss Neck, turn right on Route 615 where it exits the wildlife management area, and continue back to U.S. 17. From there you can turn left and ride to the edge of the wildlife management area near Rappahannock Academy. U.S. 17 is a busy highway, so be careful.

The Pettigrew Wildlife Management Area is mostly wooded and a haven for the likes of woodpeckers and other birds of hardwood forests. On the northeast side near the two parking areas are some large fields that are planted annually to attract doves. They also attract songbirds of various kinds. And don't overlook those beaver flowages and woodland streams for bird-watching. The bald eagle is probably the most obvious of the endangered or threatened birds here, but others include the great egret, purple finch, little blue and tricolored herons, barn owl, Caspian tern, hermit thrush, magnolia warbler, and winter wren. More common are the bittern, red-winged blackbird, eastern bluebird, indigo and snow buntings, cardinal, catbird, chickadee, crow, cuckoo, cattle egret, house finch, flicker, flycatcher, goldfinch, grackle, grebe, blue and evening grosbeak, occasional gulls, a half-dozen hawks, hummingbird, blue jay, junco, killdeer, kingfisher, lark, meadowlark, mockingbird, nuthatch, Baltimore oriole, osprey, a trio of owls, clapper, king, and Virginia rails, robin, sandpiper, several sparrows, starling, tundra swan, tern, thrush, a number of warblers, American, pileated, and red-bellied woodpeckers, and Carolina, house, and marsh wrens.

Although the big Rappahannock River is nearby, it is not accessible from this wildlife management area. There are no boating or canoeing opportunities here.

Except for the dove fields, which are in cultivation during the warmer months and high in grass and weeds through the late fall and winter, there is very little open space on this wildlife management area, but the mature forests might appeal to those who enjoy primitive camping. Or look for a spot near gurgling Ware Creek. Camping is permitted, of course, but there are no special facilities. Campers can pick a spot they like and settle in for as much as two weeks, the limit for camping on a single trip.

Fishing obviously is limited on this wildlife management area. There just isn't a lot of fishable water, but Ware Creek, which runs through the northern end of the area, offers good fishing for herring, which enter the stream from the nearby Rappahannock

River on spring spawning runs. There is also limited fishing for largemouth bass, crappie, and various sunfish. Drive across Ware Creek on U.S. Highway 17 or Route 614, and it just begs to be fished. If you are a stream fisherman by preference, it is hard to resist the temptation to pull on hip boots or waders and give the sparkling little stream a try. Less than a quarter of a mile of the stream is on the wildlife management area, but once in the stream you can continue upstream or down so long as you don't leave it and tread on private property. A major tributary of the creek forms within the wildlife management area and never leaves it before it enters Ware Creek. It might hold some fish but certainly not large ones. Mount Creek is another small-stream possibility — and check out the beaver ponds.

The hunting possibilities far exceed those for fishing, as they should, because the wildlife management area is managed primarily for hunting. Deer and turkeys offer opportunities for big-game hunting. Caroline County is one of the better deer-hunting counties in the state, and Fort A. P. Hill, which is right across U.S. Highway 17 from the area, has long had a good population of deer. Fort hunting permits can be purchased at the U.S. Highway 301 main entrance to the military reservation. The turkey population is also strong, with both fall and spring seasons open. Doves and squirrels are the most abundant small-game species. Approximately thirty acres of the area are under cultivation, planted and then allowed to remain fallow for awhile. This favors small-game species such as doves, quail, and rabbits. The mature hardwoods provide ideal habitat for squirrels, and the area gets occasional flights of woodcocks. Dove fields are planted annually, and the beaver ponds attract wood ducks and occasionally other ducks. Limited sales of hardwood timber expose the undergrowth and provide cover and food for all game.

Routes 614 and 615 plus several gated trails offer good opportunities for day hikes. One interesting possibility is to take the trail at nd of Route 719, hike the couple of miles to Route 615, and have someone pick you up there—or simply reverse your trek and hike back to Route 719. You will cross Mount Creek, of course. There are also several short hiking trails off Route 615 in the vicinity of Skinkers Corner.

The area offers the chance to view wildflowers including the scarce showy orchids. A great variety of aquatic vegetation flourishes throughout the marshy areas along Mount Creek. Opportunities to see the always busy beaver are fairly frequent. The same is true of the muskrat, and sightings of otters are fairly common. The more common critters include bullfrogs plus green, pickerel, and wood frogs and the spring peeper, red-spotted newt, a dozen salamanders, a pair of tree frogs, two dozen snakes of which only the copperhead is poisonous, several skinks or lizards, the snapping, painted, and other turtles, a half-dozen bats, several shrews, crayfish, and a wide variety of butterflies. Also expect flowering dogwoods and redbuds, rhododendron, and field flowers such as buttercups, sunflowers, and goldenrod.

A good spot for a picnic is reasonably easy to locate providing you are not too choosy. A spot along singing Ware Creek might be good, or move into the mature hardwoods and locate a spot beneath the branches of an old oak. For a more open area, check out the twin parking areas at the intersection of Routes 614 and 615.

All of the wildlife management area roads and trails are available to horsemen who are willing to trailer their mounts to the area. Don't worry about the gates at the heads of the trails. The gates are there to prohibit motorized vehicles only. Those on horseback can simply go around the gates and proceed along the trails.

There is nothing particularly spectacular about the Pettigrew Wildlife Management Area, but it does offer room to roam, stretch your legs, and enjoy the outdoors.

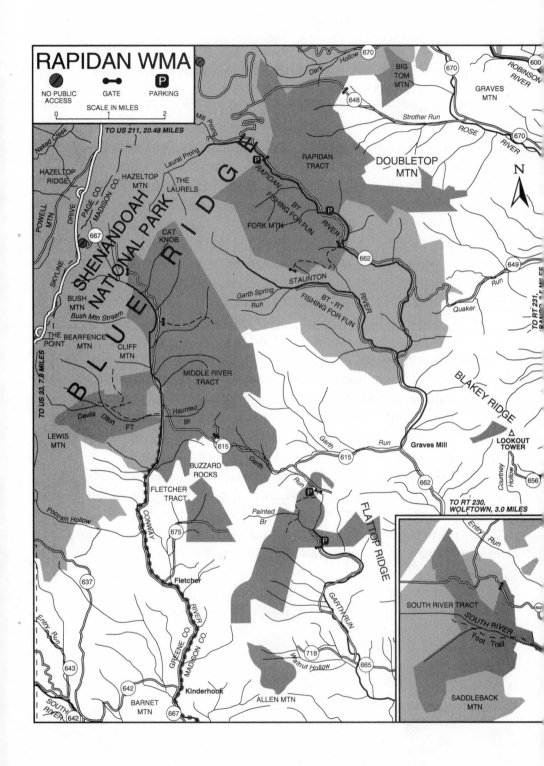

RAPIDAN WMA

- 🚫 **NO PUBLIC ACCESS**
- •—• **GATE**
- 🅿 **PARKING**

SCALE IN MILES
0   1   2

TO US 211, 20.48 MILES

Naked Creek

Mill Prong

Dark Hollow 670

BIG TOM MTN   670   600   ROBINSON RIVER

GRAVES MTN   670

Strother Run   ROSE RIVER   670

648

Laurel Prong

RAPIDAN TRACT

DOUBLETOP MTN

N

HAZELTOP RIDGE

POWELL MTN

PAGE CO.   MADISON CO.

HAZELTOP MTN

THE LAURELS

RAPIDAN

BT FISHING FOR FUN

RIVER

662   649

TO RT 231, RANGE 25 MILES

SKYLINE   DRIVE

667

SHENANDOAH NATIONAL PARK

CAT KNOB

FORK MTN

Garth Spring Run

STAUNTON

BT - RT FISHING FOR FUN

RIVER

Run

Quaker

BUSH MTN

Bush Mtn Stream

BLUE   RIDGE

BLAKEY RIDGE

THE BEARFENCE POINT   MTN

CLIFF MTN

MIDDLE RIVER TRACT

LEWIS MTN

Devils Ditch   FT

Haunted Br

615

Garth   Run   Graves Mill

△ LOOKOUT TOWER

656

TO US 33, 7.8 MILES

BUZZARD ROCKS

Garth

Courtney Hollow

662

FLETCHER TRACT

CONWAY

675

Pocosin Hollow

Run

Painted Br

🅿

🅿

FLATTOP RIDGE

TO RT 230, WOLFTOWN, 3.0 MILES

637

Fletcher

RIVER

GREENE CO.   MADISON CO.

GARTH RUN

SOUTH RIVER TRACT

Entry Run   642

643

Entry Run

718

Walnut Hollow

665

SOUTH RIVER

Foot   Trail

SOUTH RIVER   642

642   BARNET MTN   667   Kinderhook   ALLEN MTN

SADDLEBACK MTN

Rapidan Wildlife Management Area

Supervising Office: Department of Game and Inland Fisheries
1320 Belman Road
Fredericksburg, VA 22401
Telephone 540-899-4169
Location: Greene and Madison Counties
Elevation: 900 to 3,500 feet

Rugged mountain country, singing high-country streams, major trout rivers, and great black bear hunting might best sum up the Rapidan Wildlife Management Area scattered in eight separate tracts across Greene and Madison counties. The Middle River tract and Rapidan tract make up the major portion of the 10,326 acres. Next in size are Flattop Ridge and the South River tract, all of which is in Greene County. Smaller holdings include Allen Mountain, Big Tom Mountain, Blakey Ridge, and the Fletcher tract. The South River, which flows through the South River tract, is a popular put-and-take trout stream with a wild population of brook trout in its headwaters. The Conway River, which serves as part of the boundary between Greene and Madison Counties, is a special regulations trout stream. It also has a population of native brook trout in its headwaters. The Rapidan River is a popular fish-for-fun brook trout stream where all trout must be released. There is no formal access to Allen Mountain and Big Tom Mountain. Big Tom Mountain borders the Shenandoah National Park, and it can be reached by hiking through the park. Allen Mountain is sur-rounded by private land, and the permission of the landowner is needed to cross it to reach this tract. In addition to Big Tom Mountain, the Middle River, Rapidan River, and South River tracts adjoin the Shenandoah National Park. Elevations here range from 900 to 3,500 feet.

Much of the area had been logged frequently before its acquisition by the Department of Game and Inland Fisheries. The timber is predominately oak on the mountain slopes and tulip poplar at lower elevations, but there are some magnificent stands of hemlock in the deep hollows. Laurel thickets are almost impossible to crawl through, and many of the steepest mountains are faced with sheer rock cliffs. It is beautiful country, but not particularly forgiving for the inexperienced visitors who intrude. Hardy mountain people eked out livings in this beautiful but rugged country. The remains of their efforts still exist as abandoned home sites, rock fences, and traces of mountain roads. Today it is the kind of wild country that challenges the most experienced outdoorsmen. In addition to the major streams, dozens of tiny streams race down the steep mountains. Many of them all but dry up during the warm summer months.

You need a good map to find your way around this interesting wildlife management area, and a 4×4 vehicle is definitely an asset. The area is approximately thirty miles north of Charlottesville and twenty-five miles southwest of Culpeper. Routes 230 and 231 off U.S. 29 take you in the general direction of the wildlife management area, but eventually you must follow secondary roads into the area. Of the major tracts, the Middle River tract might be the easiest to reach. Take Route 230 north from Stanardsville, turn left on Route 667, and follow the Conway River deep into the area. Route 667 ends at the Shenandoah National Park border. Several trails lead off this secondary road. One follows Devils Ditch Creek to the west. Route 675 off Route 667 leads to the Fletcher tract. Another route to the Middle River tract is to take Route 662 off Route 230 at Wolftown and then take Route 615 left off Route 662. Route 615 eventually connects with Route 667 near Haunted Branch, a small tributary of the Conway River. A short road leads north off Route 615 into the tract, and another leads south to a gated trail in the Flattop Ridge tract. Possibly a better route to the Flattop Ridge Tract is to take Route 665 off Route 230 and follow Garth Run into the tract. The road is gated at the entrance to the tract. Route 718 off Route 665 leads toward the Allen Mountain tract but does not enter it.

To reach the Rapidan tract, continue on Route 662 beyond the Route 615 turnoff at Graves Mill. This takes you through a section of the Shenandoah National Park and into the tract. Another route to the Rapidan tract is to take Route 649 off Route 231 at Banco and follow Quaker Run to the Shenandoah National Park and the junction with Route 662. Still another route is to take Route 670 off 231 and follow the Rose River to Route 648 to the tract. The entrance here is gated, however, and may not always be open. To reach the South River tract, take Route 621 west off Route 230 and follow the South River to Route 637 and then to Route 642, which runs through the wildlife management area land. Route 656 left off Route 230 leads to a lookout tower near the Blakey Ridge tract. It is well to note that several of these roads and trails may be gated because of severe storm damage. At present they are open to travel on foot. The only passable route to the Rapidan River fish-for-fun area is Route 670 off Route 231 at Banco. Route 648 off Route 670 runs into Route 662, which runs along the river. Route 667 at the present ends at the Conway River just downstream from Devils Ditch. Fishermen park there and hike to the popular native trout stream.

Backpacking in the Rapidan Wildlife Management Area means either taking a compass reading and following it or taking any of the access roads that lead to just about all parts of the wildlife management area. The roads are primarily for vehicle travel, but the backpacker can make good use of them. Trails are extremely limited in the area. A trail follows the South River through the South River tract, and one leads off Route 615 into the Flattop Ridge tract. Another trail leads south off Route 662 along the southern edge of the Rapidan tract. It is gated at its entrance to the Shenandoah National Park. Finally a trail follows Devils Ditch off Route 667.

Although motorized vehicles are not allowed on these trails, they are open to bicyclists, who should be prepared to climb some steep grades. Flat country is rare here. This is mountain country, some of the most rugged in Virginia. All of the roads mentioned, however, are open to bicyclists, and they might well be the best choice for this activity.

The numerous streams in the area, none of which is particularly large, attract a great variety of birds. Remote sections of the streams where birds are most likely to be seen may require hiking through an untracked wilderness. And don't forget binoculars. Studying birds on the far side of a canyon with the aid of powerful binoculars, or even a spotting scope, is much easier than crossing that canyon for a closer look. This wildlife management area has its share of endangered and threatened birds. Included among them are the brown creeper, red crossbill, bald eagle, great egret, peregrine falcon, purple finch, northern goshawk, red-breasted nuthatch, barn owl, hermit thrush, cerulean and golden-winged warblers, and winter wren. Sighting most of these birds might be a rarity, but more frequent are sightings of several species of black-birds, the eastern bluebird, indigo and snow buntings, northern cardinal, catbird, chickadee, white-winged crossbill, cuckoo, cattle egret, flicker, flycatchers, goldfinch, grackle, several species of grosbeak, Cooper's, broad-winged, red-tailed, and red-shouldered hawks, blue jay, junco, purple martin, mockingbird, oriole, raven, robin, several sparrows, starling, swallow, tern, thrasher, thrush, towhee, warblers, whippoorwill, woodpeckers, and wrens. The area is rich in birdlife common to mountains, valleys, and racing streams.

Boating opportunities are few or nonexistent, though a kayaker might be able to run the lower stretches of the Conway or Rapidan River. Thanks to the Shenandoah National Park, a good stretch of the Rapidan River remains a public waterway even after the river leaves the wildlife management area.

The area offers numerous camping opportunities, but they are all subject to the wildlife management area regulations posted at the major entrances to the area. Pitching a tent along a singing mountain stream and allowing its music to serve as a lullaby appeal to many who love to live for awhile outdoors. At the higher elevations, which range up to 3,500 feet, the evenings should be cool enough to warrant a modest campfire. Just make sure it is thoroughly doused before breaking camp. Primitive camping is allowed for up to two weeks. Backpackers probably are responsible for most of the camping activity. They can shoulder packs and get far back into the area—far from civilization.

The Rapidan Wildlife Management Area offers good fishing for trout, and little more. The Rapidan River, made famous by President Herbert Hoover who fished there often during his years in the White House, was one of the original fish-for-fun trout streams. Thanks to the president, the beautiful little mountain stream became nationally known. It holds native brook trout only, but there is a good population of 10- to 11-inch brookies. Several of the small tributaries of the Rapidan also hold populations of native trout. The Conway River and its tributary Devils Ditch are a special regulations trout fishery with native brook trout in the upper reaches and wild brown trout downstream. An occasional brown trout may go 20 inches. The streams in the area are fast flowing over boulder- and rock-strewn beds. Cascading rapids are interspersed with deep, quiet pools. The fishing can be tough, but it is the kind of water that appeals to accomplished fly fishermen.

Hunters might know the Rapidan Wildlife Management Area best for its black bear population. Because of its proximity to the Shenandoah National Park where no hunting is allowed, the area benefits from the protected bear population that spills over from the parklands. Both deer and turkeys are present in huntable numbers, and the populations of both popular game species are growing. Ruffed grouse and squirrels are the major small game, and hunting for both can be good. Woodcocks are also found along the streams, many of them migrants on flights south. At the best, however, woodcock hunting is a hit-or-miss situation. Wildlife populations are being maintained by such management techniques as selective timber harvest and the management of wildlife clearings, old orchards, and abandoned homesites.

Day hiking along the roads and the few trails can be a way to enjoy the mountainous area. This can be done at any season, but fall and spring are delightful in this picturesque area along the eastern slopes of the Blue Ridge Mountains. The roads and trails useful for backpacking are also good for hikes. It is well to keep in mind that bear hunters may be working the area from late November until early January—primarily during the month of December. But there is no hunting on Sundays even then.

Nature watching can be a joy and a challenge. Find a comfortable seat high on a mountain peak with a commanding view of the area and work it carefully with a pair of binoculars. This is the approach often used by mountain big-game hunters. The difference is that the hunter, once he locates his quarry, has to make a stalk. If he is successful, he is then faced with getting his trophy out of the rugged mountains to his vehicle. The nature watcher merely locates something of interest, observes it for awhile, and possibly makes a few notes. The wildlife management area gives plenty of opportunities for this kind of outing. Among the critters likely to present themselves are bullfrogs, green, cricket, pickerel, upland chorus, and wood frogs, spring peeper, red-spotted newt, a variety of salamanders found mostly in the small streams, toads, both copperheads and timber rattlers and a long list of nonpoisonous snakes, a half-dozen skinks and lizards, a half-dozen turtles including the box, snapping, and painted turtles, a number of bats, coyote, shrews, a wide variety of crayfish in the streams, and many butterflies in the fields and woods. And beware the ticks. There are five different kinds.

Looking for a place for a family picnic? Load up the 4×4 and drive the open roads in the area. There are not many open meadows, but finding an idyllic spot beneath the leafy branches of a big hemlock shouldn't be a problem. Or better still, locate a spot near a sparkling mountain stream and enjoy the water. Kids might even like to go wading or skip flat stones along the surface of a glistening pool.

Many miles of wildlife management roads beckon to the horseback rider. Trailer a horse or two to the area, unload them, and head up the nearest road. Most roads lead upward to some interesting views. Gated roads limits access by motorized vehicles, particularly jeeps and ATVs, but hikers, bikers, or horseback riders can go around the gates and enjoy the roads and trails.

The Rapidan Wildlife Management Area is a spectacular chunk of mountain country within easy driving distance of much of Virginia's most heavily populated regions. Many take advantage of it.

Lower Tidewater and Eastern Shore

Counties: Accomack and Northampton, and the City of Virginia Beach

There are only three wildlife management areas in this section, Mockhorn Island, Princess Anne, and Saxis. Mockhorn is on the Atlantic Ocean side of the Eastern Shore, and Saxis is on the Chesapeake side of that interesting peninsula. The Princess Anne area is on Back Bay, a big body of brackish water separated from the Atlantic Ocean by a narrow strip of sand. Although there are other tidal-water wildlife management areas, they are on tidal rivers and are discussed elsewhere in this work.

This is coastal country. The highest point is only a few feet above sea level. The counties of Accomack and Northampton make up the Eastern Shore of Virginia, a land of truck farming and water-men who make their living from the sea. Across the mouth of the Chesapeake Bay, directly south, and connected to the Eastern Shore by the seventeen-mile-long Chesapeake Bay Bridge-Tunnel is the resort city of Virginia Beach, which hugs the coastline. South of the resort area, Virginia Beach is rich farming country all the way to the North Carolina line. The strip of sand that separates Back Bay from the ocean is also a peninsula, a land of broad ocean beaches, sand dunes, and stunted pines and other vegetation. The Back Bay National Wildlife Refuge claims the upper regions of this peninsula that runs south from the resort strip and along the ocean to the North Carolina line. Between the refuge and the North Carolina border is False Cape State Park. Also in the city of

Virginia Beach is Seashore State Park that fronts on the Chesapeake Bay at its confluence with the Atlantic Ocean.

It is interesting country that is home to these three wildlife management areas, rich in early American history and an area visited by vacationers from all over America and Canada and other countries. Land is at a premium here and costly. The Department of Game and Inland Fisheries was able to purchase this land in earlier years when the asking prices were reasonable. It would be impossible for the department to pay what these areas would command today. Outdoor people should be forever grateful that the department had the foresight to claim these priceless lands for generations to come.

Mockhorn Island
Wildlife Management Area

Supervising Office: Department of Game and Inland Fisheries
5806 Mooretown Road
Williamsburg, VA 23188
Telephone 757-253-4180
Location: Northampton County
Elevation: Mostly below sea level at high tide to approximately 5 to 10 feet at low tide

Mockhorn Island is one of many offshore islands along the Atlantic Coast, or more specifically off the Eastern Shore of Virginia. It's a land of wind and water, marshes, broad sandy beaches, and pine-covered hummocks that rise for a few feet above the marshes and ocean level. It is also a land that rolling waves can sweep over during stormy weather. Hostile during storms, the island can be a delight when the breezes are light and a warm sun shines out of the heavens. It is managed by the Virginia Department of Game and Inland Fisheries as the Mockhorn Wildlife Management Area. Despite its charm, it is not a land that should be taken lightly. Its 7,000 acres make it a vast flatland of mostly marshes, winding creeks, guts, and potholes, separated from the mainland by Mockhorn Bay to the north and Magothy Bay to the south. Its appeal is strongest among bird-watchers and rail and waterfowl hunters. The big island, ribboned by creeks and guts, is surrounded by channels and shoals. Mockhorn Island is approximately two miles wide to the north but tapers off to a narrow tip to the south. From north to south the island is approximately six miles long. From a distance it almost disappears from view, but as you approach it by water, the hummocks running north and south on the island rise from the water—and then the rest of it appears out of the sea. Except for the hummocks, much of the island disappears during

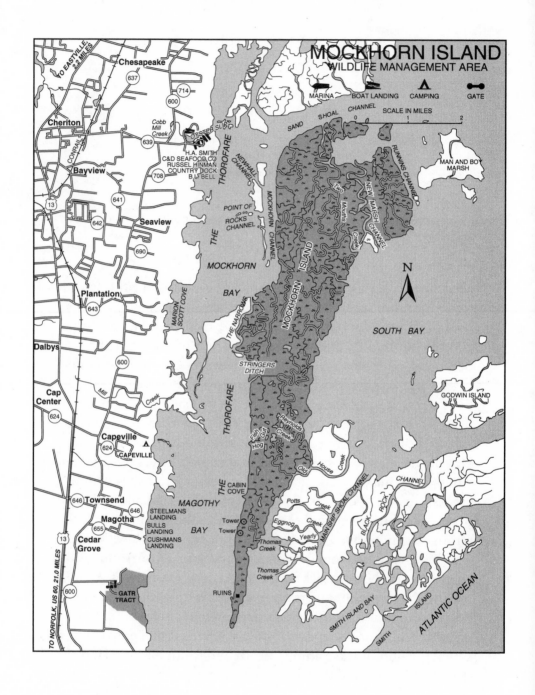

MOCKHORN ISLAND
WILDLIFE MANAGEMENT AREA

MARINA   BOAT LANDING   CAMPING   GATE

SCALE IN MILES
0   1   2

TO EASTVILLE 2.2 MILES

Chesapeake

637

714
600

Cheriton

Cobb Mill Creek

639

OYSTER SLIP

H.A. SMITH
C&D SEAFOOD CO.
RUSSEL HINMAN
COUNTRY DOCK
B.L. BELL

Bayview

708

641

13

642

Seaview

690

POINT OF ROCKS CHANNEL

NEWHALL CHANNEL

THE THOROFARE

MOCKHORN CHANNEL

SAND SHOAL CHANNEL

RUNNINS CHANNEL

MAN AND BOY MARSH

Two Mouths Creek

NEW MARSH CHANNEL

MOCKHORN ISLAND

N

Plantation

643

MOCKHORN BAY

MARION SCOTT COVE

THE NARROWS

STRINGERS DITCH

SOUTH BAY

Dalbys

Cap Center

624

600

Mill Creek

Capeville

624

CAPEVILLE

THE THOROFARE

Reynolds Creek

Fish Gut

Hog

Old

House Creek

GODWIN ISLAND

CHANNEL

646   Townsend

646

Magotha

655

Cedar Grove

600

STEELMANS LANDING

BULLS LANDING

CUSHMANS LANDING

MAGOTHY BAY

THE CABIN COVE

Tower

Tower

Potts Creek

Eggnog Creek

Yearly Creek

Thomas Creek

Thomas Creek

RUINS

BLACK

ROCK

MAIN SHIP SHOAL CHANNEL

GATR TRACT

TO NORFOLK US 60, 21.0 MILES

SMITH ISLAND BAY

SMITH ISLAND

ATLANTIC OCEAN

CONRAIL

high tide, but low tide reveals its vastness. Loblolly pines are the most conspicuous vegetation, and there is also greenbrier, honeysuckle, poison ivy, red cedar, and wax myrtle. The major vegetation in the marshes is salt-marsh cordgrass. The very nature of Mockhorn Island makes it difficult to manage — or to manipulate for wildlife habitat. Instead, those responsible for its management focus on maintaining what nature has delivered. Across Magothy Bay on the mainland is the GATR tract, 356 acres of mixed upland and marsh habitat.

Both Mockhorn Island and the GATR tract are in Northampton County just north of Cape Charles. Near the southern end of Mockhorn Island are a couple of rusting steel towers erected during World War II. To reach them from Oyster calls for a six-mile trip by boat. Virginia outdoorsmen will be forever indebted to the Virginia Department of Game and Inland Fisheries for acquiring this remarkable piece of land, marsh, and water when it was available. Today it would be all but impossible to obtain at a fair price.

Mockhorn Island is reached only by boat from the mainland. A direct route across either Mockhorn Bay or Magothy Bay is approximately two miles at most, but following the boat channels and finding open water among the many offshore marshes takes longer than the typical two-mile run in a fast boat. The Department of Game and Inland Fisheries launching ramp at Oyster is the usual point of departure from the mainland. There are other private ramps that require a shorter trip, but it is often a problem to locate and get permission to use them. The Oyster ramp is located east of Cheriton at the end of Route 639 — and directly across Mockhorn Bay from the upper end of the island. The GATR tract is reached by Jones Cove Road off the Seaside Road, or Route 600. On a calm day a canoe or kayak would take you to Mockhorn Island safely, but a sudden and unexpected storm could make the water too rough to travel back to the mainland. Ideally a seaworthy boat with an outboard in the 25-horsepower range is the safest. It should be equipped with running lights and a compass in case a thick fog envelops the island and makes travel by boat risky without these aids. But regardless of how you travel, you should consult the tide charts and determine the times of the high and low tides. And have a good map to guide you.

Sandy beaches along the hummocks might beckon to the backpacker, but backpacking opportunities are otherwise limited. At high tide the beaches may disappear. At low tide it is also possible to walk on the marshes, but only for a few hours until the tide comes back in and flood them.

Mockhorn Island, and to a less degree the GATR tract, can be a bird-watchers' dream. In addition to a wide variety of waterfowl including Atlantic brant, black ducks, buffleheads, old squaw, and scoters, there is a rich variety of other birds. Egrets and herons nest in the low shrubs and trees, and ospreys nest on buoys, channel markers, and old submarine lookout towers and man-made platforms. Additionally gulls, terns, and other sea and shore birds frequent the area. According to one authority, more than 250 species of birds use Mockhorn and other islands along the Virginia coast. The two abandoned towers are often used by bird-watchers and nature lovers to get a more commanding view of the island and its wildlife. Safety is questionable, however, as the towers are not maintained on a regular basis, and they are succumbing to rust. Among the endangered or threatened birds are the bald eagle, great egret, peregrine falcon, alder flycatcher, little blue heron, brown pelican, piping plover, Wilson's plover, salt-marsh sparrow, loggerhead gull-billed tern, roseate tern, hermit thrush, cerulean warbler, and winter wren. More common birds include American and least bitterns, the red-winged blackbird, eastern bluebird, bobolink, snow bunting, northern cardinal, gray catbird, Carolina chickadee, great cormorant, fish crow, long-billed curlew, long-billed dowitcher, cattle and snowy egrets, a number of flycatchers, several grebes and grosbeaks, over a dozen gulls, most hawks common to Virginia, great blue heron, ibis, several jaegers, several kingbirds, plovers, Atlantic puffin, a quartet of rails, over half a dozen sandpipers, black skimmer, numerous species of sparrows, mute and tundra swans, black, common, royal, and sooty terns, tufted titmouse, and a number of vireos and warblers.

The miles of winding creeks and guts are an invitation to canoeists and kayakers. Haul a couple over by bigger boat and explore the winding and interesting little inland waterways. Use a compass and keep yourself oriented, however, as getting lost out here is no fun. Mosquitoes can be a serious problem during the warmer months of the year, so go prepared.

The camping possibilities are extremely limited, though beach camping might be possible depending upon the tides. A campsite on a beach and an evening campfire could be idyllic. Finding driftwood for a fire wouldn't be a problem. The uplands of the GATR tract might offer better camping, but mosquitoes and ticks could be a problem during warm weather. For summer camping there are much better wildlife management areas.

Fishing the waters around Mockhorn Island and those adjacent to the GATR tract can produce a great variety of saltwater species. At the appropriate seasons there are black drum, channel bass, sea bass, bluefish, croaker, flounder, shark, tarpon, and gray trout. Generally these species of fish are most abundant in June through September, the top saltwater fishing months in Virginia waters. Top fishing waters include Magothy Bay between the island and the mainland and Main Ship Shoal Channel and South Bay on the ocean side of the island.

Hunters visit Mockhorn Island for its excellent hunting for clapper rails. Check the tidal charts when planning a trip as the hunting is best on a high tide. The usual approach is to pole a boat through the marshes with a hunter positioned in the bow taking the birds when they flush. A flat-bottom johnboat is probably the best craft for this kind of hunting. It might be best to cross the open water in a larger boat and tow a johnboat for the actual hunting. A great variety of ducks use the island. They feed in the marshes and rest on the potholes and creeks. Permanent blinds are illegal, but boat or floating blinds can be used; so can temporary blinds made of camouflage netting. Another approach is to jump shoot by moving a canoe up the winding creeks and hugging the inside curves to surprise birds around the bend in a creek. The GATR tract has a good population of deer. Bow hunting during the special archery season is permitted, but there is no firearms season.

Day hikers can enjoy the beaches, and at low tide they can walk on the marshes, but numerous creeks limit their travel.

In addition to the ducks and birds, there are good populations of muskrat, raccoon, and otters and a great variety of plant life. A naturalist can spend hours on the island just enjoying this rich variety of wildlife. Binoculars are an asset. Among the endangered or threatened species are a number of turtles: the Atlantic Ridley sea turtle, the Atlantic hawksbill sea turtle, the Atlantic green sea turtle, the loggerhead sea turtle, and the northern diamondback terrapin. Other turtles include the snapping, box, mud, painted, and redbelly. Also present are small numbers of the rare Delmarva Peninsula fox squirrel. More common are critters such as the bullfrog and New Jersey chorus, green, northern cricket, and southern leopard frogs. There are several salamanders and toads and a great variety of snakes including the poisonous copperhead. Also present are a half-dozen bats, muskrat, nutria, raccoon, shrew, crayfish, and a great variety of butterflies. The nature lover will never become bored on the Mockhorn Wildlife Management Area.

No other public land in Virginia offers this rare combination of land, marshes, and water. It's truly a gem in an interesting part of the state.

Princess Anne
Wildlife Management Area

Supervising Office: Department of Game and Inland Fisheries
       5806 Mooretown Road
       Williamsburg, VA 23188
       Telephone 757-253-4180
Location: City of Virginia Beach
Elevation: Sea level to approximately 5 to 10 feet

The Princess Anne Wildlife Management Area located in the city of Virginia Beach is best known for the fine waterfowl hunting it has provided for the public over the years. Thousands of hunters have spent an untold number of days in public waterfowl hunting blinds in this wildlife management area located on Back Bay. In good years modest limits of ducks can come quickly. Back Bay is a big brackish-water bay separated from the Atlantic Ocean by False Cape, a narrow strip of land running south from Sandbridge to the North Carolina border. At its widest point the distance between the western shore of Back Bay and False Cape is six to seven miles. Totaling 1,546 acres of mostly marshes, the Princess Anne Wildlife Management Area consists of three tracts, the Pocahontas tract, the Trojan tract, and the Whitehurst tract. Barbours Hill, boasting five permanent waterfowl blinds, is located on the lands of False Cape State Park on the eastern side of Back Bay. Waterfowl hunting there is possible as the result of a cooperative agreement between the Virginia Department of Game and Inland Fisheries and the Virginia Division of Parks. The Trojan tract and the Whitehurst tract are located on the western shores of Back Bay, and the Pocahontas tract is located offshore in the southern end of the bay near the North Carolina line.

  This entire wildlife management area is devoted almost exclusively to management for waterfowl hunting. The Whitehurst tract

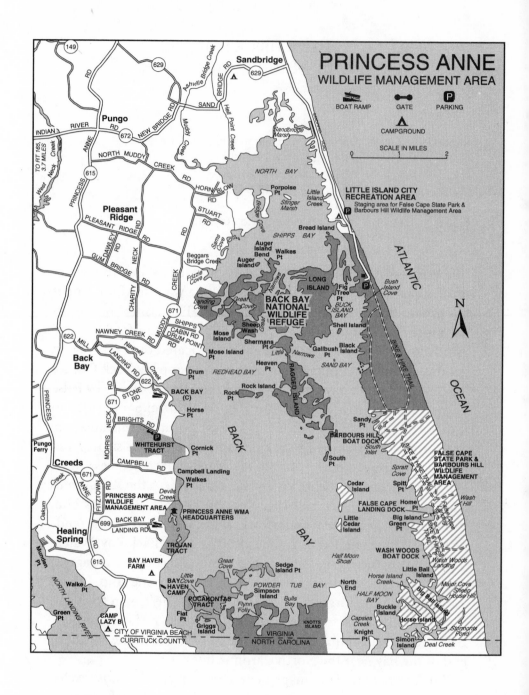

PRINCESS ANNE
WILDLIFE MANAGEMENT AREA

BOAT RAMP   GATE   PARKING

CAMPGROUND

SCALE IN MILES
0   1   2

Sandbridge

Pungo

Pleasant
Ridge

Back
Bay

Creeds

Healing
Spring

LITTLE ISLAND CITY
RECREATION AREA
Staging area for False Cape State Park &
Barbours Hill Wildlife Management Area

NORTH BAY

Porpoise
Pt

Little
Island
Creek

Stinger
Marsh

Bread Island

SHIPPS
BAY

Auger
Island
Bend

Walkes
Pt

Auger
Island

LONG
ISLAND

Fig
Tree
Pt

Bush
Island
Cove

BACK BAY
NATIONAL
WILDLIFE
REFUGE

BUCK
ISLAND
BAY

Shell Island

Sheep
Wash

Mose
Island

Shermans
Pt

Gallbush
Pt

Black
Island

Mose Island
Pt

Little
Narrows

SAND BAY

Drum
Pt

REDHEAD BAY

Heaven
Pt

RAGGED ISLAND

Rock Island

Rock
Pt

Horse
Pt

Sandy
Pt

BACK BAY
(C)

BRIGHTS RD

WHITEHURST
TRACT

Cornick
Pt

BARBOURS HILL
BOAT DOCK

South
Inlet

ATLANTIC

OCEAN

N

BIKE & HIKE TRAIL

FALSE CAPE
STATE PARK &
BARBOURS HILL
WILDLIFE
MANAGEMENT
AREA

BACK

South
Pt

Spratt
Cove

Spitt
Pt

Wash
Hill

CAMPBELL   RD

Campbell Landing
Walkes
Pt

Devils
Creek

PRINCESS ANNE
WILDLIFE
MANAGEMENT
AREA

PRINCESS ANNE WMA
HEADQUARTERS

BACK BAY
LANDING RD

TROJAN
TRACT

BAY HAVEN
FARM

Cedar
Island

FALSE CAPE
LANDING DOCK

Home
Pt

Big Island
Green

Little
Cedar
Island

BAY

WASH WOODS
BOAT DOCK

Half Moon
Shoal

North
End

Wash Woods
Landing

Little Ball
Island

Big Ball Island

Major Cove
Sheep
House Hill

Pungo
Ferry

Walke
Pt

Green
Pt

CAMP
LAZY B

POCAHONTAS
TRACT

Flat
Pt

Griggs
Island

Little
BAY
HAVEN
CAMP

Great
Cove

Cove

Sedge
Island Pt

POWDER
Simpson
Island

Flynn
Folly

TUB   BAY

Bulls
Bay

Horse Island
Landing

HALF MOON
BAY

Buckle
Island

Horse Island

Stermonts
Pond

KNOTTS
ISLAND

Capsies
Creek

Knight
Pt

Simon
Island

Deal Creek

VIRGINIA

NORTH CAROLINA

CITY OF VIRGINIA BEACH
CURRITUCK COUNTY

98

is the site of most of the management effort. The tract consists of marshes, man-made impoundments, and uplands. The impoundments are manipulated to provide vegetation for the various species of ducks that winter here. There are also duck nesting boxes for local species such as wood ducks that raise their offspring in the Back Bay area. Wildlife plots are also planted for upland wildlife, primarily in the Whitehurst and Trojan tracts. The Pocahontas tract is a group of marshy islands accessible only by boat. Private waterfowl blinds are almost impossible to come by on Back Bay. Many of them have been in the same families for years—handed down from generation to generation. These waterfowl hunting areas, obtained by the Department of Game and Inland Fisheries a number of years ago, provide the opportunity for the public to enjoy hunting on this traditionally rich waterfowling body of water. Without them many waterfowl hunters would never enjoy the opportunity.

Barbours Hill Wildlife Management Area can be reached by bicycling or hiking on a dirt road that runs through the Back Bay National Wildlife Refuge and into False Cape State Park. It is not open to motor vehicles. Waterfowl hunters, however, are met at the Little Island Recreation Area near the entrance to the Back Bay National Wildlife Refuge and transported by truck to the public waterfowl hunting blinds at Barbours Hill. The Whitehurst tract is reached by Route 622 off Route 615 (Princess Anne Road) or by taking Route 671 off Route 615 near Creeds and then turning right on Route 622. The Princess Anne Wildlife Management Area headquarters is reached by taking Route 699 (Back Bay Landing Road) off Route 615. The Pocahontas tract is reached by boat from the public boat-launching ramp at the wildlife management area headquarters.

All three tracts plus the Barbours Hill waterfowl blinds offer opportunities for watching a great variety of birds. Poisonous cottonmouth snakes are found in this part of Virginia, and wasps build nests in the blinds. Both present threats during the warm months of the year—so bird-watchers beware. Keep alert. Rather than using the blinds, bird-watchers may fare better if they launch a light boat or canoe and use it as a floating blind to watch birds. Among the endangered or threatened birds found here are the bald eagle, great egret, peregrine falcon, purple finch, little blue and tricolored herons, glossy ibis, brown pelican, black rail, piping and Wilson's migrant loggerhead shrikes, salt-marsh sparrow, several terns including the gull-billed, hermit thrush, Swainson's warbler, and the sedge and winter wrens. More common are the American and least bitterns, Brewer's, red-winged, and rusty blackbirds, eastern bluebird, indigo and lark buntings, cardinal, catbird, Carolina chickadee, cowbird, fish crow, long-billed curlew, several egrets in addition to the rare great egret, greater flamingo, several flycatchers, frigate bird, American goldfinch, grackle, several grebes and grosbeaks, a number of gulls and hawks, green heron, white ibis, Baltimore oriole, Atlantic puffin, robin, several sandpipers, black skimmer, a number of sparrows, bank, barn, and cliff swallows, a quartet of terns, several vireos, a large number of warblers, several woodpeckers, and the Carolina, house, and marsh wrens.

Boating on the broad waters of Back Bay can be a real joy. There is no tide here, and the water level is fairly stable. The bay is shallow, however, the average depth being only a few feet. Shallow water can get rough quickly if a sudden storm kicks in. Back Bay is dotted with islands of various sizes, and they are always interesting to explore. Most pleasure boats can be launched at the public launch at the Princess Anne Wildlife Management Area headquarters.

Back Bay was once one of the top largemouth bass waters in Virginia, but several environmental changes including the loss of aquatic vegetation and the reduction of the salinity of the water all but eliminated the bass populations. Bass and bluegills are now limited to the creeks feeding into the bay. There is also good fishing for channel catfish in the creeks. Back Bay does have an abundant population of white perch, a scrappy little fish that is fun to fish for and delicious on the table.

Hunting for waterfowl is the big activity in the Princess Anne Wildlife Management Area, and the management program is directed toward the ducks and geese. A great variety of waterfowl winter on Back Bay, including Canada and snow geese and tundra swans. The Barbours Hill blinds are assigned on the basis of a drawing held early in the fall well before the waterfowl hunting season, but floating blinds are assigned daily for the other locations. Permits are available daily from the Princess Anne Wildlife Management headquarters at the Trojan tract. Floating blinds are boats camouflaged to serve as blinds. This usually takes the form of netting arranged to conceal the hunters, but hunters dressed in camouflage and resting quietly in a dull-coated boat also will enjoy success. There is limited dove hunting on the Whitehurst tract, but by permit only. Check with the wildlife management area headquarters.

In addition to waterfowl and other birds, a great variety of wildlife such as the marsh rabbit, muskrat, nutria, and otter live in the rich marshlands of Back Bay. The nature lover with a boat and a good pair of binoculars can spend many pleasant hours watching the critters and studying the rich variety of flora that the wildlife management area has to offer. Endangered and threatened species such as the Atlantic Ridley sea turtle, as well as several other turtles including the loggerhead sea turtle, are always a possible sighting. Other critters, some scarce, include the bald eagle, northern diamondback terrapin, big-eared bat, canebrake rattlesnake, river otter, marsh rabbit, several species of frogs, a number of different salamanders, a great many snakes including the poisonous copperhead and eastern cottonmouth, several different skinks or lizards, crayfish, and a great variety of butterflies.

This is a fascinating wildlife management area in an interesting part of Virginia. The outdoor opportunities it offers are entirely different from those found elsewhere in the state.

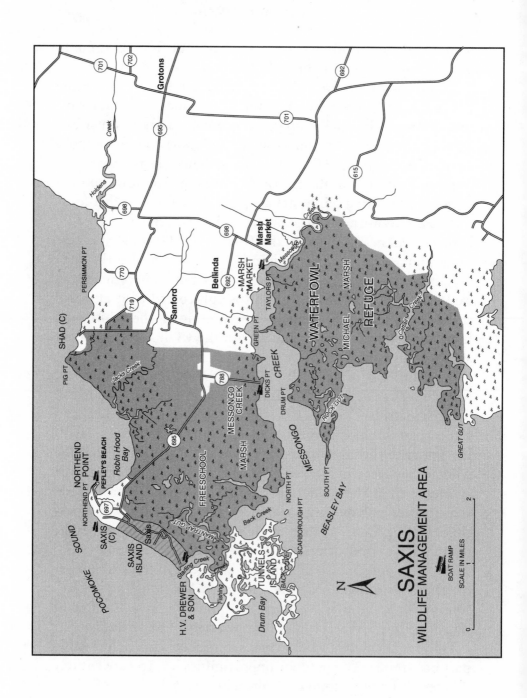

SAXIS
WILDLIFE MANAGEMENT AREA

N

BOAT RAMP

SCALE IN MILES

0   1   2

POCOMOKE

SOUND

NORTHEND
POINT

NORTHEND PT

PEFLEY'S BEACH

NORTHEND PT POINT

SAXIS
(C)

SAXIS
ISLAND

H.V. DREWER
& SON

TUNNELS
ISLAND

Drum Bay

Fishing Creek

BACK CODE

Stalling Creek

Saxis

Back Creek

MANTRAP GUT

FREESCHOOL
MARSH

MESSONGO
CREEK
MARSH

Robin Hood
Bay

Jacks Creek

695

719

770

Sanford

SHAD (C)

PIG PT

PERSIMMON PT

698

Holdens Creek

701

702

695

Grotons

701

692

615

698

698

Bellinda

Marsh
Market

MARSH
"MARKET"

692

788

DICKS PT

GREEN PT

DRUM PT

TAYLORS PT

MESSONGO   CREEK

NORTH PT

SCARBOROUGH PT

MESSONGO

BEASLEY BAY

SOUTH PT

ROCK GUT

Cattail Creek

Messongo Creek

WATERFOWL

MICHAEL
MARSH

REFUGE

GREAT GUT

Saxis Wildlife Management Area

Supervising Office: Department of Game and Inland Fisheries
5806 Mooretown Road
Williamsburg, VA 23188
Telephone 757-253-4180
Location: Accomack County
Elevation: Sea level to approximately 5 to 10 feet

The Saxis Wildlife Management Area is located on the western coast of the Eastern Shore of Virginia, and it fronts on the eastern shore of the Chesapeake Bay. It is in the far northwestern corner of the Eastern Shore close to the Maryland border—and in Accomack County. It is predominately a tidal marshland that fronts on the Chesapeake Bay, though there are forests and hummocks inland. Totaling 5,574 acres, it is divided into two tracts that are separated by tidal Messongo Creek. The tract to the south of Messongo Creek is a waterfowl refuge where waterfowl hunting is prohibited, though it is open to other kinds of hunting. The northern tract, however, is open to waterfowl hunting during the regular waterfowl hunting seasons. Both tracts are actually peninsulas in the Chesapeake Bay surrounded by water on three sides. Waterfowl hunting is the major activity here, but there is also good deer hunting. Inland there are forested high ground and hummocks, the kind of cover that is more attractive to deer than are the marshes, though they may be seen on the marshes. Very little active wildlife management is carried on, nor is it needed. The best approach seems to be to protect what nature has provided and give her a free hand. Out on the tip of the upper peninsula, there is some private land on which sprawls the quaint little waterfront town of Saxis, plus a strip of private land between the wildlife management area and the Chesapeake Bay. Tunnels Island is also private, as are several other smaller islands.

The wildlife management area is best reached by Route 695 west off U.S. Highway 13 at Temperance. Route 695 continues through the northern peninsula to the little town of Saxis. Several spur roads off Route 695 lead to various parts of the northern peninsula. Route 788 leads south to the Messongo boat-launching ramp, and Route 719 leads north to Pig Point on Pocomoke Sound. There is no road access to the southern tract, the water-fowl refuge. There are also public boat-launching ramps at Marsh Market and Saxis.

Saxis Wildlife Management Area is a dream for bird-watchers. In addition to ducks and geese, there are egrets, herons, loons, numerous shorebirds, and a rich mixture of songbirds. The marsh-lands are firm enough to walk on at low tide. That can be one approach to bird-watching, but a better one might be to take along a canoe or kayak and work your way quietly up the numerous creeks and guts that indent the shoreline, waterways like Jacks Creek and Mantrap Gut.

The list of birds that use the area is long. Endangered or threatened birds include the brown creeper, red crossbill, bald eagle, great egret, peregrine falcon, purple finch, little blue heron, glossy ibis, barn owl, brown pelican, Wilson's plover, black rail, migrant loggerhead shrike, Henslow's sparrow, salt-marsh sparrow, Caspian tern, roseate tern, hermit thrush, cerulean warbler, and sedge and winter wrens. Other birds include the American bittern, red-winged blackbird, eastern bluebird, bobolink, snow bunting, cardinal, catbird, black-capped chickadee, great cormorant, fish crow, cuckoo, long-billed dowitcher, snowy egret, house finch, greater flamingo, several flycatchers, gnatcatcher, goldfinch, the eared and horned grebes, several grosbeaks, a number of gulls, Cooper's, red-tailed, and several other hawks, great blue heron, blue jay, junco, killdeer, several kingbirds, common loon, black-tailed magpie, purple martin, nuthatch, oriole, a trio of owls, American golden plover, black-bellied plover, clapper, king, yellow, and Virginia rails, robin, a number of sandpipers, a long list of sparrows, mute and tundra swans, a half-dozen different species of terns, brown thrasher, tufted titmouse, several vireos, a long list of warblers, several woodpeckers, the Carolina, house, and marsh wrens, and the greater and lesser yellowlegs.

Pretty much surrounded by water and indented by creeks, guts, and small coves, the area is a haven for boating and canoeing, as well as kayaking. Launch a canoe or kayak and work along the shoreline until you find a creek or gut to explore—or launch a larger boat at Marsh Market and motor through Messongo Creek to Beasley Bay and the open Chesapeake Bay. Launch your vessel at the Saxis ramp and head out into broad Pocomoke Sound. North across the sound is the coast of Maryland.

Primitive camping is allowed up to two weeks. The best locations are probably inland just off Route 695, but camping is not permitted within 300 feet of any Department of Game and Inland Fisheries facility or road. In warm weather go prepared for mosquitoes and ticks. A better approach might be to load up a boat or canoe and cruise the shoreline in search of a likely camping spot. A good point where the breeze from the Chesapeake Bay keeps the mosquitoes at bay might be a better choice and probably would present less risk of ticks. A camper will have to pack in his drinking water as sources of freshwater may be difficult to locate in the wild.

Saltwater-fishing opportunities abound during the warm months from June through September. Striped bass may be found at other times of the year, but there are limited seasons and low creel limits on this popular fish. Also available in the waters that touch the wildlife management area on three sides are black drum, bluefish, channel bass, croakers, flounder, and gray and speckled trout. All are not there at the same time, but the fishing can be good at just about any season.

Waterfowl hunting, of course, is the big thing here—the purpose for which the wildlife management area was formed. Waterfowl hunting is by far the top hunting activity. The entire Saxis area is noted as a black duck breeding and wintering area. There is probably no better area along the Virginia coast to bag a black duck. The bag limit has been traditionally low, only one or two birds. Canada geese also winter on the marsh. Other puddle ducks include mallard, pintail, teal, and widgeon. On the adjacent open water, hunters will get opportunities for bufflehead, canvasback, goldeneye, mergansers, redhead, scaup, widgeon, and sea ducks such as old squaw and scoter. Deer and cottontail rabbits are common, and furbearers include gray fox, mink, opossum, red fox, and river otter. Waterfowl hunting is limited to Freeschool Marsh, the northern tract. Michael Marsh, the southern tract, is a waterfowl refuge where waterfowl hunting is prohibited—though hunting for deer and other game is permitted. As is true of all wildlife management areas, permanent blinds are not permitted. Hunters improvise with temporary blinds using camouflage netting or simply throw together skimpy blinds that serve to break up their outline. Camouflage clothing is a big help.

There are plenty of miles of roads for hiking. Even the marshes are firm enough to hike on at low tide. The area is not really big enough to warrant a backpacking trip, but a day pack with drinking water might be a good idea.

The opportunities simply to observe nature, both the critters and plants and trees, are all but unlimited. In addition to the ducks and geese, there is the wide variety of birds and the furbearing animals. The inland forests and hummocks and the expanses of salt marshes offer a rich variety of plant life. Interesting critters include a trio of sea turtles, the endangered Delmarva squirrel, northern diamondback terrapin, river otter, the bullfrog and several additional frogs, several different salamanders, a number of snakes, of which only the copperhead is poisonous, the more common turtles including the box, painted, and snapping turtles, over half a dozen bats, sika deer, nutria, flying squirrel, a number of crayfish, and a great number of butterflies.

One simple way to enjoy the wildlife management area is to pack a picnic and locate a likely place to enjoy the abundant wildlife while you munch on a tasty meal. It may be inland in the forest or on a hummock or on a sandy point where you can enjoy the tangy breezes from the Chesapeake Bay.

We are fortunate that the Department of Game and Inland Fisheries had the opportunity to obtain this delightful chunk of marshland in a remote corner of Virginia.

Southside

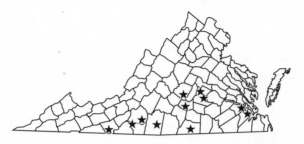

Counties: Amelia, Buckingham, Carroll, Franklin, Henry, Isle of Wight, Mecklenburg, Patrick, Pittsylvania, Powhatan, Prince Edward, and Surry

This region runs from the eastern slopes of the Blue Ridge Mountains east to the coastal counties and from the James River south to the North Carolina line. It is a transitional zone, ranging from the flat coastal plains of Isle of Wight County to the high country along the crest of the Blue Ridge Mountains. An interesting region with agriculture as its economic base, it is farming country, and the hunting here reflects that kind of land use. The traditional hunting has been for quail, rabbits, and squirrels, but deer and turkey hunting have come on strong in recent years. Dove hunting could well be more popular than quail hunting mainly because of the declining population of the long popular bobwhite quail. Despite a trend toward clear-cutting hardwood forests and replacing them with fast-growing loblolly pines, there are still enough hardwood lots to produce some good squirrel hunting. A good system of rivers and streams and the impounded waters such as Buggs Island Lake and hundreds of farm ponds produce some good waterfowl hunting. Federal lands are limited to a small section of the Jefferson National Forest in Bedford County, the Fort Pickett Military Reservation, and the U.S. Army Corps of Engineers lands around Buggs Island and Philpott lakes.

There are, however, eleven wildlife management areas in this region, and many acres of private forestlands are managed for hunting thanks to cooperative agreements between the timber companies and the Department of Game and Inland Fisheries. Obviously public lands offer numerous hunting opportunities in this vast and varied region of Virginia.

Amelia Wildlife Management Area

Supervising Office: Department of Game and Inland Fisheries
910 Thomas Jefferson Road
Forest, VA 24551
Telephone 804-525-7522
Location: Amelia County
Elevation: 200 to 300 feet

Located only twenty-five miles from Richmond, the state capital, the Amelia Wildlife Management Area provides a variety of outdoor opportunities for thousands of Virginians living in a densely populated area. Its 2,217 acres satisfy an amazing number of demands—hunting, lake and river fishing, hiking and bicycling trails, primitive camping, and picnicking. There is also a rifle range where hunters can sight in their rifles, a clay pigeons skeet range where shotgunners can sharpen their shooting, and an archery range for bow hunters. It is a popular spot for field trials and the site of scout and school outings and nature study classes. Obviously the area gets a lot of hard use. Named for the county in which it is located, Amelia Wildlife Management Area is primarily upland, gently rolling hill country with elevations ranging from 200 to 300 feet. There is, however, some bottomland along the Appomattox River, which forms its northern and eastern borders. All is in a single tract except for a small parcel of land southeast of the main body and between the Appomattox River and Route 604. This tract is reached off Route 604. The wildlife management area now encompasses what was once farmlands, and the open fields that were once grazed by livestock or planted in a variety of crops remain open. They are actively managed for small game such as doves, quail, and rabbits. Even so, there are rich stands of mature hardwoods and pines in the uplands and in the river bottoms along the Appomattox River. In addition to 100-acre Amelia Lake,

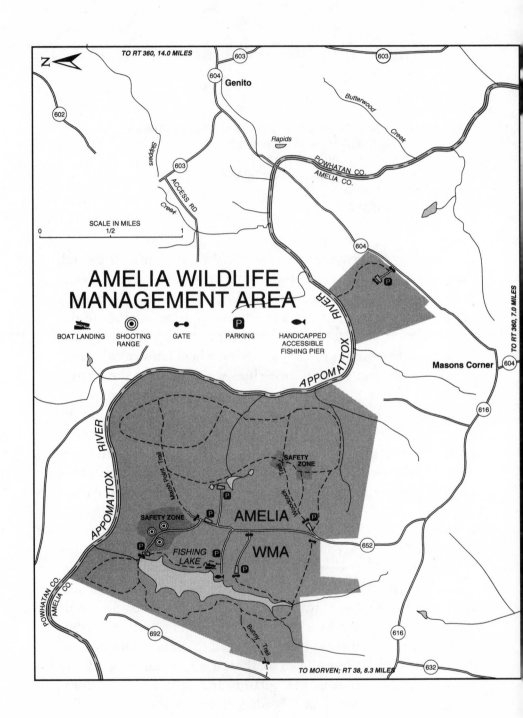

AMELIA WILDLIFE MANAGEMENT AREA

N

TO RT 360, 14.0 MILES

603
604
Genito

Butterwood Creek

602

Rapids

603

POWHATAN CO.
AMELIA CO.

ACCESS RD

Skippers Creek

SCALE IN MILES
0   1/2   1

604

TO RT 360, 7.0 MILES

Masons Corner
604

BOAT LANDING   SHOOTING RANGE   GATE   P PARKING   HANDICAPPED ACCESSIBLE FISHING PIER

APPOMATTOX RIVER

APPOMATTOX RIVER

APPOMATTOX RIVER

616

Marsh Point Trail

Woodcock Trail

SAFETY ZONE

AMELIA

652

SAFETY ZONE

FISHING LAKE

WMA

POWHATAN CO.
AMELIA CO.

Bunny Trail

692

616

632

TO MORVEN; RT 38, 8.3 MILES

there are several small ponds to the east between the lake and the Appomattox River. Several small streams drain the wildlife management area and empty into the Appomattox River.

The wildlife management area is reached by Route 652 off Secondary Route 616, which joins Route 604 at Masons Corner. Route 652 leads deep into the area and is the primary entrance. Several routes lead right and left off Route 652, the first one on the right to the resident manager's residence and the second one on the right to the three small ponds. The first one on the left leads to a parking area and to a trail which circles Amelia Lake. The second trail on the left leads to the boat-launching ramp, and the third one on the left to a trailhead and parking area near the dam of Amelia Lake. The Amelia Wildlife Management Area is approximately ten miles north of Amelia Courthouse and between U.S. Highway Routes 60 and 360. From U.S. Highway 60 turn south on Route 622, right on Route 610, and right on Route 604 at Masons Corner. From U.S. Highway 360 turn north on Route 604 and continue north to Masons Corner.

A good network of trails leads to just about all parts of the wildlife management area. A major trail circles the lake and offers the opportunity for camping with a view of the lake, though it may mean leaving the trail for short distances. Camping within 100 yards of the water, however, is prohibited. Only primitive camping is available. At several points, one near the headwaters of the lake and the other at the dam, the trail skirts the lake. It also crosses a pair of small streams that drain into the lake. Woodcock Trail, beginning at the parking area near the main entrance to the wildlife management area, skirts the small pond and then connects with Marsh Point Trail, which begins near the parking area at the end of Route 652. Using the map of the area, the backpacker can follow trails to just about all parts of the wildlife management area. Because the terrain rolls gently, the backpacker will not encounter any stiff climbs.

Any of the trails available to backpackers are also available to bicyclists, as are the main road into the area and the roads leading off of it. The nature of the terrain makes bicycling relatively easy. For overnight trips, finding a place to camp is no problem. Just pick a spot and pitch camp. Even though camping within 100 yards of the lakes and ponds is prohibited, there is nothing to prevent setting up camp along the Appomattox River. Regulations that apply to backpacking are equally applicable to bicyclists. Check the regulations posted at the entrance to the wildlife management area.

Intensive wildlife management for small game and game birds is equally as attractive to songbirds. Bird-watching can be productive and is enjoyed by many naturalists, particularly those from the Richmond area. Prescribed burning and planting wildlife food plots and thick hedgerows attract a great variety of birds. Many also are drawn to the river bottom and upland hardwood forests. One good way to observe birds is to launch a canoe on Amelia Lake and paddle slowly and quietly along the shoreline. A large beaver flowage along the Appomattox River offers a unique opportunity for watching a variety of birds. Over 150 different species of birds can be found on the wildlife management area at different times of the year. Some such as the brown creeper, dickcissel, bald eagle, purple finch, northern harrier, little blue heron, golden-crowned kinglet, moorhen, red-breasted nuthatch, barn owl, migrant loggerhead shrike, Henslow's sparrow, hermit thrush, cerulean and magnolia warblers, and winter wren are either endangered or threatened. They provide a golden opportunity to sight a somewhat rare bird. The more common birds include the rusty blackbird, eastern bluebird, indigo bunting, northern cardinal, catbird, chickadee, cowbird, fish crow, cuckoo, dowitcher, finch, flicker, flycatcher, gnatcatcher, goldfinch, grackle, grosbeak, a half-dozen hawks including the Cooper's, red-tailed, and rough-legged, green heron, hummingbird, blue jay, junco, kestrel, kingbird, lark, magpie, martin, meadowlark, mockingbird, nuthatch, oriole, osprey, ovenbird, a trio of owls, northern parula, pewee, phoebe, king rail, raven, robin, several sandpipers, siskin, a dozen sparrows, starling, barn swallow, tanager, tern, thrasher, thrush, titmouse, towhee, several vireos, over a dozen different species of warblers, waterthrush, whippoorwill, several woodpeckers, Carolina and house wrens, and the common yellowthroat. Enough possibilities to keep a bird-watcher occupied for months.

The 100-acre Amelia Lake offers opportunities for boating and canoeing. The launching ramp will accommodate both canoes and small boats, but outboard motors are prohibited, though electric trolling motors are allowed. Sailboats are prohibited, as is swimming in the lake or ponds. Carrying a light craft from the parking lot to the largest of the three ponds is no problem either. The Appomattox River, however, is the ideal water for canoeists. There is no formal access to the river, but hiking trails approach it. Portaging a light canoe along those trails might appeal to the more hardy. One possibility is to check out the stream below the dam at Amelia Lake. The Appomattox River is approximately a quarter of a mile from the dam, and even if the stream is not canoeable, it might float a light boat or canoe part of the way to the river. Drag it the rest! A trail leading from the parking area on the small detached tract of land near Masons Corner can provide exit. The trail leads to the river.

A number of opportunities are available to anglers. The major one, of course, is 100-acre Amelia Lake with a good launching ramp. It is well managed as a fishing lake and offers such species as largemouth bass, bluegill, channel catfish, crappie, redear sunfish, and walleye. Trees left standing during the construction of the dam and lake have long since rotted and fallen into the water and now offer good cover for the rich variety of fish. While the launching ramp permits anglers to launch boats, there is also a fishing pier near the ramp. Fish attractors have been positioned nearby, and they draw fish for the bank-bound anglers. The pier was also constructed to accommodate handicapped anglers. Bank fishing is also possible at various points around the lake, though shoreline brush may limit such fishing in some areas. To the east of the

and across the access road are three small ponds. The
gest offers some fishing, but the other two are flooded for
wildlife use and too shallow to hold fish.

Possibly the very best fishing is found in the Appomattox River,
which skirts the wildlife management area. The same species
found in the lake also fin the river waters—largemouth bass, catfish, and redear sunfish primarily, but no doubt a few bluegills,
crappies, and chain pickerel. During the late winter and early
spring, look for striped bass and walleyes to make spawning runs
up the river. Even though the river forms part of the boundary of
the wildlife management area, there is really no good access to it.
It might be possible to portage a canoe to the river using the trails
or the creek downstream from the lake. Portions of the river can
be waded, of course, and there is also fishing from the banks. One
possible approach is to use a tube float, which is light and easy to
transport to and from the river. Obviously there are a number of
good fishing opportunities on this wildlife management area.

Hunting, of course, is a big thing on the Amelia Wildlife Management Area. Because it is close to the Department of Game and
Inland Fisheries headquarters in Richmond, it is the site of various wildlife management research programs. For example, bobwhite quail management programs are tested here, particularly
the relationship between predators and declining quail populations. Wildlife management demonstration programs are carried
out on the area, and other practices are tested, including prescribed
burning, planting wildlife crops, and developing hedgerows, all of
which provide hunting for rabbits and quail. Dove fields are
planted annually. Dove hunting is extremely popular, with hunting limited to Saturday and Wednesday afternoons during the early
season. Probably on no other day throughout the many hunting
seasons are there more hunters on the wildlife management area
than on the opening day of the dove season. Check the hunting
regulations posted near the entrance to the area. The hardwood
offer good squirrel hunting, and there is more limited
g for deer and turkeys. Woodcock hunting can be good in

the river floodplain during the autumn migrations of the birds. And don't overlook the duck-hunting opportunities afforded by the Appomattox River. There is a large forty-acre beaver flowage on the wildlife management area side of the river that holds ducks.

Closely related to hunting are a six-station rifle range, a clay pigeon shotgun range, and an archery range. They provide golden opportunities for rifleman and archers who want to sight in their rifles or test their archery tackle in preparation for a new hunting season. The clay pigeon range offers shotgun shooters a chance to test different loads in their favorite scatterguns and sharpen their shooting before taking to the fields. Facilities for field trials are also available, including stables for horses. The use of such facilities has to be reserved in advance, of course. The field trials are particularly popular with families, providing everyone a day of competition and fun.

The various trails that loop and crisscross the wildlife management area are perfect for day hikes. Shoulder a day pack including binoculars, a camera, and lunch and strike out. The hiking is easy. An interesting half-day hike could begin in the parking area in the detached tract near Masons Corner. It is approximately a half mile to the Appomattox River. Study the map, and a hiker can plan a trip of just about any length desired.

The fact that Amelia Wildlife Management Area is a popular destination for Boy and Girl Scouts, school groups, and nature study classes attests to its value as a site for the study of nature. The lake, the ponds, the river and small streams, the well-managed open spaces, and the upland and floodplain forests make it an ideal place for those who like to study nature and photograph it. When visiting the area, nothing can be more valuable than a good pair of binoculars. Bird-watchers and nature observers should be familiar with the dates of the various hunting seasons and schedule their trips around them. After all, it is the hunters' license money that makes the wildlife management areas possible. There is no hunting on Sunday, of course, and that day is available for other uses all year long.

The variety of wildlife is rich, including over a half-dozen frogs, including the spring peeper, red-spotted newt, almost a dozen salamanders, three different kinds of toads and two tree frogs, over two dozen snakes, of which only the copperhead is poisonous, a half-dozen lizards and skinks, a half-dozen turtles including the more common box and snapping turtles, at least a half-dozen kinds of bats, beaver, bobcat, both gray and red foxes, raccoon, almost a dozen different kinds of rats and shrews, a half-dozen squirrels including the more common fox and gray squirrels and the southern flying squirrel, four different kinds of mussels, a half-dozen species of crayfish, and over thirty different kinds of butterflies. At times during the growing season there will be flowering dogwood and redbud, a limited amount of rhododendron, morning glory, yellow partridge peas, purple lespedeza, buttercups, jonquils, lady slippers, and dandelions, and in the late summer and autumn, the fields are filled with goldenrod.

Picnic sites are all but unlimited. Want to spread a blanket with a view of the lake or river, in a forest clearing, or on a grassy knoll? Chances are the picnicker will find something to please just about any taste. Just pack out your litter and leave nothing to reveal your visit.

The wildlife management area has limited horseback riding. Large groups are discouraged, but small groups of riders sometimes use the area. Check with the area's manager before mounting up. There may be restrictions riders should be aware of — or ongoing activities that riding would compete with. Gates that block motorized vehicles do not prevent bikers, hikers, or horseback riders from moving around the barriers and down the roads.

Those gates at the entrances of the various trails are often open to hunters during the open hunting seasons, but ATVs — all-terrain vehicles — and motorized bikes are always prohibited.

Offering such a wide variety of outdoor opportunities, the Amelia Wildlife Management Area could well be the busiest in the state.

Briery Creek
Wildlife Management Area

Supervising Office: Department of Game and Inland Fisheries
910 Thomas Jefferson Road
Forest, VA 24551
Telephone 804-525-7522
Location: Prince Edward County
Elevation: 200 to 400 feet

Briery Creek Lake is a household name in many Virginia angling families. The lake is noted for its big largemouth bass, and it could produce a new state record at any time. Few people probably ever realize that Briery Creek Lake is located in the Briery Creek Wildlife Management Area. The lake and the wildlife management area are named after Briery Creek and Little Briery Creek, the major feeder streams for the lake. These creeks were impounded to form the lake. But long before the land for the wildlife management area was purchased, the Briery Creek area was noted for its wild turkey populations. Hunters traveled from all over Virginia to hunt the big birds. The wildlife management area still offers good turkey hunting, and with the formation of the lake, waterfowl hunting also has become popular. Hunting and fishing are certainly the main attractions in this wildlife management area.

The 3,164-acre wildlife management area is located in Prince Edward County approximately seven miles south of Farmville and just off U.S. Highway 15. In fact, the dam is clearly visible to motorists traveling this major north-south highway. The land around the lake is mostly forested, primarily with hardwoods but also with good stands of loblolly pines that were planted by previous owners. The terrain is gently rolling hill country. Much of the land was farmed before its purchase by the Department of Game and

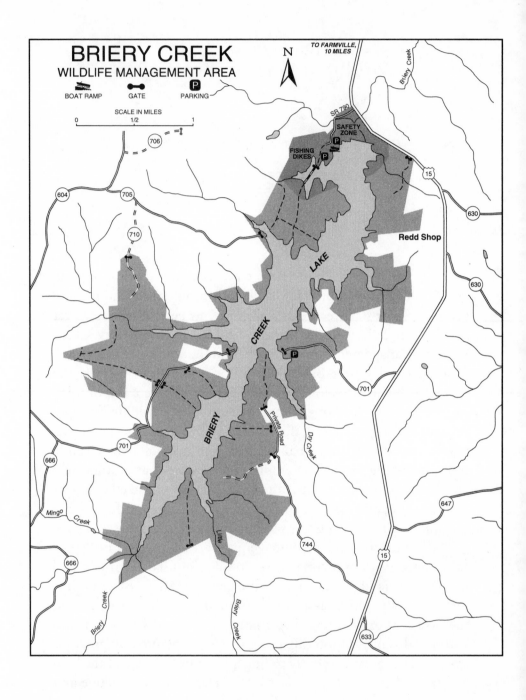

BRIERY CREEK
WILDLIFE MANAGEMENT AREA

BOAT RAMP   GATE   P PARKING

SCALE IN MILES
0   1/2   1

N

TO FARMVILLE, 10 MILES

Briery Creek

706

604   705

710

SR 790

SAFETY ZONE

FISHING DIKES

P
P

15

630

LAKE

Redd Shop

630

CREEK

P

701

701

BRIERY

666

Private Road

Dry Creek

647

Ming○ Creek

Little

744

15

666

Briery Creek

Briery Creek

633

Inland Fisheries, and some of the open fields offer hunting for small game. The major facilities include a concrete launching ramp just off U.S. Highway 15 near the dam. There is also a roomy parking area and toilet facility. A causeway at the end of Route 790 near the dam offers convenient bank fishing. Many anglers prefer to launch their boats there—and there is plenty of parking room for automobiles.

Reaching the lake is not a problem. From the north take U.S. Highway 15 off U.S. Highway 460 south to the lake, and from the south take U.S. Highway 15 off U.S. Highway 360 north to the lake. The 460 exit is in Farmville, and the 360 exit is near Keysville. Route 790 off U.S. 15 leads into the wildlife management area.

Opportunities for backpacking are somewhat limited. Most of the trails lead to the lake, and the backpacker who wants to get out for an overnight trek can find several that end on the shores of Briery Creek Lake. One possibility is to launch a canoe at the ramp off Route 790, paddle to one of the trails that end at the lake, and hike inland.

Bicyclists will find limited opportunities to ride. Both trails and roads lead generally to the lake. When the lake was formed, it flooded Route 701; the secondary route now leads to the lake off U.S. Highway 15 from the east and off Route 666 from the west. These sections of Route 701 may well offer the best bicycling opportunities.

When Briery Creek Lake was impounded, most of the timber was left standing; that above the water appeals to a wide variety of birds. There are ospreys, an occasional bald eagle, and a rich variety of waterfowl including the colorful wood duck, mallard, and various diving ducks. Different species of birds use the forested areas and the abandoned open fields. Among the endangered or threatened birds are the brown creeper, dickcissel, purple finch, harrier, golden-crowned kinglet, common moorhen, red-breasted nuthatch, barn owl, the migrant loggerhead shrike, cerulean and magnolia warblers, and winter wren. The more common birds are numerous at various times of the year. Among them are the black-bird, bluebird, indigo and snow buntings, cardinal, catbird, chickadee, cowbird, dowitcher, finch, flicker, flycatcher, goldfinch, grackle, grebe, grosbeak, several hawks, great blue and green herons, hummingbird, blue jay, killdeer, kingfisher, lark, purple martin, meadowlark, mockingbird, Baltimore and orchard orioles, osprey, a trio of owls, pewee, king rail, robin, a trio of sandpipers, a dozen sparrows, barn and northern swallows, scarlet tanager, tern, brown thrasher, thrush, tufted titmouse, several vireos, black and turkey vultures, thirteen different warblers, waxwing, downy, hairy, pileated, red-bellied, and red-headed woodpeckers, and the house wren.

Canoeists might find it fun to probe among the dead but still standing trees and back into the deep coves. Paddle quietly, and sightings of various kinds of wildlife are possible. Outboard motors are legal, but they cannot exceed 10-horsepower gasoline motors. Electric motors are also allowed. Boats can be launched at the ramp off Route 790, but light boats can be hand carried to the water from Routes 701 and 705. Boats can be cartopped to the gates at the ends of these secondary routes and carried the rest of the way—a very short distance.

The fact that camping is not allowed within 100 yards of the water limits camping opportunities, but drive along Route 701 or 705, and you might find a spot that appeals to you. Most likely you are going to be camping in a wooded area—which many campers prefer. Very few areas are accessible by automobile. For that reason the best camping might be combined with backpacking, which takes you off the roads.

Fishing, of course, is the big thing in the Briery Creek Wildlife Management Area. Popular fish include largemouth bass, bluegill, channel catfish, crappie, chain pickerel, and redear sunfish. The lunker largemouth bass is the big attraction. Florida largemouth bass, a species noted for its size, were stocked in the lake, and some big fish are being caught. The 845-acre lake gives up many citation-size bass every season. Channel catfish are the favorites of some anglers. They bite well, and catfish fillets are the favorite of many anglers who keep part of their catch. The standing and submerged timber, left when the lake was impounded, provides excellent cover for bluegill, crappie, and redear sunfish. The dead timber also attracts a great variety of insects that the fish feast on. Leaving those trees in the water was a smart move on the part of the fisheries biologists responsible for managing the lake. Fishing for panfish is excellent. Fishing from a bank is possible in several places, the most obvious being the fishing dikes at the end of Route 790, but other possibilities include the dam itself and the pier associated with the launching ramp. Probably the most popular are the trails that end on the lake at the ends of Routes 701 and 705. Chain pickerel are native to both Briery and Little Briery Creeks, and they were the most abundant fish when the lake was first formed. They still offer good fishing. The chain pickerel, Virginia's member of the pike family, is a vicious fish that hits hard and provides a thrilling battle if it decides to leap and tailwalk across the water. Anglers who want to fish for pickerel in their native water can take a boat to coves where the two streams enter the lake and get out and wade up the little streams for the fish. The coves themselves should offer good lake fishing for the chain pickerel. Briery Creek Lake is a fine fishery, one of the best in the state. The submerged timber will claim a lot of lures. Use wire hooks that bend easily; they are easier to pull free when snagged in the timber. The underwater cover is also tough on motor propellers, so proceed carefully when in this kind of water.

Waterfowl hunting could well be the most popular hunting in this water-rich wildlife management area. Waterfowl hunting is limited to Wednesday and Saturday, so plan accordingly. The standing timber seems to appeal to ducks just as it appeals to fish. The hunting seems to be best in the coves, of which there are many on the lake. The season kicks off with the colorful and tasty little wood duck being the most abundant. Later there are the mallard and several kinds of diving ducks. Permanent blinds are prohibited, but a marsh-colored johnboat and some netting to conceal it and a pair of hunters dressed in camouflage will work just as well. Put out a few decoys and wait for legal shooting time—or get there in late afternoon and plan for action during the closing minutes of the legal hunting day. The few abandoned fields offer hunting for quail and rabbits, and a managed dove field is off U.S. Highway 15 just south of the Briery Creek Lake dam. The hunting associated with woodlands—deer, squirrels, and turkeys—is probably the most extensive because, except for the lake, such cover dominates the wildlife management area.

The Briery Creek Wildlife Management Area probably has more appeal to day hikers than to backpackers. Short hikes will take hikers to the water's edge where they can unpack a lunch and pick up their binoculars to watch activities on the water as they munch on sandwiches. All kinds of things out there should be of interest—birds, beavers, and muskrat, and even the fishermen themselves. Focus those binoculars on an angler in his or her boat, and you might learn how an expert angler works.

A great variety of nature's critters are there to entertain you. Endangered or threatened species include Atlantic pigtoe mussel, the small star-nosed mole, and the river otter. The otter might well be the most likely to be spotted. The more common critters include several frogs, red-spotted newt, ten different species of salamanders, three toads and two tree frogs, two dozen snakes, of which only the copperhead is poisonous, four skinks, a half-dozen turtles including the snapping, box, mud, and painted turtles, eight different kinds of bats, eight rats and shrews, the long-tailed weasel, woodchuck, a number of crayfish, and no less than seventy-five varieties of butterflies. Conceal yourself on the shores of the lake, paddle a canoe quietly along the deeply indented shoreline, or throttle down your outboard and motor to the back end of a cove. Shut the motor off, take out your binoculars, and just watch. Ospreys or a bald eagle might entertain you for hours, but more likely it will be a great variety of songbirds that use the shoreline or visit the standing timber in the lake. A duck or two, depending upon the season, may settle down in the cover, or beavers, muskrat, or even otters may surprise you as they play nearby. Woodland flowers and shrubs provide the major color here. Look for flowering dogwoods, redbud, rhododendron, and lady slippers. The small fields sprout dandelions, buttercups, a few jonquils, and in late summer and early fall goldenrod appears.

The gated ends of Routes 701 and 705 might provide the best opportunity for a quiet picnic on the shores of the lake. Park your automobile at the gate and carry your lunch to the water's edge. A quick look along the shoreline might turn up the ideal spot. Another possibility is to launch a small boat at the ramp near the dam and cruise the shoreline in search of a spot that appeals to you.

Rides along Routes 701 and 705 might be the best possibilities for horseback riding, but even then it might be best to check with the wildlife area's manager first. Horseback riding opportunities are very limited on this area.

The fact that a popular lake dominates this wildlife management area sets it apart.

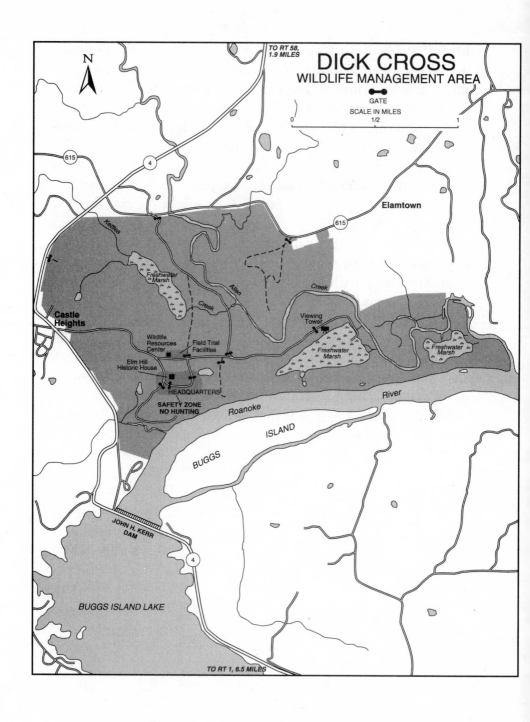

N

TO RT 58,
1.9 MILES

DICK CROSS
WILDLIFE MANAGEMENT AREA

GATE

SCALE IN MILES
1/2

0   1

615

4

Elamtown

615

Keplies

Freshwater
Marsh

Allen

Creek

Creek

Castle
Heights

Viewing
Tower

Freshwater
Marsh

Freshwater
Marsh

Wildlife
Resources
Center

Field Trial
Facilities

Elm Hill
Historic House

HEADQUARTERS

SAFETY ZONE
NO HUNTING

Roanoke

River

ISLAND

BUGGS

JOHN H. KERR
DAM

4

BUGGS ISLAND LAKE

TO RT 1, 6.5 MILES

Dick Cross Wildlife Management Area

Supervising Office: Department of Game and Inland Fisheries
910 Thomas Jefferson Road
Forest, VA 24551
Telephone 804-525-7522
Location: Mecklenburg County
Elevation: 200 to 300 feet

Honoring the late Dick Cross, former executive director of the Virginia Department of Game and Inland Fisheries, the Dick Cross Wildlife Management Area couldn't have been more appropriately named. Dick Cross devoted his entire career to the department, taking a leave of absence during World War II to serve in the U.S. Army Air Corps as a fighter pilot in the skies over Europe. Back in Virginia after the war, he began his climb to the top in the department but found time for field trials, his favorite outdoor activity. He served as a judge in many of the top field trials in the state. This wildlife management area was established as the Elm Hill Wildlife Management Area, but its name was later changed to honor Cross soon after his death. The first parcel of land was purchased in 1963. Today the wildlife management area is nationally known as the host site for national field trials. Field trial enthusiasts will find stalls for their horses, roomy kennels for their pointers and setters, and acres of open fields in which to run them. Foxhound field trials are also run here. Field trials are scheduled outside the hunting seasons to avoid conflicts. In addition to the field trials, there is some excellent dove hunting, and the freshwater marshes attract wintering waterfowl.

Driving along the entrance road, on the left you first come to the Wildlife Resources Center, an attractive building available for wildlife-related classes, conferences, and meetings. The 1,400-acre wildlife management area is located in Mecklenburg County down the Roanoke River from Buggs Island Lake and the John H. Kerr Dam. Like so much of this Southside Virginia land, the elevation ranges from 200 to 300 feet, producing gently rolling terrain. No mountain climbing here. Before its purchase by the Department of Game and Inland Fisheries, much of the land was a sprawling cattle farm, and there is evidence of that kind of land use to this day. Much of the area is open in an old-field stage or cultivated to benefit wildlife. In addition to the open uplands, there are approximately 300 acres of bottomland along Allen Creek and the Roanoke River, which serves as the southern border of the wildlife management area. Management practices include disking and prescribed burning to maintain the native vegetation in the open fields. Three freshwater marshes totaling 125 acres have been formed by impounding small streams. One was formed by impounding Kettles Creek in the northwest section of the wildlife management area, and the other two are in the Roanoke River bottomlands in the southeastern corner. Although these three freshwater impoundments are a big attraction to wintering waterfowl, the entire wildlife management area is closed to waterfowl hunting.

The Dick Cross Wildlife Management Area is an interesting creation, one of the most interesting in the wildlife management area system statewide. Those who haven't visited the area owe it to themselves to do so. The wildlife management area is bordered on the west by Virginia Primary Highway 4, on the north by Secondary Route 615, and on the south by the Roanoke River, or the headwaters of Lake Gaston. Allen Creek forms part of the eastern border, but the rest abuts private land.

Virginia Primary 4, reached off U.S. Highway 58 between South Hill and Clarksville, leads to the entrance to the wildlife management area at the community of Castle Heights. The road leading to the Wildlife Resources Center and the field trial facilities is covered with a canopy of trees and is very inviting.

Backpacking opportunities are somewhat limited. One trail leaves Route 615 and circles back on itself, a hike of less than a mile. Another trail leaves the field trial facilities area and heads north to connect with a gated road that runs a northwesterly route from Route 615 to connect with the area's main road from Castle Heights. The trail is approximately a half mile long and the gated road a little over a mile in length. The main road is approximately two miles long and leads deep into the area to the larger freshwater marsh near the Roanoke River. There is quite a bit of open country that can be explored on foot, however, for a backpacker who wants to shoulder a pack, take a compass reading, and strike out. However, as interesting as this wildlife management area is, there are better areas in the state for backpacking.

Bicyclists can enjoy a good ride by parking at Castle Heights, mounting up, and pedaling eastward into the wildlife management area. They might want to take a few minutes around the headquarters area where they'll find the Wildlife Resources Center, the Elm Hill historic house, and the field trial facilities. Continuing east in the area, they will come to the viewing tower on a high cliff overlooking the largest of the three freshwater marshes. The road is gated just before it reaches the tower, but bicyclists can go around the gate and continue to where the road leads into the marsh. On the return trip they might want to turn north and follow the gated road that parallels Allen Creek. They eventually will leave the area and hit Virginia Primary Route 4 where they can turn left and ride back to their automobile at Castle Heights. Because of the gently rolling nature of the terrain, none of the riding is difficult.

Between the three freshwater marshes, Allen Creek, the Roanoke River, and the many acres of open fields managed for wildlife, a great many birds use this area throughout the year. A bird-watcher could spend much of a day in the viewing tower overlooking the largest freshwater marsh and the Roanoke River bottomlands. In order to use this time to the best advantage, bring along a good pair of binoculars. A spotting scope might be even better. Set it up in the viewing tower and use it to complement the binoculars. Use the binoculars for general bird-watching, but when something of particular interest is sighted, move to the more powerful spotting scope for a closer look, just as many big-game hunters do. The freshwater marshes, built and managed for wintering waterfowl, can be particularly good for bird-watching. Waterfowl cannot be hunted on this waterfowl management area, so the birds will not be disturbed.

In addition to the usual ducks, a number of shorebirds use the marshes, and bald eagles winter in the area. Among the birds on the endangered or threatened list are the dickcissel, bald eagle, great egret, purple finch, northern harrier, tricolored heron, yellow-crowned night heron, golden-crowned kinglet, common moorhen, red-breasted nuthatch, barn owl, migrant loggerhead shrike, Henslow's sparrow, Caspian and Forster's terns, hermit thrush, cerulean and magnolia warblers, and sedge and winter wrens. The more common birds include the bittern, Brewer's, red-winged, and rusty blackbirds, bluebird, bunting, cardinal, catbird, yellow-breasted chat, chickadee, coot, cowbird, fish crow, cuckoo, dowitcher, house finch, flicker, flycatcher, gnatcatcher, goldfinch, grackle, grebe, grosbeak, several gulls, a half-dozen hawks, great blue and green herons, blue jay, junco, kestrel, killdeer, kingbird, kingfisher, lark, loon, purple martin, meadowlark, mockingbird, nighthawk, nuthatch, oriole, osprey, ovenbird, several owls, pewee, phoebe, pipit, plover, the king and Virginia rails, robin, several sandpipers, a dozen sparrows, starling, the barn, cliff, tree, and northern swallows, tanager, thrasher, a pair of thrushes, titmouse, towhee, several vireos and vultures, over a dozen warblers, waxwing, five woodpeckers including the downy, pileated, and red-headed, the Carolina and house wrens, and the common yellowthroat.

There are little or no boating or canoeing opportunities in this area even though the Roanoke River skirts the southern reaches of the area and Allen Creek runs through it. There is no formal access in the wildlife management area to either stream, but a knowledgeable canoeist can figure out accessing and exiting both creek and the stream. For example, he or she might enter the stream at one of the bridge crossings just upstream from the area on Allen Creek, canoe it to its confluence with the river, and then paddle downstream to the Steel Bridge Launching Area on Lake Gaston.

Although there are no campgrounds on the wildlife management area, primitive camping for up to two weeks at a time is allowed. Someone interested in camping might drive the road from Castle Heights to the viewing tower and find a spot that is appealing. Backpackers are not so limited as they can go around the gates and get to more likely campsites. They can also leave the roads and trails in search of a campsite that appeals to them.

Both Allen Creek and the Roanoke River offer fishing, even though neither has formal access within the wildlife management area. The Roanoke River and both Buggs Island Lake upstream and Lake Gaston below the Kerr Dam are noted for their striped bass fishing. Local anglers enjoy fishing for catfish in Allen Creek, but there are other species in the stream such as largemouth bass, bluegill, crappie, and chain pickerel.

Though fishing is somewhat limited on the wildlife management area, that is not the case with hunting, particularly small-game hunting. Just about every one of its 1,400 acres offers small-game hunting of one kind or another. Dove hunting might well be the best because of extensive plantings of wheat and corn as well as lespedeza, clover, and millet. Hunting for the gray ghosts can be excellent, but as is typical of public hunting areas, the pressure is heavy. The area is, however, remote from the major Virginia population centers, and this fact eases the pressure. Dove hunting is limited to the opening day afternoon and Saturday and Wednesday afternoons during the early dove season. The regulations are posted at the entrance to the wildlife management area and should be reviewed before a hunter enters the field. The rabbit hunting is good, and quail seem to be faring better in this part of Virginia than in others. Habitat for squirrels is somewhat limited, but scattered woodlots offer some good hunting. Approximately 100 acres of the area are in forest. Squirrels like hardwood ridges, and the steep one overlooking the larger of the three freshwater marshes should be worth a try. Although the management efforts on this area are directed toward small game, there is a good deer population, and wild turkeys are on the increase.

The wildlife management area is better suited to day hiking than backpacking. A hiker can shoulder a day pack including binoculars, a camera, and lunch and spend the day exploring the area, its freshwater marshes, its field trial facilities, its well-managed open fields, and the viewing tower.

The viewing tower is not limited to watching bird life. The tower covers a wide expanse of freshwater marshes and the Roanoke River bottomlands. Set up there, and in addition to birds you can watch deer feed, beavers, muskrat, and otters work and feed in the marshes, and even bald eagles soar overhead. It's a delightful place to spend an interesting day outdoors. Among the endangered or threatened critters are the Roanoke log perch, Atlantic pigtoe mussel, Carolina darter, whitemouth shiner, Roanoke bass, and river otter. The more common wildlife includes several frogs including the bullfrog and the spring peeper, red-spotted newt, a dozen different kinds of salamanders, three toads and a pair of tree frogs, water dog, almost two dozen snakes including the poisonous copperhead, a pair of lizards and a half-dozen skinks, a half-dozen of the more common turtles, a half-dozen bats, beaver, fox, mink, a pair of moles, opossum, raccoon, the gray and southern flying squirrels, two kinds of mussels, a quartet of crayfish, and over a dozen species of butterflies. There are flowering dogwoods, redbuds, and rhododendron in the limited hardwood forests, water lilies in the impoundments, and a variety of flowers in the open fields. Look to the open fields for buttercups, dandelions, Queen Anne's lace, violets, and naturalized jonquils. There may be lady slippers in the woods, and in late summer and early autumn the fields will shine with goldenrod.

For a picnic, why not pack a lunch and enjoy it in the viewing tower. Just accept the fact that other people might like to use the tower also. If so, make room for them or move your picnic somewhere else. There is plenty of space for a picnic in the 1,400-acre wildlife management area.

The area gets a lot of use by the horses of field trial participants. There are even stables for them. Probably five miles of roads and trails are available for riding. From the field trial facilities headquarters, a rider on horseback can travel all trails except the short one off Route 615 that is not accessible from any other road.

Dick Cross would be proud of this wildlife management area which bears his name.

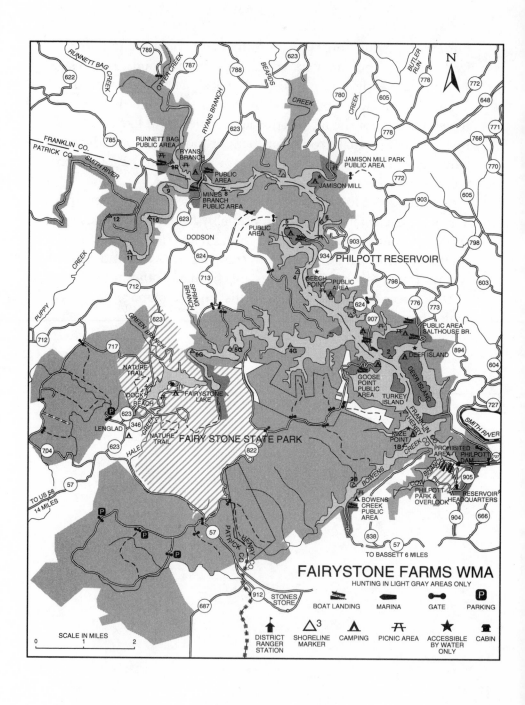

FAIRYSTONE FARMS WMA

HUNTING IN LIGHT GRAY AREAS ONLY

BOAT LANDING   MARINA   GATE   PARKING

DISTRICT RANGER STATION   SHORELINE MARKER   CAMPING   PICNIC AREA   ACCESSIBLE BY WATER ONLY   CABIN

SCALE IN MILES
0   1   2

Fairystone Farms
Wildlife Management Area

Supervising Office: Department of Game and Inland Fisheries
910 Thomas Jefferson Road
Forest, VA 24551
Telephone 804-525-7522
Location: Henry and Patrick Counties
Elevation: Approximately 900 to 1,600 feet

The Fairystone Farms Wildlife Management Area is the major part of a parcel of public recreation land that includes, in addition to the wildlife management area, Fairy Stone State Park and lands of the U.S. Army Corps of Engineers. A cooperative agreement between the federal and state agencies makes this possible. The wildlife management area offers 5,321 acres of hunting land, but thanks to the agreements with the Virginia Division of Parks and the Corps of Engineers, the total public land available for hunting and other outdoor recreation swells to over 13,000 acres. The state park alone makes up 4,561 acres of that total, with the rest being Corps of Engineers land. The legend of the fairy stone lingers from centuries ago when, according to the story, some fairies dancing around a mountain spring learned of the death of Christ. The fairies wept at the sad news, and when their tears fell to the earth, each was crystallized into a pebble forming a beautiful cross. The legend promises good fortune for those finding these little pebbles. Most of the wildlife management area lies in Patrick County, but 460 acres are located in neighboring Henry County. The wildlife management area actually surrounds the state park and borders on miles of Philpott Lake and Corps of Engineers land.

The area is in the eastern foothills of the Blue Ridge Mountains, and much of the land is steep, though there are small areas of bottomland. Many of the roads and trails in the area follow ridges that drop off quickly to deep valleys. The area is riddled with small streams, and both Otter Creek and the Smith River flow through portions of the area to form 2,800-acre Philpott Lake. Most of the area is covered with forests of hickory, oak, and pine, but there are rich stands of beech and poplar far up the narrow valleys. The primary thrust of the wildlife management plan is to provide forest habitat for deer, turkeys, and a wide variety of small game and nongame wildlife. A facet of the management plan is one that sets the stage for trophy deer. One eight-acre marsh is impounded as a refuge for migrating waterfowl. All and all, this is an interesting chunk of land in an interesting part of Virginia.

Fifteen miles northwest of Martinsville and forty-five miles south of Roanoke, the Fairystone Wildlife Management Area probably is best reached by Route 57 west from Bassett. U.S. Highway 220 is a quick route south from Roanoke to the little foothills city of Bassett. Virginia Primary Highway 122 south from Bedford to join U.S. Highway 220 at Rocky Mount is a quick route from Bedford or Lynchburg. From nearby Danville take U.S. Highway 58 west to the Bassett area. Most highway signs direct the traveler to Fairy Stone State Park instead of to the wildlife management area, but because the park is surrounded by the wildlife management area, the park signs lead to the wildlife management area also. Driving west on Route 57, you turn right on Route 623, which leads to the park entrance on Route 346. A sign indicates the entrance to the wildlife management area—to the left.

There are numerous backpacking opportunities for those who like to shoulder a pack with the essentials for living on the trail. But plan on doing some climbing; it is that kind of country. There are trails to follow, but the true outdoorsman might want to take a compass reading and strike out through the rich forest-covered hills. Several gated roads offer interesting possibilities. One off

Route 822, which serves as a boundary between the wildlife management area and the state park, leads all the way east to the Goose Point Public Area on Philpott Lake. A number of trails lead off this road, one going all the way to the Bowens Creek arm of the big lake. See the map for several interesting backpacking routes.

Bicyclists will also find this an interesting area to travel, though they may have to make some steep climbs. Parking areas near the beginning of a number of the trails serve as trailheads where a bicyclist can park an automobile, unload the bike, and take off along a trail to adventure. Gated trails prohibit only motorized vehicles. The biker can go around the gates and enter the trail.

Bird-watchers will find numerous opportunities on the lakeshore, the many tiny streams crossed by most of the trails, and the Bowens Creek, Otter Creek, and Smith River arms of the lake. Many of the hills in the area provide vantage points from which to glass for birds of many varieties. And don't overlook the impounded marsh area off Route 623, which is used by migrating waterfowl and other birds. There is also 168-acre Fairystone Lake in the park that is available for bird-watching, particularly along its shores. A number of endangered or threatened birds use this area. Among them are the brown creeper, dickcissel, bald eagle, great egret, peregrine falcon, purple finch, northern harrier, golden-crowned kinglet, moorhen, red-breasted nuthatch, long-eared owl, migrant loggerhead shrike, Caspian tern, hermit thrush, cerulean, golden-winged, magnolia, and Swainson's warblers, and winter wren. Among the more common birds are the red-winged and rusty blackbirds, bluebird, indigo bunting, cardinal, catbird, yellow-breasted chat, Carolina chickadee, chuck-will's-widow, cormorant, cowbill, crossbill, crow, cuckoo, dowitcher, finch, flicker, four species of flycatchers, gnatcatcher, goldfinch, grackle, grebe, grosbeak, a half-dozen hawks, great blue and green herons, hummingbird, blue jay, junco, kestrel, killdeer, kingbird, kingfisher, ruby-crowned kinglet, lark, purple martin, meadowlark, mockingbird, nighthawk, nuthatch, Baltimore oriole, osprey, ovenbird, a trio of owls, parula, pewee, phoebe, king and Virginia rails, raven, robin, four different kinds of sandpipers, sora, a dozen different sparrows, starling, swallow, swift, tanager, tern, thrasher, thrush, titmouse, towhee, several species of vireos, vulture, over a dozen warblers, waterthrush, waxwing, the American, downy, hairy, pileated, red-bellied, and red-headed woodpeckers, Carolina and house wrens, and the common yellowthroat.

The excellent boat access all around Philpott Lake can accommodate all kinds of pleasure boats and canoes. Many are far up the lake, one on Otter Creek, for example, and another on Smith River. Down the lake near the dam there is a ramp on Bowens Creek. The presence of so many launching ramps allows a boater or canoeist to explore just about any part of the lake desired. Try launching a canoe near the mouth of one of the several winding arms of the lake and explore far upstream. Fairystone Lake is also available to the boater or canoeist. There is a launching ramp off Route 623, which leads north off Route 346.

The Fairy Stone State Park provides camping in the very center of the entire complex, with restrooms, showers, and established campsites with picnic tables. The Corps of Engineers lands also have established campgrounds. For those who prefer to camp away from the crowd and don't object to primitive camping, the wildlife management area lands offer plenty of opportunities. A stay, of course, is limited to two weeks on a single visit.

The tailwaters below the Philpott Dam are noted for big brown trout. Icy waters released from the depths of the reservoir make the tailwaters ideal trout water. The fish thrive, and there is some natural reproduction. These waters produce some trophy brown trout every year. Trout in the 15- to 18-pound class are always a possibility. An 18-pound 11-ounce brown trout was taken from the stream in 1979. There is also good fishing well downstream from the tailwaters section, and trout are stocked regularly. The Smith River is one of Virginia's premier trout streams. The lake itself produces good fishing for largemouth and smallmouth bass, bluegills, crappies, and walleyes. The reservoir is also stocked annually with 8- to 9-inch McConaughy rainbow trout. Trout can be caught throughout the lake all year, but in the summer months the more successful fishermen fish deep and at night. The lake produces some 7- to 8-pound rainbows every season. And the angler shouldn't overlook 168-acre Fairystone Lake in the state park. It holds largemouth bass, bluegills, channel catfish, and crappies. For the angler unfamiliar with the fishing in the area, a smaller body of water can be more quickly patterned than a big, deep reservoir. This is trout-fishing country, and Patrick County has a number of trout streams.

Hunting is big in this wildlife management area, partly because of the abundance of hunting land in the complex, but also because it is located in good deer and turkey country. The deer management plan offers possibilities for some real trophy bucks. Fairy Stone State Park is one of the few in the park system that has been open to hunting for a number of years. That trend, however, is spreading to other parks. The U.S. Army Corps of Engineers generally allows hunting on its lands, but some areas are off-limits to hunting, such as Deer and Turkey Islands downlake near the dam. Also off-limits are the various recreational areas around the lake and the boat access areas. The eight-acre impounded marsh is a refuge area, of course, and there is no hunting. Otherwise the entire complex is open to hunting during all legal hunting seasons. In addition to deer and turkeys, there is good squirrel hunting for the small-game hunter. There is also more limited hunting for grouse, quail, woodcocks, and waterfowl. Of this group grouse are probably the most abundant. Weather permitting, most of the gated trails are open during the hunting seasons, allowing better access to the backcountry.

The hiker, like the backpacker, will find plenty of trails to follow. A hiker with a day pack, binoculars, and some drinking water and snacks can spend an interesting day on this complex of public lands. All of the roads and trails are open to the hiker. If the trails or roads are gated, simply go around the gate and proceed.

The tiny creeks, steep hills, deep valleys, long arms of the lake, and acres of hardwoods offer all kinds of nature to view, fauna as well as flora. Take along some pocket-size guides to identify critters and plants.

Besides the game animals, there are the likes of opossum and raccoon and water critters such as beaver, otter, and muskrat. Check out some of those small streams for beaver flowages. There are few streams in the state today that busy beavers have not discovered. Endangered or threatened species found include the Roanoke log perch, bog turtle, orangefin madtom, small-footed myotis, Atlantic pigtoe mussel, the Diana and regal butterflies, Roanoke bass, and the rustyside sucker. More common critters of interest include the bullfrog, the green, northern cricket, pickerel, upland chorus, and wood frogs, northern spring peeper, red-spotted newt, over a dozen salamanders, three toads, a pair of tree frogs, the copperhead and timber rattler and almost two dozen nonpoisonous snakes, a half-dozen lizards or skinks, the box, mud, musk, painted, and snapping turtles, eight different kinds of bats, gray and red foxes, bobcat, beaver, lemming, mink, opossum, raccoon, a half-dozen shrews, gray, red, and southern flying squirrels, several mussels, a half-dozen crayfish, and over two dozen butterflies. Wildflowers and flowering shrubs common to the southern Appalachians are found here. Among them look for dogwoods, redbud, trilliums, wild iris, wild orchids, fire pink, mayapples, mountain laurel, and rhododendron, and in the late summer and autumn goldenrod.

Sunday picnickers will find any number of likely spots to spread a blanket and enjoy an outdoor meal. Possibly along the lake or reservoir or beneath the spreading limbs of an aging oak. Or find a spot on one of those high ridges with a good view of the lake.

Horseback riders from the state park ride the wildlife management area trails as well as those in the park. In fact, the wildlife management area offers many more such opportunities than does the state park.

Before planning a trip to the Fairystone Wildlife Management Area, get some information from Virginia Division of Parks about the Fairy Stone State Park. An understanding of the park and its rules will make it possible to enjoy the wildlife management area even more.

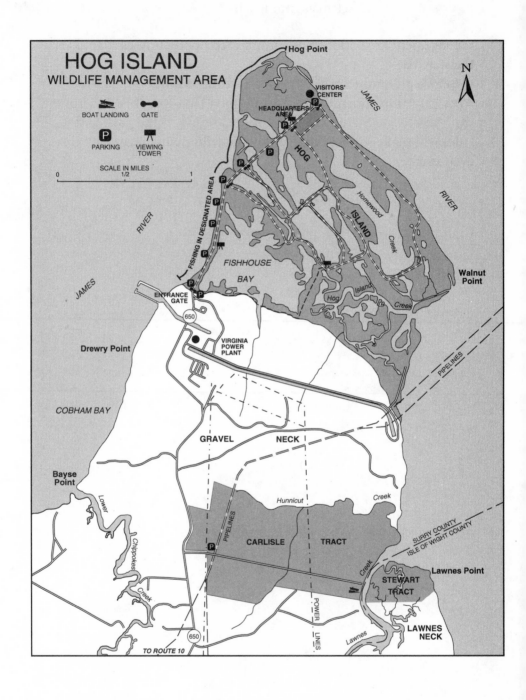

HOG ISLAND
WILDLIFE MANAGEMENT AREA

BOAT LANDING   GATE

PARKING   VIEWING
           TOWER

SCALE IN MILES
0   1/2   1

N

Hog Point

VISITORS'
CENTER

HEADQUARTERS
AREA

HOG

FISHING IN DESIGNATED AREA

ISLAND

JAMES   RIVER

Homewood

Creek

JAMES   RIVER

Walnut
Point

FISHHOUSE

BAY

Hog Island   Creek

ENTRANCE
GATE

650

VIRGINIA
POWER
PLANT

Drewry Point

COBHAM BAY

PIPELINES

Bayse
Point

GRAVEL   NECK

Hunnicut   Creek

Lower

Chippokes

PIPELINES

CARLISLE   TRACT

SURRY COUNTY
ISLE OF WIGHT COUNTY

Lawnes Point

Creek

Creek

STEWART
TRACT

650

POWER

LINES

Lawnes

LAWNES
NECK

TO ROUTE 10

Hog Island Wildlife Management Area

Supervising Office: Department of Game and Inland Fisheries
5806 Mooretown Road
Williamsburg, VA 23188
Telephone 757-253-4180
Location: Isle of Wight and Surry Counties
Elevation: Approximately sea level to 35 feet

Hog Island is more of a peninsula than an island, though a number of tidal creeks all but separate it from the mainland. At the tip of the peninsula is Hog Point, a prominent terrain feature in the James River. The name Hog Island is a carryover from centuries ago when English settlers allowed their hogs to forage on the tips of peninsulas that jutted into the James River. Farther inland on the eastern side of the peninsula are Walnut Point and Lawnes Point. On the western side of the peninsula are Drewry Point and Bayse Point. Thanks to a number of bays and creeks such as Fishhouse Bay and Hog Island and Homewood creeks, the Hog Island peninsula is about as much water as it is land. It makes up over half of the 3,908-acre wildlife management area, the other two tracts being farther inland.

The Hog Island tract is a mixture of flat, open land and pine forests interspersed with tidal marshes, numerous cuts, and controlled ponds. Probably no other wildlife management area is more intensively managed for wildlife. Several impoundments are drained annually and planted and then flooded to provide food for wintering waterfowl. A vast dike system facilitates this practice. Additionally, surrounding fields are planted in agricultural crops to help feed the birds. Dirt roads circle the impoundments to provide vehicular access to the tract. Driving into the area on Route 650, you first come to the Carlisle tract, which lies between Route 650 and the James River to the east. A paved road passes through the southern third of the tract to provide access to a boat-launching ramp on Lawnes Creek, which feeds into the James River. The Carlisle tract is approximately 35 feet above sea level, "highlands" when compared to the Hog Island tract just a foot or so above sea level. Hunnicut Creek runs north through this tract and then forms its northern boundary as it meanders slowly into the James River. The Carlisle tract has been reforested in loblolly pines, and several power-line and pipeline rights-of-way are seeded in wildlife plantings. Otherwise there are no other roads or trails to provide access to this upland tract. Across Lawnes Creek from the boat ramp lies the fifty-acre Stewart tract, an area of marshes ribboned by winding creeks and cuts. The Stewart tract is in Isle of Wight County while the remainder, and bulk, of the Hog Island Wildlife Management Area is in Surry County.

Virginia Route 650 off Route 10 between the Southside Virginia towns of Smithfield and Surry is the only access to the Hog Island Wildlife Management Area. Route 650 skirts the western edge of the Carlisle tract and passes through the Virginia Power Company property into the wildlife management area. The visitors' center is at the end of Route 650.

The Hog Island Wildlife Management Area does not lend itself to ambitious backpacking. The Carlisle tract from Route 650 to the James River is less than two miles, and south to north it is less than a mile. It's flat, of course, but the understory in the pine forest is thick and not easy to walk through. The Stewart tract is reached only by boat. The Hog Island tract has several miles of dirt roads that circle the impoundments. They are gated, but they do not prohibit travel by foot. Several observation towers overlook the marshes. A trail that begins near the entrance gate to the Hog Island tract skirts Fishhouse Bay and leads to an observation tower deep in the impoundment area. A backpacker can tackle this land of marshes and creeks, and if the going gets too tough, the trip back isn't very long. There are, however, better wildlife management areas for backpacking.

The bicyclist will find the roads into the impounded area easy to travel. There are numerous parking areas along the primary route into the area. Bicyclists can park their motor vehicles at any of these parking areas, unload their bikes, and take off into some unusual country, a land of water and low-lying fields and marshes. Most of the roads and trails are gated, which prohibits only travel by automobile. The only ungated road is the one running through the Carlisle tract to the boat-launching ramp on Lawnes Creek. As is true of the backpacker, it is doubtful that the bicyclist will want to camp in the area, even though that is possible. Mosquitoes can be vicious during the warmer months.

The Hog Island Wildlife Management Area can be a bird-watcher's dream. To that end the Department of Game and Inland Fisheries has erected three viewing towers that provide commanding locations from which to observe the wildlife on the management area. There is probably no better place in Virginia to observe and enjoy waterfowl, so great is the variety of ducks, geese, and swans, but this is just the beginning of the bird-watching possibilities. Numerous shorebirds use the area, particularly along the narrow James River beach. Cross Lawnes Creek by boat and spend some time on the Stewart tract. Be sure to wear boots or even hip boots. Several creeks meander through the small tract of marshlands. Among the endangered or threatened birds that use this area are the brown creeper, dickcissel, bald eagle, great egret, peregrine falcon, purple finch, northern harrier, little blue and tricolored herons, night heron, golden-crowned kinglet, the common moorhen, barn owl, black rail, loggerhead shrike, Caspian, Forster's, and least terns, hermit thrush, cerulean and magnolia warblers, red-cockaded woodpecker, and sedge and winter wrens. The more common birds that use or visit the area include the bittern, red-winged blackbird, bluebird, indigo and snow buntings, cardinal, catbird, yellow-breasted chat, chickadee, cormorant, cowbird, crow, fish crow, cuckoo, dowitcher, cattle and snowy egrets, finch, flicker, flycatcher, blue-gray gnatcatcher, American goldfinch, grackle, grosbeak, great black-backed, herring, laughing, and ring-billed gulls, five species of hawks, heron, night heron, hummingbird, white ibis, jaeger, blue jay, junco, killdeer, kingbird, kingfisher, kinglet, kittiwake, lark, loon, purple martin, meadowlark, mockingbird, nuthatch, Baltimore and orchard orioles, osprey, ovenbird, a trio of owls, pewee, phalarope, phoebe, pipit, clapper and Virginia rails, redhead, robin, the least, spotted, and stilt sandpipers, sapsucker, screech owl, pine siskin, sora, a dozen or more species of sparrows, starling, wood stork, bank and barn swallows, chimney swift, scarlet and summer tanagers, a trio of terns, brown thrasher, thrush, tufted titmouse, towhee, red-eyed, warbling, white-eyed, and yellow-throated vireos, vulture, black-throated, Connecticut, yellow, and a dozen other warblers, waterthrush, waxwing, a quartet of woodpeckers, the Carolina, house, and marsh wrens, and the common yellowthroat.

The boat ramp on Lawnes Creek provides access to the broad and historical James River and unlimited boating opportunities. The James River is tidal here, of course, and boaters should keep the tide in mind. A fast-dropping tide could leave them stranded until the next high tide. A watchful eye and a little caution should prevent this. A canoeist can launch at the Lawnes Creek ramp and paddle upstream or out into the James River and to the Hog Island tract where there are many tidal creeks to explore.

Like to camp on a narrow beach? This is a possibility, but it's primitive camping. There are no organized campsites. For inland camping there is the thirty-five-foot-high Carlisle tract. But it is well to bear in mind that mosquitoes can all but carry a camper away during the warmer months. Camping should be more of a pleasure here after the first killing frost or in the early spring before the final frost of the season. In addition to mosquitoes, ticks can be bad.

There are several interesting fishing opportunities on this wildlife management area, not the least of which is to bow hunt for carp during the spring when the big fish move into the shallows. The many impoundments on the Hog Island tract permit this kind of fishing. For the more conventional fisherman, the James River offers a great variety of fishing opportunities. The James River is noted for its bass fishing, for its striped bass, big blue catfish, and channel catfish. The river is a regular route for the migratory fish such as striped bass, white perch, and shad. A variety of panfish such as bluegills and crappies are found primarily in the deep coves. Launch a boat at the Lawnes Creek ramp and go fishing. Lawnes Creek itself should offer good fishing for many of the species mentioned for the James River. The designated fishing area between the entrance gate to the Hog Island tract and Hog Point should offer good white perch fishing in late April and May when the fish are moving upstream to spawning areas. Many bank fishermen also find this area productive. Another interesting possibility is to fish the mouth of the Virginia Power Company warm-water canal. The warm water it releases into the river appeals to striped bass and other fish, particularly during the cold months. This fishing is best done from a boat launched at the Lawnes Creek ramp. There are several small ponds on the right of the road to the launching ramp in the Carlisle tract. They tend to dry up, so fishing is limited. Occasionally an angler might find crappies or other fish that moved in during periods of high water.

Waterfowl hunting is the big attraction here, and hunters who draw Hog Island in the annual lottery consider themselves lucky indeed. Applications to enter the drawing are available from the Department of Game and Inland Fisheries in late summer after the seasons have been set. The drawings are made in the middle of October, and the lucky waterfowlers are advised of their selection soon thereafter. The variety of waterfowl wintering in the area is great, including many breeds of ducks plus both Canada and snow geese and tundra swans. Blinds to accommodate a pair of hunters are strategically located, and decoys and johnboats are available. The hunter who draws a permit can take a companion of his choice. Except for an archery hunt for deer, no other hunting is allowed on the Hog Island tract. Bow hunting for deer only is allowed during the special archery season.

Hunting on the Carlisle tract is open to the general public. No special permit is required. In addition to deer, the hunter may find doves, quail, rabbits, squirrels, and turkeys. The pipeline and power-line rights-of-way, which are managed for deer and small game, should not be overlooked by the small-game hunter. Any special hunting regulations are posted and should be consulted before beginning to hunt. The fifty-acre Stewart tract, accessible by boat only, might offer some hunting opportunities to those willing to transport a boat and cross Lawnes Creek. It is marshy and heavily timbered—an interesting possibility.

The day hiker with a day pack and binoculars probably will find this area more to his liking than will the backpacker. The roads around the impoundments offer a chance to watch all kinds of water-oriented wildlife. You can hike out to one of the viewing platforms, make yourself comfortable, and go to work with your binoculars. The Carlisle tract offers a two-mile hike to the boat-launching ramp; four miles round trip makes a nice hike for an afternoon.

The viewing towers, in addition to providing an opportunity to glass for birds, also offer the chance to view other wildlife such as beavers, muskrat, and otters. These critters are most active early in the day or at dusk. Get in place and settle down with your binoculars just before dawn and in late afternoon, and wildlife viewing can be rewarding. The wildlife watcher might also see deer, turkeys, and several small-game animals such as rabbits and quail. Sighting a bald eagle is always a possibility. Among the endangered or threatened critters that live on or visit the area are the diamondback terrapin, Chowanoke crayfish, Diana fritillary butterfly, blackbanded sunfish, Mabee's salamander, barking tree frog, Atlantic sturgeon, carpenter frog, oak toad, star-nosed mole, river otter, and marsh rabbit. More common are over a half-dozen frogs including the bullfrog and the northern spring peeper, red-spotted newt, a dozen different kinds of salamanders, eastern spadefoot, a number of toads and tree frogs, the poisonous copperhead and cottonmouth, and two dozen nonpoisonous snakes, a half-dozen lizards and skinks, over a half-dozen turtles including the snapping, spotted, and mud turtles, eight different kinds of bats, beaver, chipmunk, the gray, red, and southeastern foxes, mink, muskrat, opossum, raccoon, the gray, southern flying, and talkative red squirrels, woodchuck, mussels, a half-dozen crayfish, and over three dozen different species of butterflies. Plant life is somewhat limited on this wildlife management area, the predominant tree being the loblolly pine. The area supposedly is also home to the oldest holly tree in the state, a tree that bears colorful red berries in the winter. There are also wax myrtle and bayberries. The predominant marsh grass is cordgrass and some three-square grass.

Possibly the ideal spot for a picnic would be the narrow beach to the left of the road running from the entrance gate toward the visitors' center. Or a small group of hikers could pack a picnic lunch and enjoy it in one of the viewing towers while watching for birds and other wildlife.

Horseback riding is a possibility, though other wildlife management areas might be better for this activity. Check with the wildlife management area manager before riding the roads surrounding the impoundments. In any event it wouldn't be advisable during the waterfowl hunting season—except on Sunday when there is no hunting. This is a resting area for migrating waterfowl, and the manager would probably like to avoid any activity that disturbs them.

Hog Island Wildlife Management Area is an interesting 3,908 acres of public land that introduces visitors to a unique part of Virginia.

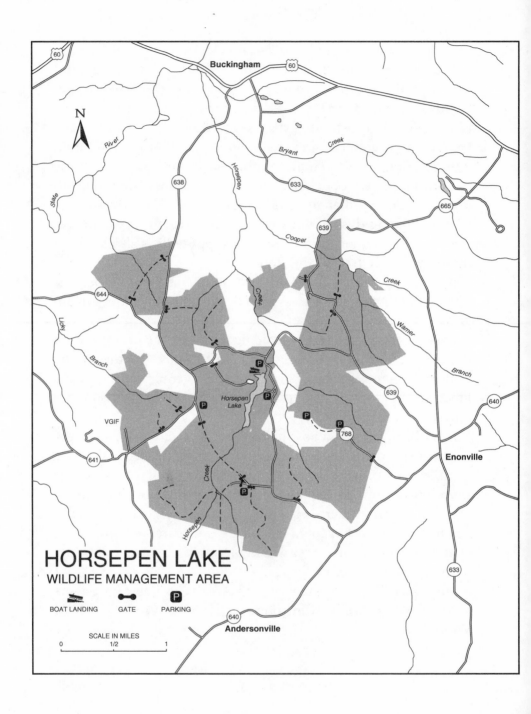

HORSEPEN LAKE
WILDLIFE MANAGEMENT AREA

BOAT LANDING   GATE   P PARKING

SCALE IN MILES
0   1/2   1

Horsepen Lake
Wildlife Management Area

Supervising Office: Department of Game and Inland Fisheries
910 Thomas Jefferson Road
Forest, VA 24551
Telephone 804-525-7522
Location: Buckingham County
Elevation: Approximately 300 to 500 feet

The first-time visitor to this wildlife management area in Buckingham County might take a quick look at the relatively small eighteen-acre Horsepen Lake and decide it is not worth considering as a hunting area. What that visitor might not know, however, is that around those eighteen acres of sparkling water are 3,065 acres of prime hunting land in one of Virginia's top hunting counties. Even the name is misleading. The small lake might prompt a visitor to feel there is nothing else to Horsepen Lake Wildlife Management Area. But don't be misled. This wildlife management area claims a good chunk of Buckingham County land. Its rolling hills are well drained and mostly covered with rich hardwoods. Numerous streams drain the area. In addition to Horsepen Creek, which was impounded to form the lake, there are Licky and Warner Branches and Cooper Creek. Several small streams are unnamed. Additionally, Horsepen Creek has several small tributaries. A number of small springs also dot the area. There is no shortage of water in this rolling hill country. The wildlife management area is located in the southeastern part of the Slate River drainage area. The Slate River is a major tributary of the James River and a good smallmouth bass stream in its own right.

At an elevation of 500 feet, this is not exactly mountain country, but those hills can be steep. They are mostly covered with a mixture of pine and hardwood forests with rich stands of mature oak and hickory. Young stands of mixed hardwoods and pine are scattered about the area. There are also good stands of bottomland hardwoods. Though the area is heavily timbered, there are enough open areas to ensure that those who hunt and visit the area will enjoy a rich diversity of wildlife.

The Horsepen Lake Wildlife Management Area is near the geographical center of Virginia, sixty-five miles west of Richmond, forty miles south of Charlottesville, and thirty-five miles east of Lynchburg. The area is reached off U.S. Highway 60. Just west of Buckingham Courthouse, take Route 638 south. The entrance to the wildlife management area is approximately two miles from the town. Several secondary roads provide access to the area from other directions. Routes 639 and 768 lead into the area from the east and south, and Routes 641 and 644 approach it from the west.

The numerous roads and trails make this area an ideal one for backpacking. There are many gated trails. The gates prohibit vehicular travel but not travel by foot, bicycle, or horseback even when they are closed. The various secondary roads that penetrate the area also offer easy travel on foot. But few wildlife management areas are more inviting to a backpacker who wants to take a compass reading and strike off across country. There are steep hills to climb or descend, but the woods are generally mature hardwoods or pine where the understory has been pretty much eliminated by nature. The Horsepen Lake Wildlife Management Area is definitely friendly to the backpacker.

The same is true of bicycling. Riders on trail bicycles will enjoy travel on the numerous secondary roads, of which there are several miles. Just plan on climbing some steep grades. Many of the trails are dead-end unless the cyclist wants to leave the trail and try traveling through a wilderness area. Most of the trails tend to cross small streams instead of running parallel to them. The trails are well maintained and get frequent use by scouts and other youth groups.

A great variety of woodland birds use the area, with their numbers peaking during annual migrations. The trails provide excellent access to good bird-watching areas—which includes most of the wildlife management area. In addition to cardinals and other woodland birds, expect sightings of hawks, owls, and even an occasional eagle. Trails that cross streams should be productive at the crossings; bird life seems to be more abundant along woodland streams than back in the hills. Among the endangered or threatened birds in this area are the brown creeper, dickcissel, purple finch, northern harrier, golden-crowned kinglet, common moorhen, red-breasted nuthatch, barn owl, migrant loggerhead shrike, hermit thrush, magnolia warbler, and winter wren. More abundant, however, are the red-winged blackbird, bluebird, bunting, cardinal, catbird, yellow-breasted chat, chickadee, chuck-will's-widow, cowbird, crossbill, American and fish crows, cuckoo, dowitcher, finch, flicker, a trio of flycatchers, gnatcatcher, goldfinch, grackle, grebe, grosbeak, a half-dozen hawks, great blue and green herons, hummingbird, blue jay, junco, kestrel, killdeer, kingbird, kingfisher, ruby-crowned kinglet, lark, purple martin, meadowlark, mockingbird, nighthawk, nuthatch, Baltimore and orchard orioles, osprey, ovenbird, the barred, great-horned, and short-eared owls, parula, pewee, phoebe, king and yellow rails, raven, American redstart, robin, sandpiper, sapsucker, screech owl, pine siskin, a dozen sparrows, starling, swallow, chimney swift, scarlet and summer tanagers, common tern, brown thrasher, thrush, titmouse, five different kinds of vireos, black and turkey vultures, over a dozen different species of warblers, the downy, hairy, pileated, red-bellied, and red-headed woodpeckers, the Carolina and house wrens, and the common yellowthroat.

Boating or canoeing is pretty much limited to the eighteen-acre lake, which is not a lot of water for extensive travel. Horsepen and the other creeks are too small for boat or canoe travel. There is, however, an excellent concrete boat-launching ramp on the lake that is available without charge to all who want to use it.

As is true of most of the wildlife management areas, only primitive camping is allowed, and stays are limited to two weeks. We are talking about woodland camping for the most part, but the woods appeal to many campers, particularly backpackers. This is an excellent area for a backpacker to shoulder a pack, take a compass reading, and head out with his eyes open for the ideal campsite. Family campers or those who tow small trailers or pitch tents in spots that can be reached by automobile should find many places that appeal to them. It behooves campers, however, to arrive early enough to locate a campsite and pitch camp before darkness. Camping is not permitted within 100 yards of Horsepen Lake. This is a general rule that applies to all wildlife management areas.

The eighteen-acre Horsepen Lake is managed for fishing by the fisheries biologists of the Department of Game and Inland Fisheries, and it offers fishing for a great variety of game fish. Among them are largemouth bass, bluegill, black crappie, pumpkinseed sunfish, and redear sunfish. The redear sunfish is better known among anglers as the shellcracker, and it grows to good size. Channel catfish and northern pike have also been introduced to the woodland lake, but whether any pike remain is dubious. Most of the small streams in this part of Virginia have good populations of chain pickerel, so don't be surprised if you land one of the toothy fish. Anglers unaccustomed to the fish may confuse it with the much larger northern pike, but it is easy to distinguish between the two. The pike's flanks are covered with beanlike markings, while those of the chain pickerel are marked by chainlike markings—hence its name. The concrete boat-launching ramp will accommodate small to medium-size fishing boats. Only electric motors are allowed, but they are completely adequate for the small lake. Horsepen and some of the other larger creeks could be an angling discovery. Many of them probably hold chain pickerel, a fish that can be a joy to tangle with. They hit savagely and leap often when hooked. And don't be surprised if you catch other fish that escape the lake. Bass, bluegills, crappies, and sunfish may escape downstream from the lake during periods of flooding. They may also move up the stream above the lake. Horsepen Lake and its tributaries may also hold some smallmouth bass that work up-stream from Slate River.

The Horsepen Lake Wildlife Management Area probably attracts more hunters than it does anglers. Covered primarily with hardwoods, the area holds good populations of deer, squirrels, and turkeys. Buckingham has traditionally reported higher than average kills of both deer and turkeys. The squirrel populations, of course, go up and down with the mast crops. They can be extremely abundant when the mast crops are high for several years in succession. Even in years of low mast crops, there will be modest populations of squirrels. Dove fields are planted annually and can provide some good shooting. Several are easily accessible from the secondary roads. Dove hunting is limited to Saturday and Wednesday afternoons. Like most Southside Virginia counties, Buckingham has a good dove population, but agricultural fields to draw them are becoming scarce. Grouse are a possibility but also a rarity. There are a few quail, and woodcocks migrate through. There is also usually a resident woodcock population, birds that breed in the area and never leave. Rabbits can be reasonably abundant where there is the proper cover in the more open areas such as the dove fields. There are opossums and raccoon for the night hunters, and other furbearers include beavers, foxes, otters, mink, and muskrat. A permit is required to trap the area—in addition to a state trapping license. Nesting boxes attract a few wood ducks, but waterfowl hunting is not strong here.

This is an excellent area for those who like to pack a picnic lunch, compass, and binoculars and head into the woodlands for a day. Numerous trails beckon to them, and high hills invite them to rest for awhile, break out their binoculars, and watch for wildlife. Or test their woodsmanship. Take a compass reading and strike out on an azimuth and then later in the day take the reverse reading and find out how good you are with a compass. No need to worry about getting lost. There are too many trails, and if you don't cross a trail, you can pick up a stream and follow it downstream. It eventually will cross a road or trail. Which way to go on the trail? Take a compass reading.

For those who like to expand their wildlife viewing beyond birds, there are obviously a great variety of game animals. Woodland flowers bloom at various times of the year, but spring could be the prime season for this activity. Climb a hill to get a good vantage point and then search for a clear view. Go to work with your binoculars, and you might be surprised. Another possibility is to locate a vantage point overlooking the lake, remain silent, and search the lakeshore with your binoculars. The only endangered or threatened critter is the river otter, but there is plenty to attract the nature watcher. Among the more common are a half-dozen frogs including the bullfrog and the spring peeper, red-spotted newt, a dozen salamanders, three toads, tree frog, the copperhead and timber rattlesnake and over a dozen nonpoisonous snakes, a half-dozen lizards and skinks, a half-dozen turtles including the box and snapping turtles, over a half-dozen bats, beaver, bobcat, coyote, gray and red foxes, lemming, mink, opossum, raccoon, the fox, gray, southern flying, and talkative red squirrels, long-tailed weasel, a couple of mussels, a half-dozen crayfish, and almost two dozen butterflies. The area holds a great variety of flowering shrubs such as dogwood, redbud, mountain laurel, and rhododendron and wildflowers such as gentian, lady slipper, squawroot, and wild ginger. Spring and early summer are the best time to view flowering plants and wildflowers. Wildlife plantings produce sunflowers, which sparkle when in bloom, and later in the summer and early autumn the fields are full of goldenrod.

There is a picnic shelter at the lake, but it might be crowded on weekends and holidays. If it is, cruise the various roads with your eyes peeled for a likely spot in the forests or in some open area.

The numerous roads and trails make excellent bridle paths for those who want to trailer a horse or two to the area and ride. Don't make it a big party. A pair of riders is ideal. The Department of Game and Inland Fisheries discourages large riding parties.

Powhatan Wildlife Management Area

Supervising Office: Department of Game and Inland Fisheries
1320 Belman Road
Fredericksburg, VA 22401
Telephone 540-899-4169
Location: Powhatan County
Elevation: 200 to 350 feet

U.S. Highway 60 runs east-west through the Powhatan Wildlife Management Area, making it easily accessible though there is limited vehicular access to the interior of its 4,462 acres. Numerous trails, however, make the entire area accessible to those who do not object to some walking. Fescue Trail, for example, runs completely through the area, leading off Route 662 near its western border and joining Route 601 at its northeastern corner. There is also the CCC Trail off U.S. Highway 60 to the north of the property, running south to Route 13, which forms the area's southernmost border.

Just twenty-five miles west of the Richmond metropolitan area, this wildlife management area is convenient to one of the state's largest population centers. It might be called the land of lakes thanks to a pair of thirty-two- and twenty-six-acre lakes north of U.S. Highway 60 and near the area's northern border. Known as the Powhatan Lakes, they are very popular among fishermen. Near the southwest corner of the property off Route 662 is a trio of ponds, Bass Pond, Bullhead Pond, and Sunfish Pond. And near the eastern border accessible from the Power-Line Trail is Bream Pond. The ponds range in size from the two-acre Bullhead Pond to nine-acre Bass Pond.

This was once thriving farm property, with the typical corn, wheat, and hay crop rotation of a past generation of farmers. Old

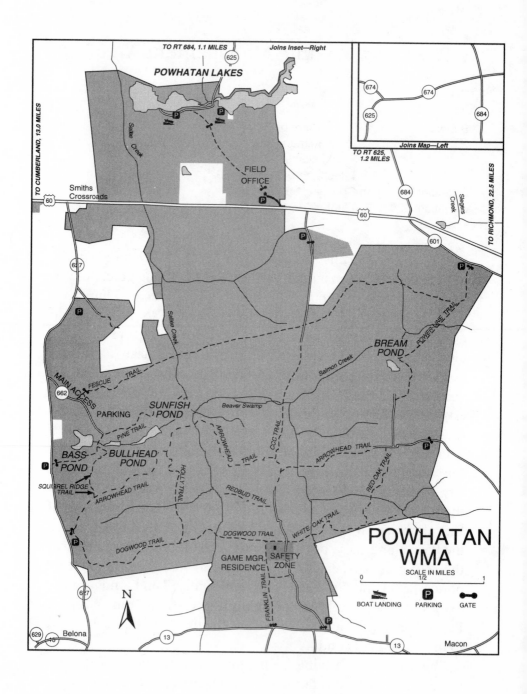

TO RT 684, 1.1 MILES
625
Joins Inset—Right

POWHATAN LAKES

674
674
625
684

Joins Map—Left

TO RT 625,
1.2 MILES

TO CUMBERLAND, 13.0 MILES

Saltee Creek

FIELD
OFFICE

Smiths
Crossroads

60

60

601

Slegers Creek

TO RICHMOND, 22.5 MILES

684

617

Saltee Creek

MAIN ACCESS

FESCUE   TRAIL

662

Parking

**SUNFISH
POND**

Beaver Swamp

Salmon Creek

**BREAM
POND**

POWERLINE TRAIL

PINE TRAIL

**BASS
POND**

**BULLHEAD
POND**

ARROWHEAD   TRAIL

CCC TRAIL

ARROWHEAD TRAIL

SQUIRREL RIDGE
TRAIL

ARROWHEAD TRAIL

HOLLY TRAIL

REDBUD TRAIL

RED OAK TRAIL

WHITE OAK TRAIL

DOGWOOD TRAIL

DOGWOOD TRAIL

**GAME MGR.
RESIDENCE**

**SAFETY
ZONE**

FRANKLIN TRAIL

POWHATAN
WMA

SCALE IN MILES
0   1/2   1

BOAT LANDING   PARKING   GATE

617

N

629
Belona
13

13

Macon

fields, cultivated wildlife areas, woodlots, and the half-dozen bodies of water make this a highly diversified 4,462 acres of land. It is gently rolling land, well drained by a number of small creeks or streams, all of which flow into Sallee Creek. Sallee Creek, which you cross on Route 13 at the southern edge of the area, flows north through the entire area and eventually into the James River. This wildlife management area is entirely within Powhatan County. In fact, it is near the center of the county, which has long been noted for its small-game hunting and more recently for its deer and turkey populations. There are numerous beaver swamps near the southern portion of the area on the headwaters of Sallee Creek. Elevations range from 200 to 350 feet.

U.S. Highway 60, which divides the wildlife management area, provides easy and quick access. Route 627 runs south along the entire western border of the area. Route 662 leads east off Route 627 and provides access to three of the ponds. Three parking areas along Route 627 also serve as trailheads to a number of trails. To the east Route 601 also leads south off U.S. Highway 60 and to the trailhead of the Power-Line Trail. From the south Route 13 skirts the wildlife management area and provides access at a parking area and a trailhead. To reach the Powhatan Lakes section, take Route 684 north near the eastern edge of the area and turn left on Route 674 and then left on Route 625, which leads to the lakes.

Numerous trails lead into the interior of the wildlife management area and offer wonderful backpacking opportunities. In fact, these trails are the only access to most of the interior. Some trails skirt beaver swamps, and one trail provides the only access to a pond. With elevations of only 200 to 250 feet, there is little climbing. The country rolls gently. There are parking areas for Arrowhead Trail, Dogwood Trail, Pine Trail, the CCC Trail, and the Power-Line Trail. One interesting trail in the northern section leads from the wildlife management area field office just off U.S. Highway 60 to the Powhatan Lakes section, with parking at both ends. Many of the trails simply serve to connect other trails. Holly

Trail, for example, connects Arrowhead and Dogwood Trails. Despite the abundance of trails, some backpackers might like to strike out through the untracked wilderness, using a compass to keep oriented. It's over three miles between the eastern and western borders of the area and over four north to south.

A sturdy trail bicycle can be put to good use in this wildlife management area because vehicular access to the interior is so limited. There are plenty of trails to accommodate a bicycle, and the terrain rolls gently. It is not demanding. Many of the trails cross streams and skirt beaver swamps where the trail might be wet. Bicyclists might have to walk their vehicles over such terrain. This wildlife management area is a good one for packing camping gear and heading off to explore a large region in a part of the state where such wilderness is rare.

A great variety of birds use the area, with its streams and small lakes being focal points for bird-watching. While vehicular access is limited, an excellent system of trails leads bird-watchers to most parts of the wildlife management area where they can take a stand and work with their binoculars and notebook. Among the endangered and threatened birds found here are the dickcissel, bald eagle, purple finch, northern harrier, little blue heron, golden-crowned kinglet, common moorhen, red-breasted nuthatch, barn owl, migrant loggerhead shrike, Henslow's sparrow, cerulean and magnolia warblers, and the winter wren. The more common birds, the ones you are more likely to see, include the red-winged and rusty blackbirds, bluebird, indigo and snow buntings, cardinal, catbird, chat, chickadee, cowbird, crossbill, crow, cuckoo, dowitcher, finch, flicker, flycatcher, gnatcatcher, goldfinch, grackle, grosbeak, five hawks, great blue and green herons, hummingbird, blue jay, junco, kestrel, killdeer, kingbird, kingfisher, kinglet, lark, magpie, purple martin, meadowlark, mockingbird, nighthawk, nuthatch, oriole, osprey, ovenbird, a trio of owls, parula, pewee, phoebe, king rail, raven, robin, four species of sandpipers, sapsucker, screech owl, a dozen different kinds of sparrows, starling, the barn, northern rough-winged, and tree swallows, chimney swift, tanager, tern, thrasher, thrush, titmouse, eastern and green-tailed towhees, the red-eyed, warbling, and white-eyed vireos, vulture, over a dozen warblers, waterthrush, waxwing, whippoorwill, the American, downy, hairy, pileated, red-bellied, and red-headed woodpeckers, the Carolina and house wrens, and the common yellowthroat.

The Powhatan Lakes and several of the ponds offer opportunities for flat-water canoeing and boating in small boats. There are good launching ramps on both of the Powhatan Lakes and a reasonably good one on Bass Pond, certainly adequate for launching a canoe or small boat. Any craft used on the others will require that it be portaged or hand carried. Good trails lead to Bullhead and Sunfish Ponds, but they cannot be used by automobiles. The carry to Sunfish Pond is only 25 or 30 yards, but the one to Bullhead is closer to 100 yards. In both cases there are places where a boat or a canoe can be launched easily. Bream Pond across the wildlife management area is a different situation. Here the portage or carry would be almost 100 yards, something few will want to undertake. Even a light canoe soon gets heavy on a carry of that length.

Primitive camping with stays limited to two weeks is permitted in the wildlife management area. Setting up camp within 100 yards of any of the six lakes or ponds is, however, prohibited. Those willing to carry their camping gear in a pack or load it on a bicycle will have the best chance of locating choice sites. For the family camper traveling by automobile the best opportunities might be found in the northern section in the vicinity of the Powhatan Lakes—but not within 100 yards of them.

The fishing opportunities are varied and abundant here. The two Powhatan Lakes probably offer the best opportunities, but the four ponds should not be overlooked. Nor should Sallee Creek. All waters except the creek are managed by the Department of Game and Inland Fisheries for fishing. Management includes the introduction of fish suitable for the water and the placement of submerged fish attractors, indicated by red and white buoys. Route 625 leads to the two lakes and also to boat-launching ramps. The fish found in the Powhatan Lakes are typical of impounded waters in Southside Virginia. Finning the lake waters are the likes of largemouth bass, channel catfish, chain pickerel, and panfish such as bluegill, black crappie, redear sunfish, and pumpkinseed sunfish. All of the fish except the chain pickerel were introduced to the lakes. The chain pickerel is native to the waters of the region, and when streams are impounded, it takes up residence quickly, feeding on the fingerlings of the various other species.

Anglers who like to fish small streams should check out Sallee Creek. It is a fair guess that it holds a good population of chain pickerel, the native fish. It could also very well hold populations of any of the species stocked in the lakes and ponds. These fish have a habit of escaping the impounded waters, usually during flooding, and taking up residence in the streams, where they flourish. Both U.S. Highway 60 and Route 13 cross Sallee Creek, offering quick access. The water is warm enough to wade during the summer months, but at other times hip boots or waders are advisable. On most of these lakes and ponds, bank fishing is also possible—and popular among local fishermen.

For years the land now claimed by the wildlife management area was prime small-game land, with doves, quail, rabbits, and squirrels the primary species. The modern comeback of deer and turkeys has changed the hunting emphasis, however, putting the hunting pressure on them more than on small game. The Powhatan Wildlife Management Area is in the heart of dove-hunting country, and it is one of the more popular dove-hunting wildlife management areas. A number of dove-hunting fields are planted just for the birds, and dove hunting is popular here. During the popular September season, hunting is limited to Wednesd Saturday afternoons. The area is also managed for quail bits, and acres of open fields, once in farmlands, blend in with this management practice. Many acres of moist soils in the vicinity of beaver ponds, the various lakes, and numerous streams are attractive to migrating woodcock. Deer and turkey hunting could well be just as popular as dove hunting. The mixed pine and hardwood forest interspersed with open fields creates edges that both deer and turkeys favor. The deer hunter who kills his animal deep in the wildlife management area may have to walk a mile or so to get it out. This is worth considering before squeezing the trigger. Trail bicycles might provide the answer.

The Powhatan Wildlife Management Area is a good choice for a day hike because of the number and lengths of the various trails. They offer all kinds of possibilities. For example, a hiker could park near the head of Arrowhead Trail, follow it to the CCC Trail, hike south on that trail to Dogwood Trail, and then hike back to the parking area. The distance is probably between four and five miles. Or for a shorter trip, the hiker could take Arrowhead Trail to Holly Trail, go south on that to Dogwood Trail, and follow it back to the parking area. There are also several through hikes where a pair of hikers could leave one vehicle at the end of a trail, drive back to the trailhead in the companion's vehicle, and then hike through to the waiting vehicle. If you prefer to hike the un-tracked wilderness, you can take a compass reading and make a circle coming back to your starting point.

Because of its proximity to a large population center, school groups and Boy or Girl Scouts use the wildlife management area often for nature walks and outdoor photography. The nature of the area lends itself to this kind of use, and it is equally available to others who want to view nature. Viewing nature is not something you can rush. Instead, learn to move quietly and spend a lot of time just watching and listening. It's the practice deer hunters use—and often on this very same wildlife management area. On the endangered or threatened species list are the Atlantic pigtoe and yellow lance mussels and the river otter. More common are a half-dozen frogs including the bullfrog and the spring peeper, red-spotted newt, almost a dozen salamanders, three toads and a pair of tree frogs, the poisonous copperhead and almost two dozen nonpoisonous snakes, the glass and fence lizard and several skinks, a half-dozen turtles including the box and snapping turtles, over a half-dozen bats, bobcat, chipmunk, mink, a number of rats and shrews, weasel, woodchuck, four additional kinds of mussels, and a half-dozen species of crayfish. Butterflies? There are over two dozen different species. Wildflowers common to fields and woods of the southern piedmont are found here. Expect to see gentian, lady slipper, squawroot, and wild ginger, rhododendron, morning glory, buttercup, dandelion, yellow partridge pea, purple lespedeza, flowering dogwood and redbud, jonquils, and in late summer and early autumn fields of goldenrod.

Climb one of the hills that surround the Powhatan Lakes and locate a good spot overlooking the lake. Sound like a good way to enjoy a picnic? Or park on the shores of Bass Pond, or lay out a picnic on the dam of Bullhead Pond, which is kept clear of heavy growth to permit fishing from the shore. You might even bring along a fishing rod and some worms and watch a bobber while you enjoy your picnic.

"We don't encourage horseback riding but allow riders in singles or pairs to ride," is the usual position of wildlife management area personnel. Limited riding is permitted, and all of the roads and trails are open to riding.

The Powhatan Wildlife Management Area provides a good chunk of outdoors in a part of the state where a growing human population needs this kind of escape.

Ragged Island
Wildlife Management Area

Supervising Office: Department of Game and Inland Fisheries
5806 Mooretown Road
Williamsburg, VA 23188
Telephone 757-253-4180
Location: Isle of Wight County
Elevation: Approximately sea level to 8 to 10 feet

The duck hunter, resting in a makeshift blind in the Ragged Island Wildlife Management Area, might be surprised to look across tidal Copper Creek to the west and see a hunter decked out in bright blaze orange moving slowly along. What he might not know is that this wildlife management area, in addition to providing good hunting for a great variety of ducks, also offers good low-country deer hunting. That orange-clad hunter is most likely still-hunting for deer. This unique area on the James River in Isle of Wight County offers both good deer hunting and good duck hunting.

But more about the hunting later. In the meantime let's take a moment to get acquainted with this outdoor prize. The broad James River forms its northeastern border, and U.S. Highway 17 passes through it, splitting it in two parts, the much larger of which is downriver. Also surprising is that just across the James River are the bustling cities of Hampton and Newport News, a pair of densely populated municipalities in the busy Hampton Roads region. The duck hunter, waiting out the final few minutes of prime duck-hunting time, might be distracted momentarily as lights begin to flicker across this broad expanse of tidewater. That far shore is the busy Newport News shoreline. Sunset is near, and the hunter's time is critically short. To the south and west, tidal Ragged Island Creek forms part of the southwestern border.

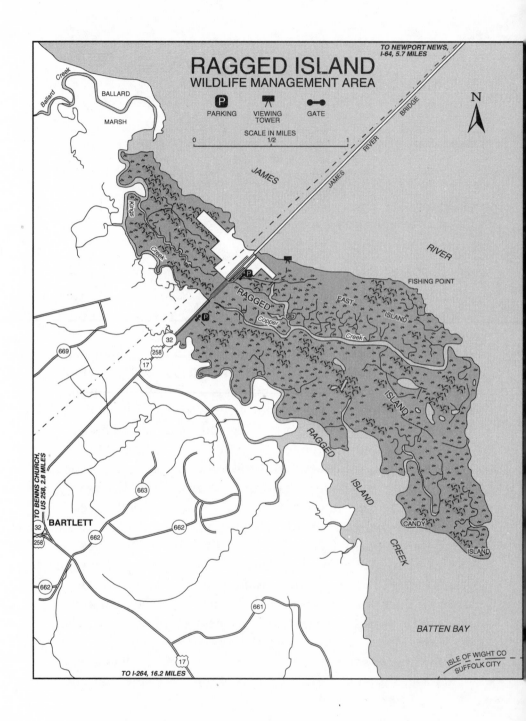

RAGGED ISLAND
WILDLIFE MANAGEMENT AREA

Upriver, across U.S. Highway 17, Kings Creek forms the western border.

This 1,537-acre wetland on the south side of the lower James River is one of water, brackish marshes, and tiny pine-covered islands. A short distance downstream the river flows into the big Chesapeake Bay. It is a largely unspoiled area that offers an amazing variety of outdoor opportunities. The major marsh vegetation includes black needlerush, salt-marsh cordgrass, and smartweed. Loblolly pine is the major forest species, but wax myrtle, often entangled with greenbrier, makes travel through much of the pine forest difficult—but that's where white-tailed deer often hang out. Copper Creek, Kings Creek, and Ragged Island Creek are the major streams, and there are numerous smaller creeks or guts and a half-dozen or more small ponds. Some are freshwater, but the major ones are saltwater. Much of the area is subject to flooding.

U.S. Highways 17 and 258 as well as Route 32 cross the James River on the long James River Bridge and provide the only land access to the wildlife management area. For much of the area, the best access is by water. Traveling from the Newport News side across the James River Bridge, the hunter will notice signs leading to a parking area on the downriver side of the highway—or to the left. This is the major access point to the area. From here two trails lead into the area, one to a viewing platform near the river's edge and the other a path to Copper Creek where hunters like to launch light boats or canoes. A short distance beyond this access point is another parking area on the same side of the highway. A short trail here leads into the upland part of the wildlife management area. It is used mostly by hunters who take advantage of the parking area to move into the upland pines to hunt. Trails at both parking areas are seasonally gated, but hunters can go around them to get into the area. Portaging a canoe around the gates is also easily done. Both gates may be open during hunting seasons.

It's hard to imagine a backpacker wanting to use this area of marshes and jumbled vegetation—even though hunters frequent it during the fall and winter hunting seasons. There are no trails in the wildlife management area, and the walking is tough, whether it be trudging through the marshes at low tide or making your way through a stand of loblolly pines where the understory is a tangle of greenbriers and wax myrtle. This is not to say there are no backpacking opportunities. They are just limited.

A low area made up of salt marshes and scattered woody hammocks of loblolly pine offers little or no opportunities for bicycling. For one thing there are no trails, and numerous creeks and guts prevent traveling very far on a bicycle.

This is an excellent area for watching birds that are attracted to a habitat of marshes, swamps, and water. A boardwalk leading to a wildlife-viewing platform offers many bird-watching possibilities. Expect to see a variety of shorebirds as well as a few upland birds, even though the pine-covered hummocks offer limited habitat. A great variety of waterfowl, particularly ducks, use this area during the winter months, but this is also the season for waterfowl hunting. There is no hunting on Sundays, however, and most waterfowl seasons are over by the end of January. February might be a good time to visit the area and watch the ducks that winter here. Among the endangered or threatened birds found on the area are the brown creeper, dickcissel, bald eagle, great egret, peregrine falcon, purple finch, northern harrier, little blue and tricolored herons, yellow-crowned night heron, glossy ibis, golden-crowned kinglet, common moorhen, red-breasted nuthatch, barn owl, brown pelican, piping plover, black rail, migrant loggerhead shrike, sharp-tailed salt-marsh sparrow, Caspian, Forster's, and least terns, hermit thrush, cerulean, magnolia, and Swainson's warblers, red-cockaded woodpecker, and wedge and winter wrens. Much more common are the bitterns, blackbird, bluebird, bobolink, cardinal, catbird, chat, chickadee, cormorant, cowbird, crossbill, the American and fish crows, cuckoo, dowitcher, cattle and snowy egrets, finch, flicker, flycatcher, gnatcatcher, godwit, grackle, grebe, grosbeak, a quartet of gulls, a half-dozen hawks, the great blue and green herons, night heron, hummingbird, jaeger, blue jay, junco, kestrel, killdeer, kingbird, kingfisher, kinglet, kittiwake, red knot, lark, loon, purple martin, meadowlark, mockingbird, nighthawk, nuthatch, Baltimore and orchard orioles, osprey, ovenbird, a trio of owls, parula, pewee, phalarope, phoebe, pipit, the clapper, king, and Virginia rails, redhead, redstart, robin, several sandpipers, sapsucker, screech owl, pine siskin, black skimmer, sora, over a dozen different kinds of sparrows, starling, several swallows, swift, a trio of tanagers, common and royal terns, thrasher, thrush, titmouse, towhee, turnstone, veery, five species of vireos, vulture, almost two dozen warblers, waterthrush, waxwing, whippoorwill, a half-dozen woodpeckers, the Carolina, house, and marsh wrens, and the common yellowthroat.

Except for hand-carried boats and canoes, there are no real launching facilities, though both anglers and hunters do launch boats across the narrow beach just downstream from the U.S. 17 Highway bridge. The sand is tricky here, and the safest towing vehicle needs 4×4 capabilities. The tidal creeks can be fun to canoe. Creep up some of the smaller creeks and watch for wildlife of various kinds—birds, ducks, muskrat, otters, and various other mammals. Again, it is best to avoid this kind of activity during the hunting seasons, particularly during the waterfowl seasons— except on Sundays.

Camping opportunities are also limited, but one possibility is to set up among the pines on one of the many hummocks. Mosquitoes can be vicious during the warm months, and hunting eliminates many of the colder months when the bugs are gone. Campers are best advised to look elsewhere to pitch their tents.

Fishing opportunities are many depending upon the season. The lower James River in which the area is located offers saltwater fishing for striped bass, bluefish, croaker, flounder, spot, and gray trout. Bluefish, croaker, spot, and gray trout leave the James River in the fall, but the striped bass fishing picks up. Channel catfish and white perch can be caught in some of the freshwater creeks feeding into the area from the uplands. Because of the somewhat limited launching facilities for larger boats here, other stretches of the James River are more easily fished—and just as productive.

Hunting is the big thing here. And well it should be because hunters' money purchased the area originally and hunters' money now pays for managing it. When the Ragged Island Wildlife Management Area comes up in a discussion, most hunters automatically think of waterfowl hunting, particularly duck hunting. A great variety of ducks visit this area during the peak of the waterfowl season. Included are black ducks, buffleheads, gadwalls, goldeneyes, mallard, ruddy ducks, and scaup. Easily accessible Copper Creek supports much of the hunting. Hunters launch canoes or light johnboats in the headwaters of the creek. Most hunters probably jump shoot in pairs, swapping back and forth the handling of the boat and the shooting. Move as quietly as possible up the winding creeks or guts that enter Copper Creek and attempt to surprise ducks feeding or resting in the area. The ideal time to expect action is as the craft rounds a curve in the stream and spooks birds just around the bend. This probably offers the best shooting opportunity. The smaller the creek or gut the better—as long as it is large enough to float the boat or canoe. Naturally there are more opportunities at high tide when more water is in the creeks and guts. This is a delightful way to hunt waterfowl in a marsh. Another possibility is to rig a crude blind alongside Copper Creek or one of the other streams and wait for passing ducks. The birds seem to follow the stream as they fly into the marsh or leave it. Those coming in often circle to land, offering classic blind shooting, but others pass so fast it's difficult to make a good shot—particularly at those leaving the marsh possibly flushed by another hunter or someone else visiting the wildlife management area. Permanent blinds are prohibited, but hunters dressed in camouflage can conceal themselves reasonably well with pieces of camouflage netting. If this is the plan, it's a good idea to take along small poles or something similar to support the netting. All, of course, should be removed when abandoning the blind. The blind hunter will need either a retrieving dog or a light boat to retrieve birds that fall on the water. One good waterfowl hunting area is Kings Creek and the little bay at its mouth. Ducks, particularly mallard, often fly down the river from somewhere upstream and swing into the bay and river to spend the night. Well-camouflaged hunters positioned along the side of the creek can get some good pass shooting as the day ends. But keep an eye on the sun. Hunting ends as it sets. Clapper rails also frequently visit the marshes, and they are best hunted at high tide when they are forced from the marshes into the open where the hunter can get a shot. One hunter poling with the shooter in the bow is the traditional way to hunt clapper rails, one of Virginia's oldest forms of hunting. Deer hunting is popular here, mainly because of the scarcity of good public deer-hunting land in the tidewater region. Deer do not often frequent the marshes, but they use the pine-covered island. Most hunting is either still-hunting or hunting from elevated stands. Permanent tree stands are prohibited, but portable stands are legal. During the waterfowl season the shooting in the marshes might drive the deer back from the river. Small-game hunting is a possibility with varying populations of rabbits and squirrels. Foxes and raccoon are also present.

As is true of backpacking, hiking is extremely limited. At low tide much of the marshland can be safely walked on, and there are the hummocks and other high ground that might be investigated. Trails here are nonexistent except for the ones leading to the headwaters of Copper Creek and to the boardwalk.

The wildlife management area is a designated Watchable Wildlife Area with interpretive signs and limited trails. The boardwalk with the viewing tower at its end offers a unique area to watch and photograph nature. Among the endangered or threatened critters here are the Atlantic Ridley sea and leatherback sea turtles, Dismal Swamp southeastern shrew, northern diamondback terrapin, eastern big-eared bat, Arogos skipper and Diana fritillary butterflies, eastern tiger and Mabee's salamanders, barking tree frog, carpenter frog, oak toad, barn owl, small star-nosed mole, river otter, and marsh rabbit. More likely to be sighted are the likes of the two-toed amphiuma, any one of a half-dozen frogs, including the spring peeper, red-spotted newt, several of almost a dozen kinds of salamanders, greater and lesser sirens, a trio of toads and a quartet of tree frogs, the poisonous copperhead and cottonmouth and two dozen other nonpoisonous snakes, several lizards and skinks, the box and snapping and a half-dozen other turtles, over a half-dozen bats, beaver, fox, mink, nutria, opossum, raccoon, gray and flying squirrels, weasel, woodchuck, a couple of mussels, a half-dozen crayfish, and several dozen species of butterflies. Loblolly pines are the major tree of the limited forest area, and the major marsh vegetation is marshmallow, smartweed, salt-marsh cordgrass, and black needlerush. There are also wax myrtle, bayberry, and water lilies.

Likely picnic spots in this wildlife management area are extremely limited. Probably the best opportunity might be the narrow James River beach. And hope that there is an onshore breeze to keep the mosquitoes away.

Trails to ride horseback on are, as is the case with picnic spots, either nonexistent or very limited. Not worth trailering a horse to the area for a ride.

Located just across the river from a major metropolitan area, the Ragged Island Wildlife Management Area is a good example of how wildlife and a bit of wilderness can be compatible with modern civilization.

Stewarts Creek
Wildlife Management Area

Supervising Office: Department of Game and Inland Fisheries
Route 1, Box 107
Marion, VA 24354
Telephone 540-782-9051
Location: Carroll County
Elevation: 1,580 to 2,955 feet

At only 1,087 acres, the Stewarts Creek Wildlife Management Area in Carroll County is one of the smaller ones. Few, however, can match it in pure wilderness. It is all but inaccessible except by foot. Located high in the Blue Ridge Mountains, its westernmost land is less than a half mile from the Blue Ridge Parkway. Most of the area is forestland, with tulip poplar and yellow birch the predominant species at the lower elevations and in the creek hollows and hickory and oak taking over as the elevation rises. The height above sea level rises from 1,580 feet at the lower parking lot near the eastern side of the area to 2,955 feet at the upper parking lot near the western end. The distance between the two parking lots is approximately a mile, providing an indication of the steepness of the grade.

The headwaters of several delightful streams form within the area or flow through it, the most noteworthy being Stewarts Creek, for which the wildlife management area was named. Stewarts Creek proper and the North and South Forks of the stream offer fishing for native brook trout high on the eastern slopes of the Blue Ridge Mountains. Outdoorsmen desiring to explore the wildlife management area have to ford the main stem of Stewarts Creek to reach the lower parking area. Clear mountain streams, rhododendron thickets, and scenic beauty await the outdoors

173

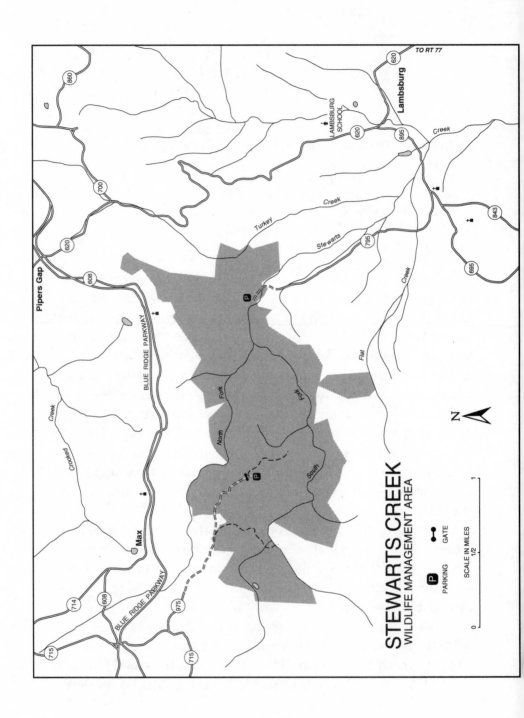

STEWARTS CREEK
WILDLIFE MANAGEMENT AREA

P PARKING   ●—● GATE

SCALE IN MILES

0   1/2   1

N

TO RT 77

Lambsburg

LAMBSBURG SCHOOL

Pipers Gap

Max

BLUE RIDGE PARKWAY

Crooked Creek

North Fork

South Fork

Turkey Creek

Stewarts Creek

Flat Creek

860

700

620

608

714

608

715

975

715

620

895

620

795

695

843

person who visits this wildlife management area in Carroll County. It is approximately seven miles southeast of Galax.

The Stewarts Creek Wildlife Management Area is probably best reached from the Blue Ridge Parkway. Its northern border runs roughly parallel to the parkway. To reach the upper or western parking area, turn south on Route 715, drive a short distance, less than a half mile, and turn left onto Route 975, which dead-ends in the wildlife management area. To reach the lower or eastern parking area from the parkway, take the Interstate 77 exit south to the Route 620 exit and proceed northeast on Route 620, left on Route 895, and right on Route 795 which dead-ends in the wildlife management area. To reach the end of Route 795, you have to ford the main stem of Stewarts Creek within the wildlife management area.

The backpacker who does not like to leave the roads or trails won't get far in the Stewarts Creek Wildlife Management Area. A trails extending Route 975 goes a half mile at the most. Department signs on routes to the area guide the traveler into it. There are no trails leading from the eastern parking area. For the backpacker who prefers a true wilderness experience, however, this can be a challenging wildlife management area. A backpacker can take a compass reading at the western parking area, for example, and hike to the eastern area to meet a pickup. Or do the reverse: take a compass reading from the eastern parking area and hike to the western. Or hike to either, take a reverse reading, and hike back. Just remember that the elevation at the upper, or western, parking area is almost 3,000 feet, nearly 1,500 feet higher than the lower or eastern one. That means a climb of 1,500 feet in little over a mile. For an easier backpacking trip, do the reverse, hike from the higher to the lower area. There are, of course, other backpacking trips, but the longest, from the western boundary to the eastern, or vice versa, is going to be approximately three miles. The backcountry, however, offers much to explore, such as the headwaters of the North and South Forks of Stewarts Creek. Or a stretch of Turkey Creek, which flows through an eastern corner of the wildlife management area. The only way to reach it is on foot. The backpacker will find many delightful spots to camp overnight. There are the singing mountains streams high on the eastern slopes of the Blue Ridge Mountains where rushing waters and deep pools hold special charm.

Trails suitable for mountain bicycles are extremely limited in this wildlife management area, three or four miles at the most. Any other travel by bicycle is over wilderness and often steep terrain. Bicyclists are best advised to look to other nearby wildlife management areas for their recreation.

Bird-watching opportunities are more or less unlimited here, though access to good observation points is limited because of the absence of an extensive system of trails. The rich hardwood forests and miles of mountain streams attract a variety of birds. Wild grapes are abundant, and wildlife management practices at the upper elevations, including the creation of linear strips for the production of brood range, attract a variety of birds. The steep terrain also creates natural observation points at the higher level. They offer views of much of the wildlife management area. Good binoculars are definitely an asset. Despite its small size, the wildlife management area hosts a variety of endangered or threatened birds, including the brown creeper, dickcissel, bald eagle, peregrine falcon, purple finch, alder and yellow-bellied flycatchers, northern harrier, golden-crowned kinglet, common moorhen, red-breasted nuthatch, barn owl, migrant loggerhead shrike, loggerhead shrike, hermit thrush, and the cerulean, golden-winged, magnolia, and Swainson's warblers. More common are eastern and red-winged blackbirds, bunting, cardinal, catbird, chat, chickadee, cormorant, cowbird, crossbill, crow, cuckoo, dowitcher, finch, a quintet of flycatchers, gnatcatcher, goldfinch, grackle, grebe, grosbeak, the Cooper's, broad-winged, red-shouldered, red-tailed, rough-legged, and sharp-shinned hawks, great blue and green herons, hummingbird, blue jay, junco, kestrel, killdeer, kingfisher, lark, purple martin, meadowlark, mockingbird, nighthawk, nuthatch, oriole, osprey, ovenbird, the barred, great horned, and short-eared owls, parula, pewee, phoebe, raven, redstart, robin, sandpiper, sapsucker, screech owl, pine siskin, a dozen different kinds of sparrows, swallow, swift, scarlet and summer tanagers, tern, thrasher, thrush, titmouse, towhee, veery, a quintet of vireos, black and turkey vultures, over a dozen warblers, waterthrush, waxwing, whippoorwill, five different kinds of woodpeckers, the Carolina and house wrens, and the common yellowthroat.

There are absolutely no boating or canoeing opportunities in this mountainous wildlife management area.

Camping here is primitive, but delightful spots along the streams or at the higher levels will appeal to many. Most camping probably is done by backpackers accustomed to wilderness travel. Just remember the wilderness traveler's motto, "Pack it in and pack it out." Leave no evidence of your presence. If all campers practice this, the area will remain attractive for generations.

This wildlife management area can be a trout fisherman's dream come true. Various sections of different streams total 4.8 miles. There are eight trout streams in Carroll County, one of which is Stewarts Creek, a special regulations wild trout stream. Native brook trout are abundant, and fishing is limited to single-hook artificial lures only. This generally means fly-fishing, but spinning tackle is permitted so long as it meets the single-hook, artificial-lures-only criteria. This is catch-and-release water. All trout must be released. Stewarts Creek is a high-gradient native brook trout stream with numerous plunge pools, rock ledges, and a dense rhododendron canopy for cover from overhead prey. Year-round fishing is allowed in the stream, first opened to the public in 1989. The trout population is healthy, and nine-inch fish are common. The special trout waters include the main stem of Stewarts Creek and both its North and South Forks. Anglers fishing these waters must have no bait in their possession. Both forks begin high in the mountains and tumble down through steep rocky gorges. Pool habitat is abundant. Each fork has tributaries of its own that hold trout. A section of Turkey Creek, another tributary of Stewarts Creek, flows through the wildlife management area near its eastern border.

Forest game—deer, grouse, turkeys, and squirrels—are the species hunted in this wildlife management area. The grouse hunting is particularly good because of an abundance of wild grapes and young forests in parts of the area. The best grouse hunting is in the upper part of the wildlife management area, near the Blue Ridge Parkway. A strip of private land, however, separates the wildlife management area from the parkway lands. The permission of the landowner or owners is needed to hunt this narrow strip of high country; the hunting, however, could be well worth the effort to locate those owners. The creation of linear strips at the higher elevations is designed to boost the brood range of the grouse. The turkey hunting is also very good during most seasons. Possibly the most hunted critter using the wildlife management area is the little gray squirrel, but the quality of the hunting varies from season to season depending upon the mast crop. Two successive seasons of good mast production translate into good squirrel hunting, particularly during the second season. A favorite time for squirrel hunting is September when the little critters are "cutting nuts," or gnawing on ripe hickory nuts. Few kinds of hunting are more popular than squirrel hunting in Carroll County.

There are no formal viewing platforms or towers as on many of the wildlife management areas, but the very nature of the land, rising as it does rapidly in elevation, provides good places from which to take binoculars and hope for a parade of wildlife. There are the popular game critters such as deer, grouse, turkeys, and squirrels, but also expect the likes of raccoon, opossums, and maybe a fox or two. The list goes on. There are also delicate wildflowers in early spring and blooming rhododendron along the steep stream banks in July. In September the hickory nuts ripen, and the squirrels are busy in the hickory groves gnawing on ripe

t's a time squirrel hunters look forward to. Creep quietly

along one of the forks of Stewarts Creek, and you might get a glimpse of a colorful brook trout finning lazily in the crystal clear water.

Endangered or threatened critters found here include the Indiana bat, Kanawha minnow, eastern hellbender, small-footed myotis, green floater mussel, Howe's dragonfly, and the regal fritillary butterfly. The more common kinds of wildlife include the bullfrog and several other frogs, including the spring peeper, the red-spotted newt, over a dozen salamanders, eastern spadefoot, American, and Fowler's toad, tree frog, the poisonous copperhead and timber rattlesnake and a dozen other nonpoisonous snakes, the fence lizard and a pair of skinks, the common musk, eastern box, and snapping turtles, over a half-dozen bats, beaver, black bear, bobcat, cottontail, coyote, fox, mink, opossum, raccoon, a half-dozen shrews, the spotted and striped skunks, the gray, red, and southern flying squirrels, long-tailed weasel, elliptio mussel, a half-dozen crayfish, and over three dozen species of butterflies. Wildflowers and flowering shrubs common to the southern Appalachians are found here. Among them are mountain laurel and rhododendron, dogwood, redbud, trillium, wild iris, wild orchids, fire pink, mayapple, and in late summer and early fall goldenrod in the few open spaces.

Those interested in picnicking will have to look no farther than one of the two parking areas. If they prefer, a short walk into the forests certainly will offer them what they want. There are no picnic tables or tap water, just nature in the raw, which appeals to many who love the outdoors—even if it is just picnicking.

Horseback-riding opportunities are very limited here unless a rider wants to take off through an untracked wilderness. The nature of the terrain limits that.

That's the Stewarts Creek Wildlife Management Area, small but loaded with surprises.

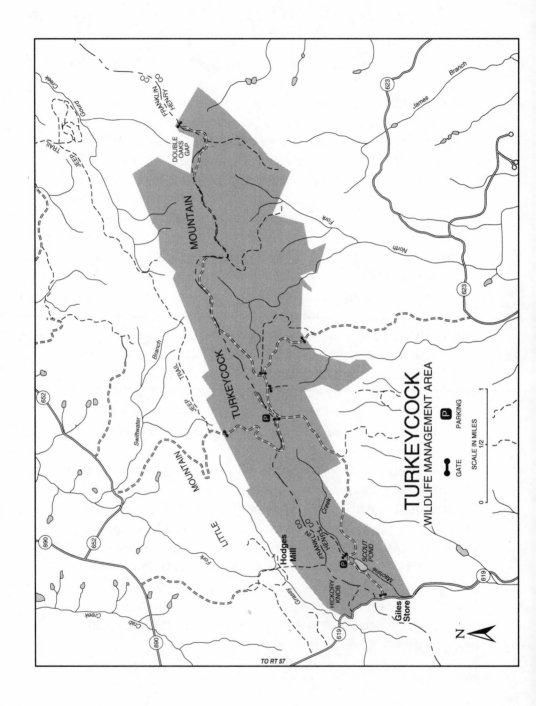

TURKEYCOCK
WILDLIFE MANAGEMENT AREA

P PARKING

⬤▬⬤ GATE

SCALE IN MILES

0   1/2   1

N

Turkeycock Mountain
Wildlife Management Area

Supervising Office: Department of Game and Inland Fisheries
910 Thomas Jefferson Road
Forest, VA 24551
Telephone 804-525-7522
Location: Franklin and Henry Counties
Elevation: 1,100 to 1,700 feet

Turkeycock Mountain rises out of the eastern foothills of the Blue Ridge Mountains, and riding the ridge of that range of mountains is Turkeycock Mountain Wildlife Management Area. Predictably, the wildlife management is long and narrow. It runs northwest from Giles Store where Route 619 forms its narrow southern border to Double Oak Gap. It straddles the ridge that also forms the Franklin-Henry county line. Interesting country, much of the area is all but inaccessible except on foot. Its 2,679 acres sprawl over portions of both Franklin and Henry Counties. It is a high, heavily forested area with elevations ranging from 1,100 to 1,700 feet. Wildlife management on the area consists almost exclusively of improving the quality of the timber and the habitat for forest game by the selective sale of timber. The headwaters of several small streams form within the wildlife management area including Gourd and Machine Creeks and the North Fork of Turkeycock Creek. A dirt road runs the length of the wildlife management area, beginning with a seasonal gate near Giles Store and exiting with a seasonal gate just north of Double Oaks Gap. Four trails lead off this road down the southern slope of the mountain. A couple of short ones enter the area near the western end of the wildlife management area, but they don't connect with the dirt road. Still another trail follows Machine Creek east from Scout Pond for a short distance. Many of these trails are gated, but only motorized vehicles are blocked. Anyone on foot, bicycle, or horse can go around the gate and proceed along the trail.

The primary access to the area is off Route 619 near Giles Store. The entrance there is seasonally gated, but when it is open, it's possible to drive a 4×4 vehicle all the way to the entrance near Double Oaks Gap, a distance of approximately six miles. If the gate is closed, hikers, bicyclists, and those on horseback can skirt the gate and travel the entire length of the wildlife management area or take one of several trails leading off the dirt road. From the south there is also access by a dirt road off Route 623 and from the north by a dirt road off Route 652. Both of these dirt roads are gated at the entrance to the wildlife management area. Hickory Knob and Scout Pond are prominent terrain features near the western entrance of the wildlife management area. To reach the area from Martinsville, take Route 108 north through Figsboro, Route 890 north to the community of Snow Creek, and then Route 619 south to the western entrance of the area.

The Turkeycock Mountain Wildlife Management Area can be a backpacker's dream. A six-mile winding trail along the crest of a 1,700-foot-high mountain with commanding views of the foothills is exciting to contemplate. Backpackers can park their vehicles in the parking area near Scout Pond and head northeast along the winding trail, and if they leave early enough, they will hike into the dawn and a rising sun. A good two-day backpacking trip would include hiking to the eastern end of the wildlife management area and camping in the Double Oaks Gap area, enjoying a leisurely breakfast, and hiking back the next day. Alternative hikes include descending the mountain on one of the several trails leading down the southern slopes of Turkeycock Mountain. Another possibility for the backpacker who prefers a more wilderness experience is to take a compass reading near the western entrance and hike northeast. To return, take the reverse compass reading and follow it back west. It should bring the hiker to the general vicinity of the western parking area.

The dirt road beginning at the entrance of the wildlife management area near Giles Store and ending at the eastern end near Double Oak Gap offers an excellent opportunity for a long bicycle ride, up and back in a long day, or up for an overnight camp and back the next morning. The dirt roads leading into the wildlife management area from Routes 623 and 652 also offer unique biking trips. Both are gated at the entrance to the area but can be skirted. And both connect with the long six-mile dirt road that leads east and west along the crest of Turkeycock Mountain.

The well-managed hardwood forests, the small streams that drain the area, beaver ponds, and Scout Pond offer a rich habitat that attracts a variety of birds at the right seasons. Wildlife management practices that encourage the wild turkey also offer a unique opportunity to observe these magnificent birds feeding and at play. Ideally the bird-watcher should wear camouflage such as hunters use for concealment. The bird-watcher who gets within viewing distance of a big flock of turkeys should also see a number of songbirds, none of which is as wary as the wild turkey. Ravens, rarely seen in the lowlands, are fairly common in Virginia's high country. Listen for their croaking call. They look like big crows, but their call is entirely different. Hear it once, and you will recognize it the next time you hear it. Among the endangered or threatened birds found here are the brown creeper, dickcissel, bald eagle, great egret, peregrine falcon, purple finch, northern harrier, yellow-crowned night heron, golden-crowned kinglet, the common moorhen, red-breasted nuthatch, barn and long-eared owls, migrant loggerhead shrike, loggerhead shrike, Caspian tern, hermit thrush, cerulean and magnolia warblers, and winter wren. Among the more common birds are the red-winged and rusty blackbirds, bluebird, bunting, cardinal, catbird, chat, chickadee, chuck-will's-widow, cormorant, cowbird, crossbill, crow, cuckoo, dowitcher, finch, flicker, a quartet of flycatchers, gnatcatcher, goldfinch, grackle, the blue, evening, and rose-breasted grosbeaks, a half-dozen hawks including the Cooper's, red-tailed, and sharp-shinned, great blue and green herons, hummingbird, blue jay, junco, kestrel, killdeer, kingbird, kingfisher, kinglet, lark purple martin, meadowlark, mockingbird, nighthawk, nuthatch, Baltimore and orchard orioles, osprey, ovenbird, the barred, great horned, and short-eared owls, parula, pewee, raven, redstart, robin, sandpiper, sapsucker, screech owl, siskin, an even dozen sparrows, starling, barn and northern swallows, swift, tanager, tern, thrasher, thrush, titmouse, towhee, a quintet of vireos, vulture, over a dozen warblers, waterthrush, waxwing, a half-dozen woodpeckers, wren, and the common yellowthroat.

Boating and canoeing are all but nonexistent in this wildlife management area, with the possible exception of Scout Pond, and that is not large enough to be much of a boating attraction.

As in all wildlife management areas, camping here is primitive only, and it is limited to a two-week stay. A primitive campsite high on the ridge of Turkeycock Mountain can be a joy. From that vantage point a camper can enjoy the sun rising out of the foothills and as the day ends watch it sink behind those foothills and mountains to the west. The evenings can be cool at the higher elevations, and the joy of relaxing around a sparkling campfire is a good way to end a long and eventful day of hiking, hunting, watching birds, photographing wildflowers, and in general just being outdoors in an invigorating setting.

Fishing can be hard to find in this mountainous wildlife management area. The streams are not cool or high enough to hold native brook trout. Most of the North Fork of Turkeycock Creek is outside the wildlife management area. There may be a few rock bass or sunfish in Machine Creek, on which Scout Pond was impounded, and there may be limited fishing for bluegill or crappie in the pond. The best fishing in this general area will be found beyond the boundaries of the wildlife management area.

Turkeycock is a good name for this mountain and the wildlife management area that straddles it. The turkey hunting can be good, and there is plenty of remote area where a hunter can get away from the crowd for some spring gobbler hunting or even fall turkey hunting when hens as well as gobblers are legal. Both Henry and Franklin Counties produce high deer kills, and some of that kill comes from this wildlife management area. There is plenty of food and cover for the whitetails here as well as remote country where wise old bucks can hang out once the shooting starts. Because the wildlife management area is so elongated, most of it is easily accessible from the long ridge road that rides the crest of the mountain. The trails leading off this road make the area even more accessible, but a hunter should plan on how to get that big buck back to the road before squeezing the trigger. We are talking about having to drag a deer a mile or more when the road is opened for the hunting season. The gates are open seasonally depending on the weather. Of course where there are hardwoods, acorns, and hickory nuts, there are squirrels. Squirrel hunting has long been a favorite in this part of Virginia where the season opens in early September when the little critters are feeding on ripe hickory nuts. There are also plenty of raccoon for the night hunters, and even a few grouse for the wing shooter, though the area is not noted for its grouse hunting. A few woodcocks should migrate through in the fall, and a hunter might just sneak up on a mallard or wood duck on Scout Pond. That, however, would be a bonus of more productive hunting for other species. Hunting is probably the major activity on this unique wildlife management area.

Those who prefer day hikes, as opposed to overnight backpacking trips, will find plenty of opportunities here. A hike from Scout Pond to Double Oaks Gap and back in the single day might be more than many hikers desire, but it's a possibility for a long-day hike. Other hikes might begin at the gated entrances off Route 623 and 652. From either point it's a short hike to the dirt road along the ridge of Turkeycock Mountain. There a hiker can turn east or west along the road or hike from one entrance to the other and back.

Nature viewing is a possibility worth considering for a day outing. In addition to the various birds that pass through or use the area, there are the possible sightings of deer and turkeys and small mammals such as raccoon and squirrels. Watching turkeys eat and play can be fascinating, and try locating a viewing spot near a ripe hickory tree and watch the squirrels scamper about. Note how a squirrel gathers a nut from the tree and rests on its haunches as it gnaws on this meal. If you are close enough, you might hear the nut fragments drifting down through the leaves. At various seasons wildflowers add their charm to the wildlife management area.

Among the endangered or threatened critters here are Roanoke log perch, orangefin madtom, small-footed myotis, Atlantic pigtoe mussel, and Roanoke bass. Much more common are a half-dozen frogs including the bullfrog, pickerel frog, and spring peeper, the red-spotted newt, over a dozen salamanders, eastern spadefoot, a trio of toads, two tree frogs, the poisonous copperhead and timber rattler and almost two dozen nonpoisonous snakes, the fence lizard and five skinks, several turtles including the box and snapping turtles, eight different kinds of bats, chipmunk, gray and red foxes, mink, opossum, raccoon, a half-dozen shrews, skunk, five species of squirrels, weasel, several mussels and a half-dozen crayfish, over a dozen butterflies, and almost a dozen gnats. Most flowers common to the southern Appalachian Mountains are found here. Included are flowering dogwoods, redbud, both mountain laurel and rhododendron, trillium, wild iris, wild orchids, and mayapples.

Picnickers generally like to travel by automobile to picnic sites, and here they should have little trouble finding a wooded site near the four entrances to the wildlife management area.

A horseback ride from one end of the elongated wildlife management area to the other should be an enjoyable event. Round trip it is about twelve to fifteen miles.

Turkeycock Wildlife Management Area is one of the least accessible in the system, and that makes it unique.

White Oak Mountain
Wildlife Management Area

Supervising Office: Department of Game and Inland Fisheries
910 Thomas Jefferson Road
Forest, VA 24551
Telephone 804-525-7522
Location: Pittsylvania County
Elevation: 550 to 900 feet

The White Oak Mountain Wildlife Management Area is a small-game hunter's dream. Though called a mountain, the area might best be described as a plateau. The country here is gently rolling with elevations ranging from 550 to 900 feet, not exactly mountain country in the true sense of the word. The hunter may have to climb a few hills, but certainly no mountains. Walking behind a pair of English setters or following a pack of little beagle hounds harks back to the days when family farms supported the very best in small-game hunting. The access to the area is excellent. Roads or trails lead to just about all parts of the area, making it easy to put down a brace of bird dogs or a small pack of beagles. Approximately two-thirds of the 2,712 acres are wooded, the forest cover being primarily hardwoods and pine. Loblolly and Virginia pine comprise most of the pine forests. Hardwood cover is primarily oak—black, chestnut, southern red, and white oak. Sprinkled among the hardwoods are groves of nut-laden hickory trees, to the delight of squirrels and those who hunt them. Managing these rich forests is an important part of the wildlife management plan. In addition, the open areas, roughly a third of the area, are planted with annual and perennial wildlife cover and food, and prescribed burning is done periodically. A hunter cruising the area in his vehicle will be impressed with the results of a carefully planned and

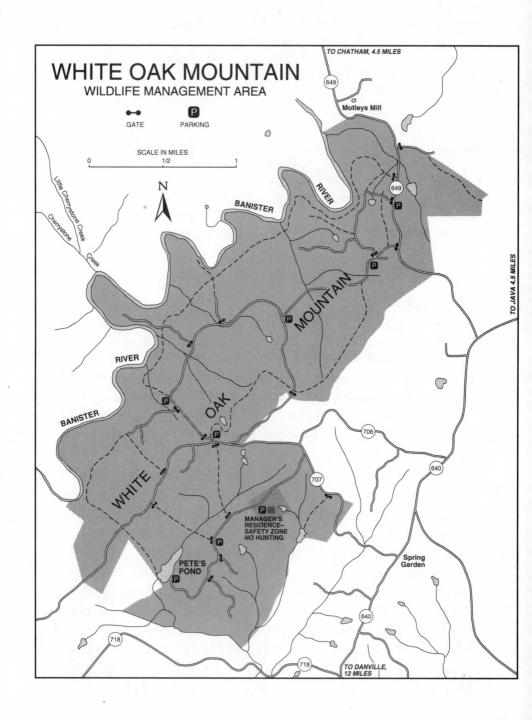

carried-out program to create ideal habitat for small-game hunting. The Banister River, a major tributary of the Dan River, forms the meandering northwest boundary of the wildlife management area. The area is dotted with ponds ranging in size from a half acre to six-acre Pete's Pond, the largest. Most used to be farm ponds during the days when the area was privately owned and actively farmed. This interesting wildlife management area is located near the center of Pittsylvania County, approximately five miles southeast of Chatham.

From Chatham on U.S. Highway 29, two routes lead to the Whiteoak Mountain Wildlife Management Area. Take Route 832 east of Chatham to Route 649, which leads south into the northeastern corner of the wildlife management area near Motleys Mill. South of Chatham, Route 640 north through Spring Garden leads to the main entrance near the manager's residence.

The backpacker enjoys a lot of options in this wildlife management area. Five miles of dirt and gravel roads touch much of the area and probably equally as many miles of trails. The trails hold more appeal to most backpackers because they lead off the beaten path. One trail begins near the southwestern corner of the area and roughly follows the Banister River to the northeastern corner near Motleys Mill. A dirt road crosses it near its southwestern corner, and a bit farther on it intersects with another trail. Another trail begins near the manager's residence across the wildlife management area from the Banister River trail and heads northeast through the area. Several small streams also cross this trail. A backpacker could park near the manager's residence, take the trail northeast to the Motleys Mill area, and then head back by way of the Banister River trail and a combination of roads and trails that lead back to the parking area. Study of the map will reveal all kinds of backpacking opportunities. There are numerous small streams in the area, and the backpacker should plan on crossing several of them regardless of which trail is chosen.

The gently rolling hill country holds a lot of appeal to bicyclists. Good dirt roads lead all over the wildlife management area, and trails lead to parts not reached by the roads. Strapping on a backpack, the bicyclist will find many attractive places to camp for the night. Trails lead to the banks of the Banister River where the murmur of the river calms your nerves or welcomes you for a quick swim in its gentle waters. Study the map carefully, pick out parts of the wildlife management area you want to visit, and peddle off.

The mixed hardwood and pine forests, the numerous small ponds, the well-managed open areas, the Banister River, and the many small streams offer almost unlimited bird-watching opportunities. There are no observation towers or wildlife-viewing platforms, but this does not deter the avid bird-watcher. The Banister River offers a variety of bird-watching opportunities at the points formed by the sharply meandering route it takes. Get on one of these points, locate a spot that gives a good view of the river both upstream and down, and you will be kept busy making notes in your book. Cherrystone Creek enters the river across from one of the points, and the combination of the two streams should attract a variety of birds. Don't overlook the dozen ponds, mostly small. All kinds of birds water at these little ponds of still water, particularly if there are bare spots along the shoreline. The wildlife management area is a popular dove spot, and doves particularly like to gather on clear spots near ponds to water. They won't use the ponds, however, if there is high vegetation right down to the shoreline: too much opportunity for predators to make a meal out of one of them. Spend some time near where a trail crosses one of the many small creeks—a good place for birds. Food plots in the open fields also attract a variety of birds. Take a stand at the edge of one of the fields and go to work with your binoculars.

Among the endangered or threatened birds found here are the brown creeper, dickcissel, bald eagle, great egret, purple finch, northern harrier, yellow-crowned night heron, golden-crowned kinglet, common moorhen, red-breasted nuthatch, barn owl, migrant loggerhead shrike, loggerhead shrike, Caspian tern, hermit thrush, cerulean and magnolia warblers, and winter wren. More common, however, are birds such as the red-winged and rusty blackbirds, bluebird, bunting, cardinal, catbird, chat, chickadee, cowbird, crossbill, crow, cuckoo, dowitcher, cattle egret, finch, flicker, flycatcher, gnatcatcher, goldfinch, grackle, grosbeak, a half-dozen of the more common hawks, great blue and green herons, black-crowned night heron, hummingbird, blue jay, junco, kestrel, killdeer, kingbird, kingfisher, lark, purple martin, nuthatch, Baltimore and orchard orioles, osprey, ovenbird, three kinds of owls, parula, pewee, phoebe, king and Virginia rails, raven, redstart, robin, a pair of sandpipers, sapsucker siskin, a dozen sparrows, starling, a trio of swallows, swift, tanager, tern, a trio of different kinds of thrush, titmouse, towhee, five different species of vireos, vulture, over a dozen species of warblers, waterthrush, waxwing, whippoorwill, pileated, red-headed, and four other woodpeckers, Carolina and house wrens, yellowlegs, and the common yellow-throat.

Canoes or small boats can be launched on Pete's Pond for some limited boating, but stay well away from fishermen. Their license money helped pay for the wildlife management area you are using. There is also the winding Banister River that skirts the area, a good stretch of river to canoe or float in a light boat. The wildlife management area offers access to the river, but there are no formal launching ramps. Several trails or dirt roads will get a boater or canoeist within a hundred yards or so of the river, but after that he is on his own.

As is true of all of the wildlife management areas, there are no formal campgrounds here, but this area's ready access makes it ideal for campers who want to pick out a likely site and set up on their own. There are plenty of opportunities for primitive camping—the preference of many experienced campers. About the only restrictions are a limit of two weeks at a time and no camping within 100 yards of any of the ponds. The excellent system of dirt and gravel roads makes it fairly easy for the camper to locate a site that meets his needs.

Five of the dozen or more ponds on the wildlife management area are available for fishing. The others are generally inaccessible except on foot. The largest, Pete's Pond, six acres of fishing water, holds largemouth bass, bluegills, channel catfish, and redear sunfish. The four smaller ponds hold bluegills and largemouth bass. There may be special regulations on some of the ponds from time to time. If so, they are well posted. Check them before you fish. In addition, several miles of the Banister River skirt the northwestern edge of the wildlife management area. The river is best known for its population of rough fish such as catfish, carp, eels, and suckers, but there are also sunfish and a few largemouth bass. This is not one of the better wildlife management areas for fishing, but the angler who gives it a hard try most likely will be rewarded.

Most of the wildlife management areas were obtained for hunting, and hunters' license money pays for managing them for hunting. The White Oak Mountain Wildlife Management Area offers a rich variety of hunting opportunities, be it small game, big game, or even waterfowl. Small game, however, is the big thing. Wildlife management programs here are pitched toward hunting for doves, quail, rabbits, and squirrels. Prescribed burning, which encourages new young shoots that are tender and exposed, gets a lot of attention. So does field planting in lespedeza and other food-bearing plants. Together with strip disking in the open fields, these practices make the wildlife management area attractive for small game. Game populations vary from year to year, but not because there is a scarcity of food, a condition that frequently affects small game birds and mammals.

Rabbit hunting is predictably good in most years, but quail hunting is not always. That popular bird is barely holding its own in Virginia, but there are always a few coveys on this wildlife management area. The dove hunting can be excellent—or only fair.

Excellent feeding conditions draw the birds to the area, but sometimes farming operations elsewhere in the region prove more attractive and tough competition for the wildlife management area. There is always fair hunting at the worst, however. Hunting is limited to Wednesday and Saturday afternoons during the early season. Check the current dove-hunting regulations posted on the wildlife management area. With two-thirds of the wildlife management area in forests, the squirrel hunting is generally good. Wildlife management practices directed toward doves, quail, and rabbits don't do a lot for squirrels, which look to the forests for cover and food. When two good hard masts seasons occur in a row, the squirrel hunting should be excellent the second season. It might even pick up the first season as the critters move in to share the abundance of food. Woodcocks are always a possibility, either the migrants that move through Virginia during the fall and winter hunting seasons or resident birds that nest locally and produce a hatch of young. The Banister River and the numerous ponds favor the wood duck, and nesting boxes erected near or on the ponds have helped boost the wood duck populations. Don't be surprised to see a few mallard, larger ducks that also tend to breed locally. Although the wildlife management plan is pitched toward small game, there is also good white-tailed deer and wild turkey hunting. Both feed in the open fields and are attracted to tender young shoots that spring up following a prescribed burning session. The hardwoods support turkeys just as they do squirrels, and deer feed on white oak acorns.

Nature viewing, like bird-watching, is done on an informal basis in the absence of viewing towers or platforms. In addition to the songbirds, there are the game birds and mammals discussed above plus the likes of beaver, foxes, muskrat, raccoon, and even mink and otter. Among the endangered or threatened critters are the Roanoke log perch, spirit supercoil snail, Roanoke bass, speckled killifish, rustyside sucker, and river otter. Much more common are frogs including the bullfrog, green and pickerel frogs, and the spring peeper, the red-spotted newt, a dozen different kinds of salamanders, eastern spadefoot, several toads and tree frogs, the poisonous copperhead and timber rattler and almost two dozen nonpoisonous snakes, the fence lizard and a quartet of skinks, five turtles including the better-known box turtle and the snapping turtle, over half a dozen bats, beaver, chipmunk, gray and red foxes, mink, opossum, raccoon, several shrews, striped skunk, weasel, woodchuck, a quartet of crayfish, eastern elliptio mussel, and the carus skipper, orange sulphur, wild indigo, and Zarucco duskywing butterfly. And don't overlook an abundance of wildflowers, many of which are encouraged by the wildlife management practices. Flowering plants such as yellow partridge pea and purple lespedeza, even though not exactly wildflowers, are the result of management practices encouraging wildlife. They are there for visitors to enjoy, however, along with a host of wildflowers found in the deep woods and open fields. Look for the likes of gentian, lady slipper, squawroot, wild ginger, rhododendron, morning glory, buttercup, dandelion, flowering dogwood, and redbud, and in late summer and early fall fields glorified by goldenrod.

Picnickers can pack a lunch or dinner and drive the gravel and dirt roads until they find a suitable spot, probably beneath the spreading branches of a big oak at the edge of a hardwood forest. You will have the place to yourself as others looking for a spot to picnic are not likely to seek a crowd. They can do that by journeying to a city or state park.

The five miles of gravel and dirt roads offer an excellent opportunity to unload a horse or two at the parking area and ride the trails. Generally, large parties are discouraged, but pairs of riders are welcome—or single riders, or very small parties.

The White Oak Mountain Wildlife Management Area is a well-managed one, and the manager who lives with his family on the area is in a position to keep an eye on it. He is doing a good job for hunters and others who enjoy the out-of-doors.

Southwest

Counties: Carroll, Roanoke, Russell, Smyth, Tazewell, and Washington

For the true outdoorsman Southwest Virginia could well be the most interesting part of Virginia. This was Virginia's last frontier. Modern civilization came late to Southwest Virginia though it has long since caught up with the rest of the state in that respect. Early settlers fought the Indians and lived off the land in this enchanting area of rugged mountains, green valleys, and racing streams long after civilization had claimed the eastern part of the state. One of Daniel Boone's several sons was killed during an Indian raid near the Clinch River years after Indian raids were no longer a threat in most of Virginia. While Thomas Jefferson was drawing plans for his mansion, Monticello, hardy frontiersmen were chinking their crude log cabins against the bitter Southwest Virginia winters, and Daniel Boone was seeking a pass through the rugged mountains to Kentucky. He found it at Cumberland Gap in the far southwest corner of the state in what is now Lee County.

The modern hunter takes pride in hunting the mountains and valleys that Daniel Boone, probably the most famous hunter ever, roamed. The same game that Boone hunted, bears, deer, and turkeys, still challenge modern hunters. The state's highest mountains, 5,729-foot Mount Rogers and just to the east 5,520-foot Whitetop Mountain, reach toward the heavens to challenge hikers, bicyclists, and others. And the New River, one of the oldest rivers in the world, flows through Southwest Virginia. Today it is a fine smallmouth bass stream, as are the Clinch, the Holston River system, and other well-known Southwest Virginia streams. In addition to the wildlife management areas found here, the Jefferson National Forest provides over 600,000 acres of public land available for backpacking, biking, fishing, hiking, hunting, and other outdoor activities. Finally, the Claytor, John W. Flannagan, North Fork of the Pound, and South Holston Lakes offer big-water boating and fishing. There is plenty to hold the outdoorsman's attention in this fascinating land.

Clinch Mountain
Wildlife Management Area

Supervising Office: Department of Game and Inland Fisheries
Route 1, Box 107
Marion, VA 24354
Telephone 540-782-9051
Location: Russell, Smyth, Tazewell, and Washington Counties
Elevation: 1,600 to 4,700 feet

At 25,477 acres the Clinch Mountain Wildlife Mountain area is the second largest in Virginia. Only Goshen–Little North Mountain at 33,697 acres is larger. Measured east to west it stretches for almost fifteen miles across Virginia's southwest highlands and claims parts of four big Southwest Virginia counties—Russell, Smyth, Tazewell, and Washington. It is mostly rugged mountain country with deep hollows and tall mountains. Elevations range from 1,600 to 4,700 feet, only a thousand feet lower than the highest point in Virginia. The peak of Beartown Mountain near the northwestern corner of the wildlife management area provides the highest elevation. The large differences in elevation make this wildlife management area the most biologically diverse. Tree species representative of both northern and southern forests are present. Somewhat unique to this area is a turkey brood area just off Route 747, which leads to Laurel Bed Lake and the developed camping area. The area now claimed by the wildlife management area was mostly virgin forest well into the late 1880s when it was heavily logged. Evidence of the old narrow-gauge railroad used in the logging operations is still visible, and some of the old railroad bed is now part of the management area road system.

In addition to the vast mixed hardwood and evergreen forests that all but blanket the area, there is an amazing amount of water

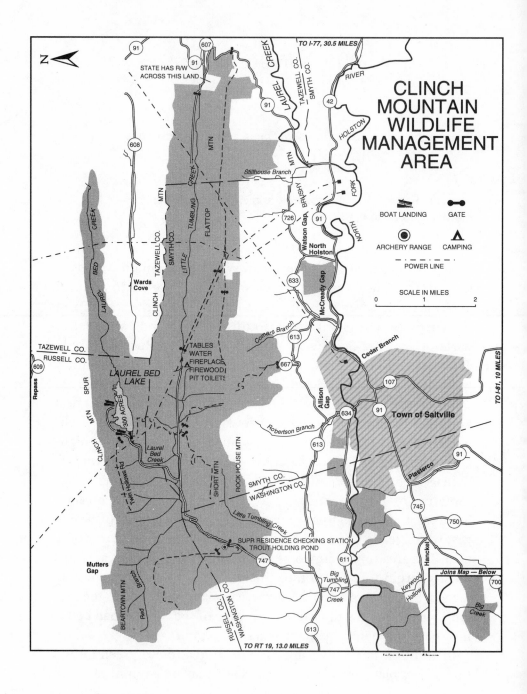

CLINCH MOUNTAIN WILDLIFE MANAGEMENT AREA

N

TO I-77, 30.5 MILES

BOAT LANDING   GATE

ARCHERY RANGE   CAMPING

POWER LINE

SCALE IN MILES
0   1   2

STATE HAS R/W
ACROSS THIS LAND

LAUREL CREEK

RIVER

HOLSTON

Stillhouse Branch

Watson Gap

North Holston

BRUSHY

FORK

NORTH

McCready Gap

Wards Cove

CLINCH MTN

SMYTH CO.

TAZEWELL CO.

LITTLE TUMBLING CREEK

FLATTOP MTN

LAUREL BED CREEK

LAUREL MTN

TAZEWELL CO.
RUSSELL CO.

Repass

LAUREL BED LAKE

300 ACRES

Twin Hollows Rd

Laurel Bed Creek

CLINCH MTN SPUR

Corners Branch

Cedar Branch

107

91   Town of Saltville

Allison Gap

634

Robertson Branch

613

667

613

SHORT MTN

ROCK HOUSE MTN

SMYTH CO.
WASHINGTON CO.

Little Tumbling Creek

SUPR RESIDENCE CHECKING STATION
TROUT HOLDING POND

Mutters Gap

BEARTOWN MTN

Red Branch

RUSSELL CO.
WASHINGTON CO.

747

TABLES
WATER
FIREPLACE
FIREWOOD
PIT TOILETS

611

Big Tumbling

747

Creek

Plasterco

745

750

Hancket

Keywood Hollow

TO I-81, 10 MILES

Joins Map — Below

700

Big Creek

613

TO RT 19, 13.0 MILES

Joins Inset — Above

in the form of tumbling mountain streams and a big lake on the top of Clinch Mountain. Laurel Bed Lake is a 300-acre impoundment on Laurel Bed Creek. Blindfold a couple of visitors, put them on the shores of the sparkling mountain lake, remove the blindfolds, and they could be convinced they were standing on the shores of a northern wilderness lake. It is surrounded by forest, with no sign of human habitation—except for a couple of boat-launching ramps. Little Tumbling Creek and Laurel Bed Creek thread their ways east to west almost the entire length of the area. Laurel Bed Creek eventually forms Laurel Bed Lake and then flows into Big Tumbling Creek, noted for its fine trout fishing. Route 747 follows Big Tumbling Creek deep into the area and provides fishing access to the stream. Little Tumbling Creek eventually joins Big Tumbling Creek after both have left the wildlife management area, and it eventually flows into the North Fork of the Holston River. In addition to the lake and the three major streams, there are a number of smaller streams, some of them tributaries of the major streams. Red Branch, which rises along the flanks of Beartown Mountain, flows into Big Tumbling Creek, and Comers Branch rises in the wildlife management area to flow out of it and into the North Fork of the Holston River. Farther east, Stillhouse Branch also forms in the area to flow into the North Fork. Big Creek flows through a detached plot of the area and into the North Fork also.

Rugged mountains and plenty of water—and there are also the deep valleys. In addition to Beartown Mountain, other major mountains include Flattop, Rock House, and Short. Several utility lines cross the area. In addition to the main tract, there are also several smaller parcels of land along the North Fork of the Holston River. Obviously the Clinch Mountain Wildlife Management Area has a lot going for it. Route 747, which enters the area off Route 613 where Big Tumbling Creek flows beneath the secondary road, is the major entrance to the area, leading to the lake and the campground. Far to the east Route 91 and Route 607 provide access to the area though the routes are seasonally gated. The manager's residence is just inside the area off Route 747.

The town of Saltville is the closest municipality and the jumping-off point to the Clinch Mountain Wildlife Management Area. It is reached north off Interstate 81 by Route 107 at Chilhowie or by Route 91 off the interstate through Glade Springs. From Saltville go north on Route 634 through the hamlet of Allison Gap and turn left on Route 613. The entrance to the area is approximately two miles from Allison Gap. It is well marked. In addition to the roads, a number of trails lead to various parts of the wildlife management area.

The Clinch Mountain Wildlife Management Area can be a backpacker's dream, offering a variety of trails that climb mountains and cross valleys and streams. Some of the utility rights-of-way may also provide improvised trails for backpacking into the more remote parts of the 25,477 acres. There is ample parking space at most of the entrances to the trails, all of which are gated. Motorized vehicles are prohibited, but not travel by foot. Some of the trails are seasonally gated to protect them during unusually wet weather. This, however, does not prohibit foot travel. Many of the trails dead-end, the one going up Short Mountain, for example. This means returning by the same route or taking a compass reading and striking out across untracked country. Several trails, however, provide for through hiking; the one at the end of Route 667, for example, connects with Route 747. A backpacker might like to follow Little Tumbling Creek from the developed campground east to Route 607, which enters the area at a seasonal gate near the eastern boundary of the area. The opportunities for backpacking across wilderness country, however, are all but unlimited.

Although motorized vehicles are prohibited on the trails; mountain or trail bicycles can be used. Those same trails that appeal to backpackers also will be enjoyed by bicyclists. Like the hikers they can go around the gates and proceed along the trails.

Blowdowns that the management area personnel haven't had an opportunity to clear away may create obstacles, but a seasoned hiker or bicyclist can get through or around these. The bicyclist should plan on some steep climbs, however, ones that might make it wise to get off the bicycle and walk it uphill. Even the ride along Route 747 to the campground or Laurel Bed Lake will test the best-conditioned bicyclist. For a ride along Little Tumbling Creek, the bicyclist can take Route 607 west from the extreme eastern edge of the wildlife management area. This offers a ride along approximately two miles of dirt road, but there is no trail leading off it. The only way out is to return by the same route. The trail at the end of Route 667 that terminates near Route 647 also connects with a long six- to seven-mile trail that leads east through the southern reaches of the wildlife management area to terminate on Route 91.

Just as some trees are typical of both northern and southern forests, some birds are attracted to both kinds of habitat. Laurel Bed Lake even attracts a few shorebirds. The bird-watcher could launch a canoe on the lake, paddle quietly and slowly along the shoreline, and get numerous opportunities to view birds that are attracted to this high-altitude mountain lake. The trails that lead to or along the many streams are another possibility. And why not hike to a high vantage point and study the picturesque mountain country with a pair of binoculars. Sightings of various hawks and birds of prey are always a possibility. Even the sight of a bald eagle soaring against a blue sky is a possibility. The wildlife management practices directed toward game species also attract a variety of birds; the wildlife clearings, for example, should be productive. Several are readily available along Route 747. And don't overlook the high-country wetlands, marshes, and swamps along the streams. Several are visible from Route 747.

Among the endangered or threatened birds found on this area are the brown creeper, red crossbill, bald eagle, great egret, peregrine falcon, purple finch, the alder and yellow-bellied flycatchers, northern harrier, golden-crowned kinglet, red-breasted nuthatch, the barn, long-eared, and northern saw-whet owls, loggerhead migrant shrike, loggerhead shrike, Bachman's sparrow, hermit thrush, the cerulean, golden-winged, magnolia, and Swainson's warblers, and the Appalachian Bewick's and winter wrens. More common are such birds as the Brewer's and red-winged blackbirds, bluebird, bobolink, bunting, cardinal, catbird, chat, the Carolina and black-capped chickadees, cowbird, crow, cuckoo, dowitcher, the cattle and golden egrets, finch, flicker, a quintet of flycatchers, gnatcatcher, goldfinch, grackle, the blue and evening grosbeaks, ring-billed gull, over a half-dozen hawks, the great blue and green herons, hummingbird, blue jay, junco, kestrel, killdeer, kingbird, kingfisher, kinglet, lark, martin, meadowlark, mockingbird, nighthawk, nuthatch, oriole, osprey, ovenbird, a trio of owls, parula, pewee, phoebe, raven, redstart, robin, three species of sandpipers, sapsucker, screech owl, siskin, a dozen different sparrows, starling, stork, the barn, cliff, and northern swallows, swift, tanager, tern, thrush, towhee, veery, a quintet of vireos, vulture, over a dozen warblers, waterthrush, waxwing, a quintet of woodpeckers, the Carolina and house wrens, and the common yellowthroat.

Laurel Bed Lake offers opportunities for boating as well as canoeing. On the lake are a pair of well-maintained boat-launching ramps, both off Route 747. The downlake ramp is made of concrete, and the uplake one is well graveled. Both offer ease in launching a boat. This is primarily a trout-fishing lake, and it is managed as such, though smallmouth bass have been introduced to control an expanding rock bass population. Boaters should respect the rights of fishermen, whose license money built the lake and the launching ramps and pays for managing and maintaining them. Only electric motors may be used. Trailering a large heavy boat up the winding and steep Route 747 access route is not recommended.

A developed campground is unique to this wildlife management area. Its facilities are primitive, but there are picnic tables, water, fireplaces, firewood, and pit toilets. It is open only during the hunting and fee-fishing seasons. Primitive camping outside the campground, however, is allowed all year, but not within 100 yards of Laurel Bed Lake. Stays are limited to two weeks. Camping in the developed campground is limited to those who obtain camping permits at the checking station on Route 747 near the entrance to the area. Backpackers and bikers can pack light camping equipment and camp in remote parts of the wildlife management area, an excellent opportunity to experience wilderness camping.

The Clinch Mountain Wildlife Management Area and Laurel Bed Lake offer fishing for brook trout, possibly the best lake fishing for brook trout in Virginia. The lake lies in what was once a boggy depression on the top of Clinch Mountain, and it is rich in nutrients. Fingerling trout released in the lake feed on natural forage and grow to good size. A daily permit is required to fish the lake during the fee-fishing season, usually from the first Saturday in April through the end of September. At other times only regular fishing and trout licenses are required. In addition to Laurel Bed Lake, the fee-fishing season also includes seven miles of Big Tumbling Creek and its major tributaries, Briar Cove Creek and Laurel Bed Creek. Trout, mostly rainbows, are stocked daily in the streams during the fee-fishing season. Route 747, which follows Big Tumbling Creek up the mountain, provides access to the stream fishing. Many of the smaller streams also have good populations of native brook trout. An angler could spend a week fishing the fee-fishing lake and streams and the native brook trout streams and not get to all of them.

While the trout fishing is good in the Clinch Mountain Wildlife Management Area, the hunting can be just as good or better. Good wildlife management practices, which include maintaining forest clearings and the selective harvest of timber, are producing good game populations, particularly deer, grouse, turkeys, and squirrels. Both fox and gray squirrels are present, with their numbers tied to the mast crop. Several successive years of mast crops result in good squirrel hunting. There is also fair hunting, but the populations fluctuate. Rabbits are found at the lower elevations, and the squirrel hunting is often good in hardwoods near water. The deer herd produces some quality antlered bucks. The black bear populations are increasing. Bears are not hunted at the present, but this could change. A high population of beavers has created beaver flowages on most of the streams, and the wood duck hunting can be good, particularly during the early October season. The hunting can be demanding because of the steep terrain—deep valleys and high mountains.

The network of roads and trails can be very attractive to day hikers who shoulder a light pack and strike out for a long day in the mountains. The numerous short one-way trails should appeal to them—or they can strike out on a through trail and have someone pick them up at the other end. One good example is to take the seasonally gated trail near the Route 747 branch to the campground, hike down the mountain, and have someone pick you up at the Route 667 gate off Route 613. A longer hike would begin at the same spot and have a pickup at the eastern end of the trail that threads east near the southern border of the area.

Nature viewing and bird-watching are hard to separate. Move quietly along the trails, particularly early or late in the day, and sightings of big-game animals such as bears, deer, and turkeys are a strong possibility. Or listen carefully, and you may hear a deer snort or an old tom turkey gobble—and maybe the answering yelp of a hen. Listen carefully in the fall, and you may hear the pitter-patter of nut fragments drifting down through the leaves of a tree, sure sign of a squirrel feeding up there on a ripe hickory nut. You may have to look hard to spot it in the green foliage. Sometimes the movement of the leaves when it moves gives it away. Like to watch the busy beaver at work? Follow one of the small streams until you locate a beaver pond. Then back off, make yourself comfortable, and you won't have to wait very long. Alarm the critter, and it will dive, slapping the water with its broad tail. The report can be alarming to the uninitiated. Get out there, walk the trails, canoe the lakeshore, or follow some of the streams, and the opportunity to view nature is almost unlimited. Try to do so outside the busier hunting seasons, the deer and turkey seasons, for example, so your activities will not conflict with serious hunters.

Among the endangered or threatened forms of wildlife found here are the gray, Indiana, Rafinesque's, and Virginia big-eared bat, dusky northern flying squirrel, nineteen different kinds of mussels, the slender and spotfin chubs, the yellowfin, madtom, ashy, and longhead darters, bluestone sculpin, eastern hellbender, Appalachian cottontail, small-footed myotis, spiny riversnail, Diana and regal fritillary butterflies, Tennessee dace, the bluebreast, channel, greenfin, slippershell, and Tippecanoe darters, emerald and steelcolor shiners, blotchside log perch, fatlips minnow, river redhorse, mirror and popeye shiners, stonecat, and the pigmy, shovelnose, and Weller's salamanders. Much more common are such critters as the bullfrog and a number of other frogs, including the spring peeper, red-spotted newt, over two dozen salamanders, including the mudpuppy, spadefoot, a trio of toads, tree frog, the poisonous copperhead and timber rattlesnake and a number of nonpoisonous snakes, the northern fence lizard, the five-lined skink, a number of turtles, eight bats, bobcat, coyote, gray and red foxes, mink, a number of mice and shrews, the fox, gray, and southern flying squirrels, over two dozen mussels and crayfish, and over four dozen species of butterflies. In addition to the trees representative of both the northern and southern forests, there are flowering dogwoods, redbuds, mountain laurel, rhododendron, lady slippers, trillium, and in the open areas buttercups, dandelions, violets, and other wildflowers.

Drive along Route 747 from the south or Route 607 from the east, and you are sure to find an inviting site for a family picnic. Look for a wildlife clearing along the road or a spot beneath a spreading oak or another forest tree. There is plenty of room for a picnic on the shores of Laurel Bed Lake.

Routes 607 and 747 offer many opportunities for horseback riding, but for safety and other reasons it is best to do so outside the deer and turkey hunting seasons. Grouse and squirrel seasons present less of a problem. Some of the trails might be a possibility, but it might be a good idea to talk to the area manager first.

That's the Clinch Mountain Wildlife Management Area, a jewel for those who love the outdoors.

Crooked Creek
Wildlife Management Area

Supervising Office: Department of Game and Inland Fisheries
Route 1, Box 107
Marion, VA 24354
Telephone 540-782-9051
Location: Carroll County
Elevation: 2,400 to 3,000 feet

Most outdoorsmen probably know Crooked Creek Wildlife Management Area best for its fine trout fishing. It is named for Crooked Creek, which enters the area midway on its narrow southern border, to meander through the wildlife management area and exit at its extreme northwestern corner. Unlike most of the Southwest Virginia wildlife management areas, which are located in rugged mountain country, this one sprawls over the more gentle mountains of Carroll County. Elevations range from 2,400 feet to over 3,000, still high country for Virginia, when over half of the state is at elevations of less than 1,000 feet. Its 1,796 acres were once farming country, and the remains of old homesteads still exist. The land is a mixture of forests and open areas, many of which were once pastures. The forests are primarily mixed hardwood, but there are scattered stands of pines. Rhododendron thickets border much of the two major streams that thread through the area, Crooked Creek and East Fork, which flows into Crooked Creek near the manager's residence and the concession stand. The wildlife management area is actually in two sections, the major section being the one through which Crooked Creek flows and on which is located the headquarters buildings. The smaller section is in the northeast corner, and East Fork Creek flows through it.

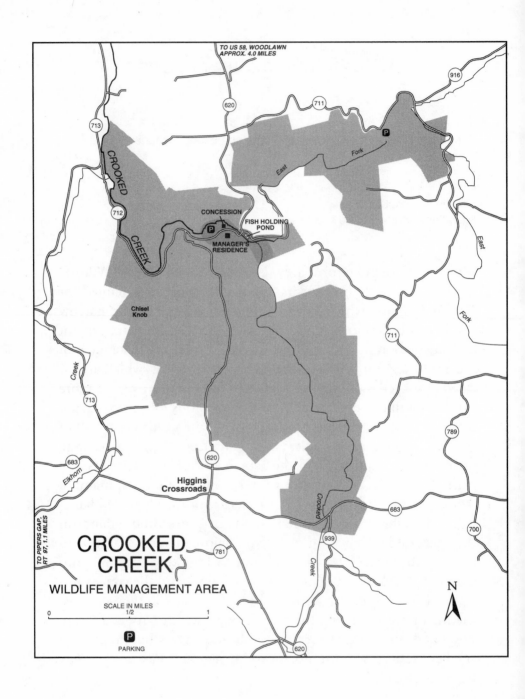

TO US 58, WOODLAWN
APPROX. 4.0 MILES

916

620

711

713

712

CROOKED

CREEK

East

Fork

P

East

CONCESSION

FISH HOLDING
POND

P

MANAGER'S
RESIDENCE

Fork

711

Chisel
Knob

Creek

713

789

683

Elkhorn

620

Higgins
Crossroads

Crooked

683

700

TO PIPERS GAP,
RT 97, 1.1 MILES

781

939

CROOKED
CREEK

WILDLIFE MANAGEMENT AREA

Creek

Crooked

N

SCALE IN MILES
1/2

0   1

P

PARKING

620

While trout fishing is the primary emphasis here, the hunting opportunities are also excellent on land that offered good small-game hunting for many years even before the Department of Game and Inland Fisheries acquired it. The concession stand, located across Secondary Route 712 from the manager's residence, offers drinks and snacks during the fee-fishing season. Public restrooms and picnic tables are also available.

The wildlife management area is located four miles east of Galax and four miles south of Woodlawn, both on U.S. Highway 58. Route 620 south from Woodlawn is the most popular route into the area. It leads to the concession stand across the road from the manager's residence. Another possibility is to take Route 620 north from Higgins Crossroads where Routes 620 and 683 cross. This route will also take you to the concession stand. Route 683 passes through the southern tip of the wildlife management area and crosses Crooked Creek near its headwaters. Route 939 also leads in from the south to join Route 683 near Crooked Creek. A possible route from the west means taking Route 712 off Route 713 at the northwestern corner of the area and following it to Route 620. To reach the East Fork section, take Route 711 east off Route 620 just before it enters the wildlife management area from the north. Route 711 skirts the northern edges of the East Fork section, where a parking area provides easy access to the stream. It then turns abruptly south along the eastern border of the area, following East Fork.

There are no trails in the wildlife management area, but Routes 620, 683, 711, and 712 offer backpacking opportunities. Probably a better possibility is to follow Crooked Creek downstream and north off Route 683. A two- to three-mile hike will take you to Route 620 and the concession stand. Another possibility is to follow East Fork west from Route 711 to its confluence with Route 620 near the concession stand. Backpacking opportunities are somewhat limited here except for those who like to take a compass reading and head off through open country.

The absence of trails pretty much limits the bicyclist to the roads in the area, Routes 620, 683, 711, and 712. The owner of a rugged mountain bicycle might want to take a compass reading and strike off through the untracked wilderness, though there is little true wilderness in this wildlife management area. Traveling across country might reveal interesting traces of the farm life that existed here before the land's purchase for wildlife management.

Mixed hardwood forests, pastures that now serve as wildlife clearings, and several miles of singing trout steams attract a variety of birds. The bird-watcher can roam this wildlife management area with a pair of binoculars and a bird identification book and probably add to his or her list of sighted birds. Check on the time of the hawk migrations that can expand the exciting bird-watching opportunities. Check out the beaver ponds on the pair of major creeks. Trout fishermen know where they are—or ask the area manager who lives on the property. Endangered or threatened birds are more limited here than on most wildfire management areas, but included are the brown creeper, dickcissel, bald eagle, peregrine falcon, purple finch, the alder and yellow-bellied flycatcher, northern harrier, golden-crowned kinglet, common moorhen, red-breasted nuthatch, barn owl, migrant loggerhead shrike, loggerhead shrike, hermit thrush, the cerulean, golden-winged, magnolia, and Swainson's warblers, and winter wren. More common, however, are birds such as the red-winged blackbird, bluebird, bunting, cardinal, catbird, chat, chickadee, cowbird, crossbill, crow, cuckoo, dowitcher, finch, flicker, a quartet of flycatchers, gnatcatcher, goldfinch, grackle, grebe, the blue, evening, and rose-breasted grosbeak, the Cooper's, red-tailed, and four other hawks, great blue and green herons, hummingbird, blue jay, junco, kestrel, killdeer, kingbird, kinglet, lark, martin, meadowlark, mockingbird, nighthawk, nuthatch, oriole, osprey, ovenbird, a trio of owls, parula, pewee, phoebe, raven, redstart, robin, sandpiper, sapsucker, screech owl, a dozen different species of sparrows, starling, swallow, swift, tanager, tern, thrasher, thrush, titmouse, towhee, veery, a quintet of vireos, vulture, over a dozen different species of warblers, waterthrush, waxwing, whippoor-will, a quartet of woodpeckers, the Carolina and house wrens, and the common yellowthroat.

Obviously there are no boating or canoeing opportunities here. The trout streams are too small and shallow. A canoeist would spend more time dragging the craft through shallow water than actually canoeing.

Camping, as is the case with all of the wildlife management areas, is primitive only. The camper simply locates an appealing site and pitches the tent. Just bear in mind that there are no camping facilities, but many experienced campers prefer this. It offers them the solitude they can't find in developed campgrounds.

Trout fishing is the big attraction here, with fishing for both native brook trout and stocked browns and rainbows. The area was first developed and managed as a fee-fishing area but now also offers several miles of stream fishing for native brook trout. The fee-fishing waters get the majority of the angling attention. Trout are stocked every day except Sunday throughout the fee-fishing season, which runs from the first Saturday in April through September. Anglers pay a modest daily fee to fish the fee-fishing waters. The permits are sold at the concession stand, and an attendant is there early to accommodate early-rising anglers. Fishing is legal from 6:30 A.M. until 6:00 P.M. when the stream is closed for re-stocking, the only exception coming in April when fishing doesn't begin until 7 A.M. The trout are kept in a holding pond near the concession stand and removed from there to the stream daily. The pond, of course, has to be replenished frequently from the trout hatcheries. There are five miles of fee-fishing waters, and the stream is rarely crowded. In addition to the permit, the angler needs a basic state fishing license. The stream is open all year, however, and outside the fee-fishing season, the angler needs the basic fishing license plus a trout fishing license. The daily permit is needed only during the fee-fishing season. The stream holds trout well, and trout should be present much of the year, holdovers from the stocking season.

Crooked Creek is a wide, fairly low-gradient stream with a gravel bottom. The country through which it flows is mixed forests and open fields, not characteristic of typical mountain trout country. There are some rock ledges, but wading is much easier than in the more typical boulder-studded mountain stream with a rocky bottom. It's a pleasure to wade. Although there are no specific parking areas along the stream, there is plenty of parking room along the side of Route 620. Crooked Creek above Route 620 and all of the East Fork are managed as a wild trout fishery. Over two miles of these two streams offer fishing for wild trout, mostly brook trout but also naturally reproducing browns. Crooked Creek rises outside the wildlife management area. It offers fishing for wild trout, but there the permission of the landowners is needed. The angler who wants to take the time to get permits might enjoy some excellent fishing.

Because of its history as farming country where much of the land was in open fields and agriculture, the Crooked Creek Wildlife Management area offers both big-game and small-game hunting and limited waterfowl hunting. With only 600 feet between its lowest and highest elevations, the area is relatively easy to hunt. It rolls gently. Long noted for its small-game hunting, the area could well be more popular today for its deer and turkeys. The populations of both are on the increase. The mixed hardwood forests with their mast crops and large open fields that function as wildlife clearings serve the hunter well. The deer and turkey hunting are probably the most popular, with squirrel hunting close behind. Squirrel hunting is very popular in Southwest Virginia where traditionally the season has opened in early September. Forest management is directed toward these three game species. Den trees are protected, and timber harvesting is done on a selective basis. The mature hardwood forests favor both squirrels and turkeys. Deer also feed on the hardwood mast, particularly white oak acorns. The old agricultural fields are also managed for wildlife by creating hedgerows and manipulating native vegetation and permanent wildlife plantings. Good wood duck populations use Crooked Crook, and the work of beavers favors the colorful little duck with the flowages that the always busy rodents create.

The day hiker probably will find this area more appealing than the backpacker, who looks for areas to pack into and set up an overnight camp. Routes 620, 683, 711, and 712 are all available for day hikes. Ideally, I suppose, a hiker should hike through and arrange for a pickup on the other end. Route 620 would be perfect for this. It leads through the forested area and along Crooked Creek, interesting areas to hike. Pack a lunch and binoculars and make a day of it. Another possibility is to pick up Crooked Creek where it is crossed by Route 683 and follow it through to the headquarters area.

The mature hardwood forests, creeks, wildlife clearings, and beaver ponds on the creeks all provide opportunities to watch nature, deer, rabbits, squirrels, and turkeys in addition to the rich variety of birds. Take along binoculars for close-up viewing. One unique opportunity is the wide array of wildflowers that color the old fields in spring and summer. While the flowers themselves are worth enjoying, the fact that they provide nectaring areas for butterflies makes them even more appealing. As is true of birds, a few endangered or threatened critters live in the area or visit it. Among them are the Indiana bat, bog turtle, Kanawha minnow, eastern hellbender, small-footed myotis, green floater mussel, Howe's dragonfly, and regal fritillary butterfly. More common, however, are half a dozen frogs including the bullfrog, green and pickerel frogs, and spring peeper, the red-spotted newt, over a dozen salamanders, spadefoot, a pair of toads, tree frog, the poisonous copperhead and timber rattlesnake and over a dozen nonpoisonous snakes, fence lizard and a pair of skinks, box, musk, painted, and snapping turtles, over a half-dozen bats, bobcat, coyote, fox, mink, a half-dozen shrews, skunk, woodchuck, mussel and a half-dozen crayfish, and fields full of butterflies—over four dozen different species. The open fields and hardwood forests offer the opportunity to enjoy a wide variety of flowering shrubs and wildflowers. Wild-flowers in the open fields provide summer nectaring areas for the four dozen butterflies, and rhododendron thickets along Crooked Creek add color during the spring months. There are also blooming dogwoods and redbuds, and possibly some mountain laurel back in the hills. Look for trillium, wild iris, wild orchids, fire pink, mayapples, morning glory, lady slippers, violets, buttercups, dandelions, and in the late summer and early fall fields of colorful goldenrod.

The picnic tables near the concession stand offer a fine opportunity to enjoy a picnic, but some might prefer to drive along the road and look for the sprawling branches of a big oak or a spot along Crooked Creek.

All of the secondary roads, 620, 683, 711, and 713, offer opportunities for horseback riding. It might be a good idea to check with the manager beforehand to make sure riding won't conflict with other activities.

The Crooked Creek Wildlife Management Area is somewhat unique because it was purchased for trout fishing, but it also offers good hunting and public land for other outdoor activities.

Havens Wildlife Management Area

Supervising Office: Department of Game and Inland Fisheries
910 Thomas Jefferson Road
Forest, VA 24551
Telephone 804-525-7522
Location: Roanoke County
Elevation: 1,500 to 3,200 feet

Approximately 6,000 of the 7,190 acres of rugged mountain land that make up the Havens Wildlife Management Area were purchased back in 1930 at the Great Depression bargain basement price of $2.61 per acre. The remainder, a little over 1,000 acres, has been added since. Located in the Appalachian highlands, it occupies a portion of Fort Lewis Mountain and is in Roanoke County approximately five miles west of the populous Roanoke-Salem metropolitan area. To the northeast is Little Brushy Mountain and to the southwest Catawba Mountain.

The terrain is steep and generally inaccessible except on foot, bicycle, or horseback. Elevations range from 1,500 to 3,200 feet. Those on foot likely will fare the best, though bicyclists and horseback riders should be able to handle it. Generally only the hardiest of hunters or hikers are willing to tackle it. It is a true wilderness region, one amazingly close to a major population center. The soil on the area is generally shallow and poor. Water is scarce with only a small intermittent stream that disappears in dry weather. The Department of Game and Inland Fisheries has constructed several water holes for wildlife, but they are generally dependent upon rainfall. Like the intermittent stream, they too can disappear during extended periods of dry weather. Ninety-nine percent of the area is covered with mixed forests of oaks, hickories, and pines. Before its purchase by the Department of Game

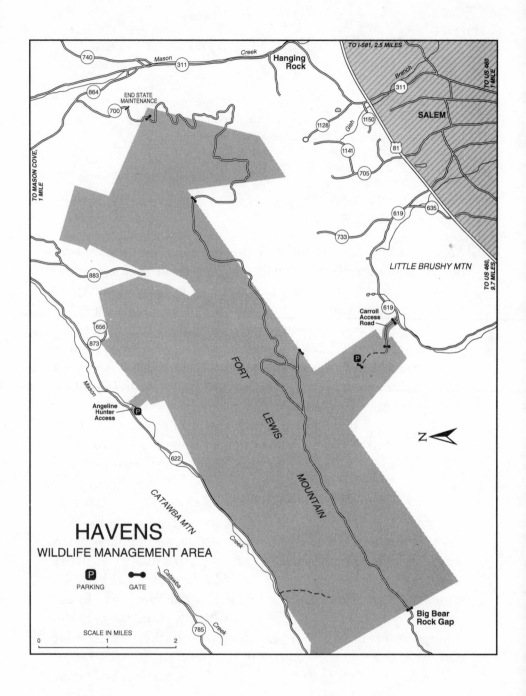

TO I-581, 2.5 MILES
TO US 460, 1 MILE

740 Mason Creek Hanging Rock
311
864 311 Branch
END STATE MAINTENANCE SALEM
700 1128 Gish 1150
81
TO MASON COVE, 1 MILE 1141
705
619 635
883 733
LITTLE BRUSHY MTN
TO US 460, 9.7 MILES
656
873 619
Carroll Access Road
Mason P
Angeline Hunter Access P
FORT
622 LEWIS
CATAWBA MTN MOUNTAIN
N

HAVENS
WILDLIFE MANAGEMENT AREA

Creek Big Bear Rock Gap

P
PARKING GATE

Catawba

SCALE IN MILES
0 1 2 785 Creek

and Inland Fisheries, much of the region was logged, and because of the poor soil and limited water, the forestlands have been slow to recover. Despite this, few other wildlife management areas in Virginia offer a better opportunity for hunters or backpackers to escape the crowds and find solitude in a high-country setting. Escaping the crowds is possible because few outdoors people are willing to tackle this somewhat hostile environment. Travel within the area is generally through untracked country, so a good compass and the ability to use it are very important. Probably no other wildlife management area in the statewide system is more inaccessible.

The wildlife management area is best reached off Interstate 81 at Salem, by taking the Route 311 exit. Follow Route 311 to Route 864 (Bradshaw Avenue), turn left onto Route 864 and left again on Route 622, and look for the wildlife management area signs on the left. Route 622 skirts the area. Mason Creek follows Route 622 and dips into the wildlife area for a short distance. Another possibility is to take Route 619 off Interstate 81 in Salem and follow it north to Carroll Access Road on the south side of the area. The access road goes a short distance into the wildlife management area. It is seasonally gated, but hikers, bicyclists, and horseback riders can use the road and trail at any season. Another possibility is to continue southwest on Route 622, which skirts the north side of the wildlife management area, and look for the Angeline Hunter Access. You might find a trace of a trail leading into the area. An old dirt road passes through the wildlife management area from Big Bear Rock Gap running northeast near the southern border and exiting near the northeast corner to join Route 864. It meanders in and out of the area but is gated at all of the wildlife management area borders. It also winds onto private land occasionally, and the permission of the landowners should be sought before continuing. Otherwise the only option is to reverse your route and exit back at Big Bear Rock Gap. Within the gates the area is accessible by foot, bicycle, or horseback only.

Backpacking can be tough in this wildlife management area, but the kind of challenge the more hardy backpackers like. The dirt road leading from Big Bear Rock Gap to Bradshaw Road is reasonably well maintained, but the problem is that to get through it the hiker has to pass through private land. Wisely, the backpacker will clear this up before beginning the trip—getting permits if necessary. Trails from the Carroll Access Road and the Angeline Hunter Access are short and will not take the hiker far into the area. You could, of course, take a compass reading and hike through to the dirt road that runs the length of the area. This would call for some stiff mountain climbing but would not expose you to private land. Backpacking opportunities are there, but they should not be taken lightly. Study the map of the area thoroughly before beginning a trip.

Since the area is 99.9 percent forestland, the bird-watcher should concentrate on forest birds. Taking the trails that lead inward from the Angeline Hunter Access and Carroll Access Road is the easiest way to watch birds. Climbing the steep Fort Lewis Mountain is tough, but the reward could be a high point overlooking miles of the surrounding country. Use your binoculars and study the forest slopes before you. Another possibility is to locate one of the water holes and take a stand nearby. Numerous birds will fly in to drink because water is very limited on this wildlife management area. Another possibility is to pick up Mason Creek where it dips into the area along Route 622. Follow it upstream or down until it swings back on private land. We're talking about possibly a mile of a high-country stream. There should be bird life along the creek.

As is true of all of the wildlife management areas, endangered or threatened birds are found here. Among them are the brown creeper, crossbill, dickcissel, bald eagle, great egret, peregrine falcon, purple finch, alder flycatcher, northern goshawk, northern harrier, yellow-crowned night heron, golden-crowned kinglet, common moorhen, red-breasted nuthatch, barn owl, migrant loggerhead shrike, loggerhead shrike, Henslow's sparrow, hermit thrush, cerulean, golden-winged, magnolia, and Swainson's warblers, the Appalachian Bewick's wren, and the winter wren. More likely to be sighted are birds such as the bittern, red-winged and eastern blackbirds, bunting, cardinal, catbird, chat, chickadee, cowbird, crossbill, crow, cuckoo, dowitcher, finch, flicker, a quartet of flycatchers, gnatcatcher, goldfinch, grackle, grebe, grosbeak, the Cooper's, broad-winged, red-tailed, and several other hawks, great blue and green herons, hummingbird, blue jay, junco, kestrel, killdeer, kingbird, kingfisher, kinglet, kite, lark, longspur, magpie, martin, meadowlark, mockingbird, nighthawk, nuthatch, oriole, ovenbird, a trio of owls, parula, pewee, phalarope, phoebe, raven, redstart, robin, sapsucker, screech owl, siskin, a number of different sparrows, starling, four different swallows, swift, the scarlet and summer tanagers, tern, thrasher, thrush, titmouse, towhee, veery, a number of different species of vireos, vulture, over a dozen different kinds of warblers, waterthrush, a half-dozen different species of woodpeckers, the Carolina and house wrens, and the common yellowthroat.

There is obviously no boating or canoeing opportunity here. Leave your boat or canoe at home.

The camping is entirely primitive but convenient for someone living in the Roanoke-Salem area who wants to get out for an overnight camping trip. Get a copy of a map of the wildlife management area from the Department of Game and Inland Fisheries and spend some time poring over it. A camping family could park their vehicle at either of the two access areas, the Angeline Hunter Access or Carroll Access Road, and find a camping spot close by. Another possibility is camping near Mason Creek where it dips into the wildlife management area alongside Route 622. Camping stays are limited to two weeks.

This is the only wildlife management area on which there is absolutely no fishing. The few streams that exist dry up in during periods of drought. They do not support fish populations.

Hunting is tough here, but it can be rewarding. Big game includes bears, deer, and turkeys—and within a stone's throw, approximately five miles, of a major population center. The very nature of the terrain discourages a lot of hunters, but those who do accept the challenge can find some good hunting and little or no competition. Ruffed grouse and both fox and gray squirrels are the major small-game critters. And there are sure to be opossums and raccoon for the night hunter who is brave enough to try following his dogs over the almost forbidding terrain and through thick forests. The poor soil and rugged terrain make wildlife management difficult, but improved access is alleviating this problem to a degree. Power lines are seeded with wildlife food plants, and several acres of wildlife clearings are maintained to provide grassy areas for wildlife. Additionally, a number of areas have been planted with food-producing shrubs, and several water holes have been created. The hunter does not have to venture far off the roads to find good hunting. Squirrel hunters park along Route 622 and enjoy good hunting. So do grouse hunters. But before squeezing the trigger on that big buck or even bear, give some thought to how you will get it back to your vehicle. Dragging a bear or a big deer for a mile or so through the forest and over rugged terrain is not something for the faint of heart. Slinging a turkey over your shoulder is much easier, but before you do so, tag it well with blaze orange. Despite the nature of the country, some other hunters are going to get into it also, and you don't want to risk someone sighting that moving turkey and mistaking it for a live one.

The day hiker is generally limited to following one of the trails into the area and then returning by the same route. A more ambitious hiker might want to follow the unnamed trail off Route 622 near the northwestern corner of the area to its end, take a compass reading, and continue on to the dirt road that leads northeast from Big Bear Rock Gap.

Nature viewing includes, in addition to the usual forest songbirds, such game animals as bears, deer, grouse, squirrels, and turkeys. You might also see an occasional raccoon, and it is almost a certainty that you will stumble on a roaming opossum and have it fake sleep when you approach. This area has its endangered and threatened species including the Roanoke log perch, Indiana and Virginia big-eared bats, James spiny mussel, orangefin madtom, roughhead shiner, bluestone sculpin, northern pine snake, Appalachian cottontail, small-footed myotis, Atlantic pigtoe mussel, Diana, grizzled, and regal fritillary butterflies, and the rusty-side sucker. Much more common, however, are critters such as the bullfrog, green and pickerel frogs, and spring peeper, red-spotted newt, over a dozen different kinds of salamanders, spadefoot, a couple of toads, tree frog, the poisonous copperhead and timber rattlesnake and over a dozen nonpoisonous snakes, the fence lizard and a couple of skinks, the eastern box, musk, and snapping turtles, over a half-dozen different kinds of bats, bobcat, chipmunk, coyote, fox, mink, mole, over a half-dozen shrews, skunk, weasel, a trio of mussels, a half-dozen crayfish, over a hundred different species of butterflies, and a half-dozen different gnats to pester the summer visitor. Wildflowers are abundant at the proper seasons, and don't miss the opportunity to view or photograph mountain rhododendron when it is in full bloom. As is the case with bird-watching, good binoculars are a true asset. Among the wildflowers and shrubs are flowering dogwood, redbud, mountain laurel, trillium, wild orchid, lady slipper, violets, and other woodland flowers of the high country.

Picnicking opportunities are pretty much limited to openings in the forest. Good picnic spots should be available within easy reach of your automobile in one of the designated parking areas. Another possibility is to find a spot near Mason Creek where it passes through the wildlife management area. You should be able to park along the shoulders of the lightly traveled Route 622.

The long dirt road leading northeast through the area from Big Bear Rock Gap should offer good horseback riding. Ideally, I suppose the mounts should be the popular and surefooted quarter horses so popular in the mountains of the western United States. But the rider who knows his horse should experience no trouble. The road is rocky and steep in places, and if there is a chance your horse might lose its footing, the safest approach is to get off and lead the horse instead of riding it. The road curves into private land approximately three miles from the gap. Unless you have permission to enter the private property, it is best to turn around and reverse your route.

The Havens Wildlife Management Area is challenging and rugged, and it has a personality of its own — as does each of the twenty-nine wildlife management areas.

Hidden Valley
Wildlife Management Area

Supervising Office: Department of Game and Inland Fisheries
Route 1, Box 107
Marion, VA 24354
Telephone 540-782-9051
Location: Washington County
Elevation: 2,000 to in excess of 4,000 feet

To reach the Hidden Valley Wildlife Management Area, you take Route 690 off U.S. Highway 19, follow Little Moccasin Creek, and head almost straight up the mountain. There is probably not another route to a Virginia wildlife management area that is steeper. If you are driving a 4×4 vehicle, shift into low 4×4 and drive slowly until you reach the top. As you enter the wildlife management area, the road forks at Low Gap. If you take the right fork, you climb even higher up the mountain—up Brumley Mountain, over 4,000 feet high. If you take the left fork, you drop down from Low Gap into Hidden Valley, and there before you is Hidden Valley Lake, a sixty-one-acre jewel that rests in the valley at 3,600 feet. Hidden Valley and Hidden Valley Lake are appropriately named. Surrounded by rugged mountains, the little mountain valley and the lake are an improbable pair.

This picturesque 6,400-acre wildlife management area is located in Washington County, with the Russell-Washington county line forming its long northwestern border. It is rugged country with elevations ranging from 2,000 to over 4,000 feet at its highest elevation. The area was logged soon after the turn of the century when most of it was covered with a virgin forest. The predominant forest cover now is mixed hardwoods, though some hemlock is found at the lower elevations, and there is some red spruce at the higher elevations near the crest of Brumley Mountain. Except

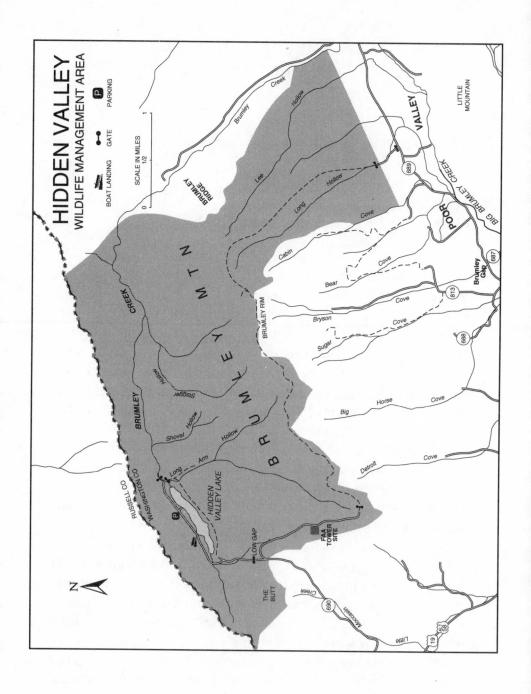

HIDDEN VALLEY
WILDLIFE MANAGEMENT AREA

P PARKING

● GATE

BOAT LANDING

SCALE IN MILES

0   1/2   1

N

for scattered wildlife clearings developed by the Department of Game and Inland Fisheries and the sixty-one-acre lake, the area is completely covered with forests. Rugged but beautiful might best describe this westernmost wildlife management area. Compare this rugged, high-elevation wildlife management area with Mockhorn Island Wildlife Management Area at sea level off the coast of the Eastern Shore, and you get an idea of the great variety of outdoor opportunities the twenty-nine wildlife management areas offer.

Brumley Creek, which originates near the western border of the area, flows eastward across its northern reaches. It was impounded near its headwaters to form Hidden Valley Lake. A number of small streams, mostly intermittent, form high on Brumley Mountain to flow into Brumley Creek. Among them are streams flowing down through Long Arm Hollow, Shovel Hollow, and Stagger Hollow. Brumley Creek flows out of the area and then turns south to skirt the wildlife management area at its southeastern corner. Big Brumley Creek flows east through Poor Valley just to the south of the wildlife management area. Several small intermittent streams form along the southern slopes of the wildlife management area and flow into Big Brumley. Among them are streams flowing from Cabin Cove, Lee Hollow, and Long Hollow. Big Brumley Creek is a Category C trout stream. Several long hiking trails provide access to the interior of the area.

To reach the area you take U.S. 19 north from Abingdon or south from Lebanon and exit east on Route 690. You will follow Little Moccasin Creek approximately a half mile, and then it will disappear to your left. The road forks as you enter the area, the left fork dropping down to Hidden Valley Lake and the right fork continuing up the mountain. There is an FAA tower site on the right of the right fork, and just beyond that, the road ends at a gated trail.

The backpacker will find much that is appealing here, not the least of which is an eight- to ten-mile combination dirt road and trail that leads to the crest of Brumley Mountain and down the other side. The first mile or so is mostly a dirt and gravel road that ends at the gated trail. From the gated entrance the trail follows along the southern edge of the wildlife management area and exits the area on Route 689, which follows Big Brumley Creek through Poor Valley. Ideally someone should be there to meet the backpacker—or the reverse, with the backpacker leaving a vehicle there and getting a ride to the entrance to Route 690 on U.S. Highway 19, so that no specific time has to be set for the pickup at the other end. Another possibility is to drop over Low Gap and hike to Hidden Valley Lake. The backpacker can follow the road to the far end of the lake where a gated trail provides a hike back along the south side of the lake to the dirt road. A short trail of less than half a mile leads up Long Arm Hollow, a small diversion before heading back toward Low Gap. These are the only trails on the Hidden Valley Wildlife Management Area, but there is plenty of room for cross-country backpacking. One such possibility might be to follow Brumley Creek downstream from Hidden Valley Lake. The going could be tough, but it is downhill. The creek eventually leaves the wildlife management area, and approximately a mile beyond the boundary, the creek runs parallel to a secondary road that eventually joins Route 689. This is a good area for a backpacker to spend several days in wilderness travel—and in high country up there among the stands of red spruce.

Climbing Brumley Mountain on Route 690 can be a real test of a bicyclist's endurance, but once you reach Low Gap, the going gets easier regardless of whether you take the fork to the right and climb farther up Brumley Mountain or the one to the left and drop down to Hidden Valley lake. You can circle the lake by taking the gated trail to the right, riding to the end of the lake, and returning by the road on the northern side of the lake. The trail is gated at both ends, but there are no gates on the road. The road to the right up Brumley Mountain continues down the southern side of the mountain as a trail that eventually leaves the area and joins

Route 689, which skirts the southern boundary of the wildlife management area. You can have someone pick you up there, or you can continue on a secondary road that leads back to U.S. 19 and Route 690. Or you can reverse the route, peddling back up the trail to Low Gap.

Probably the best place for bird-watching is Hidden Valley Lake and the road and trail that circle it. Hike along the road or trail until you find a spot that offers a good view of the lake and shoreline, make yourself comfortable, and go to work with your binoculars. Another possibility is to launch a canoe at the boat-launching ramp and slowly circle the lake. Paddle slowly and as quietly as possible. Water is scarce in much of this wildlife management area, and the lake is a real drawing card. Keep your eyes on the shoreline. The stream below the lake should also be productive, but the going is tough in the absence of a trail. For forest birds or birds that frequent higher elevations, take the road to the right at Low Gap, the one that leads to the FAA tower site and beyond.

Endangered or threatened birds here include the brown creeper, red crossbill, bald eagle, great egret, peregrine falcon, purple finch, alder and yellow-bellied flycatchers, northern harrier, golden-crowned kinglet, common moorhen, red-breasted nuthatch, the barn, long-eared, and northern saw-whet owls, migrant loggerhead shrike, loggerhead shrike, Bachman's sparrow, hermit thrush, cerulean, golden-winged, magnolia, and Swainson's warblers, and Appalachian Bewick's and winter wrens. More common, however, are the Brewer's and red-winged blackbirds, bluebird, indigo bunting, cardinal, catbird, chat, Carolina and black-capped chickadees, chuck-will's-widow, cowbill, crossbill, crow, cuckoo, dowitcher, golden eagle, cattle egret, house finch, flicker, a quintet of different flycatchers, gnatcatcher, goldeneye, goldfinch, grackle, grebe, blue, evening, and rose-breasted grosbeaks, over a half-dozen hawks, great blue and green herons, hummingbird, blue jay, junco, kestrel, killdeer, kingbird, kingfisher, kinglet, lark, martin, meadowlark, mockingbird, nighthawk, nuthatch, oriole, osprey, ovenbird, barred, great horned, and short-eared owls, parula, pewee, phoebe, rail, raven, redstart, robin, a trio of sandpipers, sapsucker, screech owl, siskin, a dozen different species of sparrows, starling, stork, the barn, cliff, northern rough-winged, and tree swallows, chimney swift, scarlet and summer tanagers, tern, thrasher, thrush, titmouse, towhee, veery, a quintet of vireos, vulture, over a dozen and a half warblers, waterthrush, waxwing, whippoorwill, the downy, hairy, pileated, red-bellied, and red-headed woodpeckers, the Carolina and house wrens, and the common yellowthroat.

The lake offers sixty acres of flat water for boating or canoeing, and a good boat ramp facilitates the launching of watercraft. Keep in mind that gasoline outboard motors are prohibited, but electric-powered ones are no problem. Canoeing at this high elevation on a warm summer day could be a real joy.

Primitive camping is permitted throughout the wildlife management area, but not within 100 yards of Hidden Valley Lake. For campers who do not want to backpack, the best solution might be to look for a spot along the road leading to the FAA tower site. With most of the area covered with mixed hardwood forests, it is almost a certainty that camping here means setting up in a woodland environment. Camping stays are limited to two weeks.

One might expect the 3,600-foot-high Hidden Valley Lake to be a trout lake, but surprisingly it is home to a rich variety of warmwater fish, namely, rock bass, smallmouth bass, bluegills, and walleyes. The boat-launching ramp on the north side of the lake facilitates the easy launching of a boat.

A rich variety of game is found on this mountainous wildlife management area, but bears, deer, grouse, squirrels, and turkeys are the game species most sought after. Local hunters consider the grouse hunting excellent. There are also raccoon for the night hunters. And don't overlook the possibility of waterfowl on Hidden Valley Lake, mostly wood ducks. The hunting can be demanding because of the mountainous nature of this wildlife management area. Getting a deer out of the area could be tough if it is taken far from the road. And a big bear could be even more so. Give this some consideration before squeezing off that shot.

The day hikers who like to shoulder light packs and hang binoculars around their necks should be able to enjoy a good outing here. They might want to park their vehicle at Low Gap or at Hidden Valley Lake and hike around the lake or take the longer hike along the right fork at Low Gap. Maybe they would like to hike for two or three hours along the road and on the trail beyond the gate, eat lunch, and then return by the same route.

In addition to songbirds, there is a great variety of game animals as well as nongame species. Keeping in mind that most critters like to look for water at some point during the day, an observation point on Hidden Valley Lake might be a good spot to view a great variety of wildlife as it comes to the lake for a drink of water. A close examination of the shoreline should reveal the more popular watering spots. Look for footprints in the soft earth near the lake. An ability to read tracks can be very valuable. A number of endangered and threatened creatures are found on this area. They include the Indiana, gray, and Rafinesque's bats, northern flying squirrel, nineteen different kinds of mussels, the spotfin chub, yellowfin madtom, ashy, bluebreast, channel, and longhead darters, eastern hellbender, the Appalachian cottontail, small-footed myotis, spiny river snail, the Diana and regal fritillary butterflies, Tennessee dace, bluebreast, channel, greenfin, sharphead, and Tippecanoe darters, the emerald and steelcolor shiners, blotchside log perch, fatlip minnow, river redhorse, mirror and popeye shiners, stonecat, and the pigmy, shovelnose, and Weller's salamanders. More common creatures include the bullfrog, green, pickerel, and wood frogs, and spring peeper, the red-spotted newt, over two dozen salamanders, including the mudpuppy, spadefoot, cooter, the copperhead and timber rattlesnake and over a dozen nonpoisonous snakes, fence lizard, skink, Cumberland slider, the box, spiny softshell, snapping, and several other turtles, over half a dozen bats, bobcat, chipmunk, coyote, fox, mole, almost a dozen shrews, skunk, seven different species of squirrels, weasel, almost two dozen mussels, a half-dozen crayfish, and over three dozen different kinds of butterflies. With limited open areas the wildflowers and flowering shrubs are mostly those associated with woodlands. Trees representative of both the northern and southern forests are found here. A good example is the northern red spruce. Look for flowering dogwood, redbud, mountain laurel, and rhododendron, lady slippers, trillium, violets, and in the few open spaces buttercups, dandelions, and other field flowers.

For a picnic you have a choice of a spot on Hidden Valley Lake or in the forests off the road leading to the right and up the mountain to the FAA tower site. Thanks to the high elevation of this wildlife management area, it holds appeal on a hot summer day when the temperatures are more inviting at high altitudes. Even the lake is 3,600 feet high.

Route 690 and the several trails offer limited horseback riding, but it might be best to check with the wildlife management area manager first. A telephone call will clear the way. Otherwise there might be other activities that would conflict with horseback riding. It might also be a good idea to drive up to Low Gap and decide for yourself whether the grade is too steep to pull a horse trailer up — or too steep for a horse.

So ends this little guide to Virginia's wildlife management areas. Hidden Valley is a good note to end on. It leaves you with the description of an exciting place to explore. It's last only because the alphabet and arrangement of the book placed it there.

Index

Angeline Hunter Access, 217, 218, 219
Atlantic Coast, 91
Atlantic Ocean, 89, 90, 91

Back Bay, 89, 97, 99, 100, 101
Back Bay Landing Road, 99
Back Bay National Wildlife Refuge, 89, 99
Barbours Hill, 97, 101
Bass
    channel, 95, 105
    largemouth, 12, 37, 45, 51, 64, 78, 100,
        115, 116, 119, 122, 131, 139, 147, 154,
        162, 192
    Roanoke, 186, 193
    rock, 20, 28, 202, 228
    smallmouth, 12, 20, 28, 37, 57, 64, 71,
        139, 155, 196, 202, 228
    striped, 46, 51, 105, 116, 131, 147, 169
Bass Pond, 157, 161, 164
Bayse Point, 143
Bear, black, 3, 20, 28, 58, 84, 85, 179, 195,
    204, 220, 228, 229
Beasley Bay, 105
Beaver, 46, 48, 52, 65, 66, 75, 85, 124, 125,
    132, 140, 148, 155, 172, 179, 193, 194,
    204, 213
    flowage, 11, 20, 21, 66, 79, 117, 140, 159, 204
    ponds, 48, 78, 163, 183, 204, 210
Blakey Ridge, 81, 83
Bluefish, 95, 105, 160
Bluegill, 37, 45, 64, 71, 100, 115, 116, 122, 123,
    131, 139, 147, 154, 162, 184, 192, 228
Blue Ridge Parkway, 1, 7, 31, 173, 175, 178
Bobcat, 13, 156, 179
Bolar Flats Marina, 12, 14

Boone, Daniel, 195
Bowfin, 51
Bradshaw Road, 218
Bream Pond, 161
Buck Hill Road, 26
Bullhead Pond, 157, 161, 164
Bullpasture Gorge, 25, 28
Bullpasture Mountain tract, 24, 28, 29, 30
Bullpasture River tract, 25

Carlisle tract, 143, 144, 145, 146, 147, 148
Carp, 146, 192
Carroll Access Road, 217, 218, 219
Catfish, 12, 51, 64, 115, 192
    blue, 45, 147
    channel, 37, 45, 57, 71, 100, 115, 122, 123,
        139, 147, 154, 162, 192
    white, 45
Chesapeake Bay, 31, 89, 90, 102, 105, 107, 167
Chesapeake Bay Bridge-Tunnel, 89
Cities and towns
    Abingdon, 225
    Allison Gap, 200
    Amelia Courthouse, 113
    Augusta Springs, 17
    Banco, 83
    Basset, 136
    Bedford, 136
    Big Bear Rock Gap, 217, 218, 220, 221
    Bremo Bluff, 63, 64
    Buckingham Courthouse, 152
    Castle Heights, 128, 129, 131
    Charlottesville, 82, 152
    Chatham, 189
    Cheriton, 93

Index

Cities and towns (*cont.*)
  Chilhowie, 200
  Creeds, 99
  Culpeper, 82
  Danville, 136
  Double Oak Gap, 181, 182, 183, 185
  Farmville, 119, 121
  Figsboro, 182
  Forest, 111, 119, 127, 151, 181, 187, 215
  Fredericksburg, 37, 53, 61, 75, 76, 81, 157
  Galax, 175
  Giles Store, 181, 182, 183
  Glade Springs, 200
  Glasgow, 19
  Goldvein, 35
  Graves Mill, 83
  Hampton, 165
  Higgins Crossroads, 209
  Keysville, 121
  Lebanon, 225
  Lexington, 17, 19
  Linden, 55
  Lovingston, 69
  Lynchburg, 136, 152
  Marion, 173, 197, 207, 223
  Markham, 55
  Martinsville, 136, 182
  Masons Corner, 112, 113, 115, 117
  McDowell, 25, 26
  Millboro Springs, 26
  Monterey, 62
  Moss Neck, 75, 76
  Motleys Mill, 189
  Newport News, 49, 165, 167
  Oyster, 93
  Paris, 55
  Providence Forge, 43, 49, 51
  Remington, 35, 37
  Richmond, 32, 111, 116. 152, 157
  Roanoke, 7, 136
  Rocky Mount, 136
  Rustic, 41, 43, 44
  Salem, 217
  Saltville, 200
  Sandbridge, 97
  Saxis, 102, 104
  Scottsville, 62, 64, 71
  Skinkers Corner, 76, 78
  Smithfield, 144
  Snow Creek, 182
  Sounding Knob, 23
  Spring Garden, 189
  Stanardsville, 82
  Sumerduck, 35
  Surry, 144
  Tappahannock, 76
  Temperance, 104
  Verona, 9, 15, 23
  Virginia Beach, 89, 97
  Williamsburg, 49, 91, 97, 102, 143, 165
  Williamsville, 23, 25, 26, 28
  Wingina, 69, 71, 72
  Woodlawn, 209
Cobbs Road, 26
Coles Point, 12
Comers Branch, 199
Coyote, 156, 179
Counties
  Accomack, 89, 102
  Alleghany, 9, 10
  Amelia, 111
  Amherst, 31
  Augusta, 15
  Bath, 9, 10, 15, 23
  Buckingham, 61, 67, 151
  Caroline, 75, 78
  Carroll, 173, 175, 177, 178, 207
  Charles City, 41, 46
  Clarke, 53, 58
  Culpeper, 33
  Fauquier, 33, 53, 58
  Fluvanna, 61
  Franklin, 181, 185
  Greene, 81
  Henry, 135, 181, 185
  Highland, 23
  Isle of Wight, 109, 143, 144, 165
  Lee, 195

Index

Counties (*cont.*)
  Louisa, 31
  Madison, 81
  Mecklenburg, 127, 128
  Nelson, 67
  New Kent, 49
  Northampton, 89, 91, 93
  Orange, 31
  Patrick, 135, 139
  Pittsylvania, 187, 189
  Powhatan, 157, 159
  Prince Edward, 119
  Roanoke, 215
  Rockbridge, 15
  Russell, 197
  Smyth, 197
  Spotsylvania, 31
  Surry, 141, 144
  Tazewell, 197
  Warren, 53, 58
  Washington, 197, 223
Crappie, 12, 45, 51, 64, 78, 115, 116, 122, 123, 131, 139, 147, 154, 162, 184
Creeks
  Allen, 128, 129, 131
  Back, 12
  Big Brumley, 225, 226
  Big Tumbling, 199, 203
  Bowens, 137, 138
  Briar Cove, 203
  Briery, 119
  Brumley, 225
  Cherrystone, 190
  Clover, 25, 26
  Cooper, 151
  Copper, 165, 167, 170, 171
  Crooked, 207, 209, 211, 213, 214
  Davis, 30
  Devils Ditch, 81, 83
  Dobby, 62, 66
  East Fork, 207, 209
  Gourd, 181
  Horsepen, 151

Hunnicut, 144
Jacks, 104
Laurel Bed, 199, 203
Lawnes, 143, 144, 145, 146, 147, 148
Little Moccasin, 223
Little Tumbling, 199, 200, 201
Long Hollow, 225, 226
Kettles, 128
Kings, 167, 171
Machine, 181, 184
Mason, 217, 218, 219, 221
Messongo, 102, 105
Mill, 10, 12, 13, 14
Morris, 41, 43, 44, 45, 46
Mount, 75, 76, 78, 79
North Fork of Turkey, 181, 184
Otter, 136, 137, 138
Ragged Island, 165, 167
Sallee, 159, 161, 162
Stagger Hollow, 225
Stewarts, 173, 175, 176, 178, 179
Turkey, 175, 178
Ware, 75, 77, 78, 79
Croaker, 95, 105, 169
Cross, Dick, 127
CSX Railroad, 61, 63, 69
Cumberland Gap, 195

Davenport Tract, 53, 55
Davis Run, 28, 29
Deer, white-tailed, 3, 12, 20, 21, 28, 38, 39, 46, 57, 58, 65, 72, 72, 78, 85, 96, 102, 106, 109, 116, 124, 132, 136, 139, 148, 155, 162, 163, 165, 171, 178, 185, 193, 195, 203, 204, 205, 212, 220, 228, 229
  doe, 72
Deer Island, 139
Denfield Hunter Access, 17
Department of Game and Inland Fisheries, 1, 2, 4, 5, 9, 28, 32, 33, 36, 62, 63, 67, 71, 82, 90, 91, 93, 97, 99, 105, 107, 110, 116, 119, 127, 128, 145, 147, 154, 156, 209, 215, 219, 225

Index

Division of Forestry, 2, 49
Division of State Parks and Recreation, 2,
    97, 135, 141
Double Roads Hunter Access, 17
Dove, mourning, 3, 35, 36, 38, 46, 65, 69, 71,
    72, 77, 78, 101, 109, 111, 116, 131, 148,
    155, 162, 163, 190, 192 , 193
Drewry Point, 143
Drum, black, 95, 105
Ducks, 65, 72, 95, 99, 104, 117, 145, 165, 168,
    169, 170, 171, 213
    Atlantic Brant, 94
    black ducks, 94, 106, 170
    bufflehead, 94, 106, 170
    canvasback, 106
    gadwall, 170
    goldeneye, 106, 170
    mallard, 38, 72, 106, 121, 124, 170, 171,
        185, 193
    merganser, 106
    old squaw, 94, 106
    pintail, 106
    redhead, 106
    ruddy, 170
    scaup, 106, 170
    scoters, 94, 106
    teal, 106
    widgeon, 106
    wood, 18, 20, 27, 38, 46, 52, 63, 72, 99,
        121, 123, 185, 193, 204, 228
Dump Road Hunter Access, 17

Eagle Nest Road, 43
Eastern Shore, 89, 91, 102
Eels, 192
Endangered and threatened species, 11, 19,
    27, 36, 44, 51, 56, 63, 70, 77, 84, 94,
    96, 100, 101, 104, 106, 114, 121, 124,
    130, 132, 137, 140, 145, 148, 153, 156,
    160, 163, 168, 171, 176, 179, 183, 184,
    185, 190, 191, 193, 201, 205, 210, 213,
    218, 219, 221, 227, 229

FAA Tower, 225, 227, 228, 230
Fairy Stone State Park, 135
Fallfish, 37, 64
False Cape, 97
False Cape State Park, 89, 99
Field trials, 117, 127, 132
Fish and Wildlife Restoration Programs, 2
Fishhouse Bay, 143
Fishing Run, 35
Flattop Ridge Tract, 81, 82 , 83
Fletcher Tract, 81, 82
Flora, 10, 14, 15, 21, 23, 30, 35, 39, 41, 48, 51,
    52, 58, 61, 63, 65, 72 , 73, 75, 79, 82, 91,
    93, 101, 106, 118, 119, 125, 132, 133, 136,
    140, 149, 151, 156, 164, 167, 168, 171,
    173, 178, 179, 186, 187, 194, 197, 201,
    205, 207, 213, 214, 220, 221, 223, 230
Flounder, 95, 105, 169
Fort A. P. Hill, 75, 78, 79
Fortney Branch, 12, 59
Fort Pickett, 109
Fox, 65, 155, 171, 172, 179, 193
    gray, 106, 156, 194
    red, 106, 156, 186, 194
Freeschool Marsh, 106

Gar, 51
Garth Run, 82
Gathright, T. M., 9
Gathright Dam, 9, 10
GATR tract, 93, 95, 96
Geese, 65, 104, 145
    Canada, 20, 28, 57, 72, 101, 147
    snow, 65, 85, 147
Goose Point Public Area, 137
Grouse, ruffed, 139, 155, 178, 185, 203, 206,
    220, 228
Guys Run, 18, 20
Guys Run Hunter Access, 17

Haunted Branch, 82
Herring, 77
Hidden Valley, 223

Index

Hog Island, 143
Hog Island Point, 143, 147
Hog Island Tract, 144, 146, 147
Hogue tract, 33, 35, 38
Homewood Creek, 143
Hupman Valley Road, 25, 26, 27
Hupman Valley tract, 25

Jack Mountain tract, 26, 28, 29
Jefferson National Forest, 1, 7, 109, 196
John H. Kerr Dam, 128
Jones Cove Road, 93

Kellys Ford rapids, 33, 35, 37, 39
Kentucky, 195
Kettle Run, 55, 56
Kids Mill Road, 62, 63

Lakes
  Amelia, 111, 112, 115
  Anna, 31
  Briery Creek, 119, 121, 123, 124
  Buggs Island, 109, 127, 131
  Chickahominy, 49, 51
  Claytor, 196
  Fairystone, 137, 138, 139
  Flannagan, John W., 196
  Gaston, 128, 131
  Hidden Valley, 223, 225, 226, 227, 228,
      229, 230
  Horsepen, 151, 154
  Laurel Bed, 197, 199, 201, 202, 203, 204
  Moomaw, 7, 9, 10, 11, 12, 13, 14
  North Fork of the Holston, 199
  North Fork of the Pound, 196
  Philpott, 109, 135, 136, 137, 138
  Powhatan, 157, 159, 161, 162, 164
  South Holston, 196
  Thompson, 55, 56, 57, 58
Laurel Run, 18
Lawnes Point, 143
Licky Branch, 151
Little Doe Hill tract, 29

Little Island Recreation Area, 99
Little North Mountain Tract, 15
Low Gap, 223, 226, 227, 229, 230

Magothy Bay, 91, 93, 95
Main Ship Shoal Channel, 95
Mantrap Gut, 104
Marsh Market, 105
Marsh Market boat ramp, 104
Marsh Run, 35, 38
Meadow Ground, 15
Messongo boat ramp, 104
Michael Marsh, 106
Middle River Tract, 81, 82
Mine Run, 35
Mink, 65, 106, 155, 156, 172, 179, 186, 193, 194
Mockhorn Bay, 91, 93
Mockhorn Island, 93, 95
Monticello, 195
Mosquitoes, 47, 95, 105, 145, 146, 169, 172
Motts Landing, 37
Mountains
  Allegheny, 7, 10, 11
  Allen, 78, 81, 83
  Beartown, 197, 199
  Big Tom, 81
  Blue Ridge, 7, 31, 53, 56, 67, 85, 109, 136,
      173, 176, 181
  Bolar, 10, 13
  Bratton, 15
  Brumley, 223, 225, 226
  Bullpasture, 23, 26, 29
  Catawba, 215
  Clinch, 199, 203
  Coles, 10, 11, 13
  Elliott Knob, 7
  Flattop, 199
  Forge, 15
  Fort Lewis, 215, 218
  Hickory Knob, 182
  Hogback, 15
  Jack, 7, 23, 26, 27, 29
  Little Doe Hill, 23, 25, 27

235

Index

Mountains (*cont.*)
  Little North, 15, 17, 18, 20, 21
  Massanutten, 7
  Mount Pleasants, 31
  Mount Rogers, 7, 195
  Ragged, 22
  Rock House, 199
  Short, 199, 200
  Turkeycock, 181, 182, 183, 185
  Whitetop, 195
Muskie, 64, 71, 132
Muskrat, 65, 79, 96, 101, 124, 125, 140, 148,
    155, 169, 193

National Forest Service, 12
Nongame species, 11, 12, 14, 19, 21, 27, 28,
    29, 30, 36, 39, 44, 45, 48, 51, 52, 56, 57,
    58, 59, 63, 64, 65, 66, 70, 71, 72, 73,
    77, 79, 84, 85, 94, 95, 96, 99, 101,
    104, 106, 114, 118, 122, 124, 130, 132,
    137, 138, 140, 145, 146, 148, 152, 153,
    156, 160, 161, 164, 168, 169, 171, 176,
    177, 179, 183, 186, 191, 193, 194, 201,
    205, 210, 211, 213, 219, 221, 227, 228,
    229, 230
Nutria, 101, 172

Old Road, 62, 63
Opossum, 65, 106, 140, 155, 156, 172, 179,
    186, 194, 220, 221
Otter, 79, 96, 101, 125, 132, 140, 148, 155, 169,
    193
  river, 66, 73, 106, 156

Perch
  yellow, 12, 46, 52
  white, 46, 51, 101, 147, 169
Persimmon Run, 35, 37, 39
Pete's Pond, 189, 191, 192
Phelps, Chester F., 33, 36
Pickerel, chain, 12, 37, 46, 51, 64, 116, 122,
    123, 131, 154, 162
Pig Point, 104

Pike, northern, 52, 154
Pocahontas tract, 97, 99
Pocomoke Sound, 104, 105
Poor Valley, 225, 226
Princess Anne Road, 99

Quail, bobwhite, 38, 46, 65, 72, 78, 109, 111,
    116, 124, 132, 139, 148, 155, 162, 192,
    193
Quaker Run, 83

Rabbits
  Appalachian cottontail, 29, 73, 229
  cottontail, 20, 28, 38, 46, 57, 65, 72, 78,
    106, 109, 111, 116, 124, 132, 148, 155,
    162, 171, 179, 192, 193, 204, 213
  marsh, 101
Raccoon, 13, 65, 72, 96, 140, 155, 171, 172,
    179, 185, 186, 193, 194, 220, 221, 228
Rails, 46, 77, 95, 171, 191
Range
  archery, 117
  rifle, 111, 117
Rapidan tract, 81, 83
Rappahannock Academy, 75, 76
Red Branch, 199
Reese, Tom, Jr., 38
Rivers
  Appomattox, 111, 112, 113, 114, 115, 116,
    117
  Banister, 189, 190, 191, 192, 193
  Bullpasture, 23, 25, 26, 27, 28, 29, 30
  Chickahominy, 41, 43, 44, 45, 46, 47, 49
  Clinch, 195, 196
  Conway, 82, 83, 84
  Cowpasture, 7, 25, 26, 28
  Dan, 189
  Hardware, 62, 63, 64, 66
  Jackson, 7, 9, 10, 12, 28
  James, 7, 19, 28, 31, 41, 45, 61, 62, 63, 64,
    65, 66, 67, 69, 70, 71, 72, 109, 143,
    144, 145, 146, 147, 159, 165, 167,
    169, 172

Index

Rivers (*cont.*)
  Holston, system, 196
  Liberty, 25
  Maury, 7, 15, 18, 19, 20, 21
  Middle, 81
  New, 195
  North Fork of the Holston, 199
  North Fork of the Shenandoah, 7
  Potomac, 31
  Rapidan, 31, 81, 83, 84
  Rappahannock, 31, 33, 35, 36, 37, 39, 72,
    75, 77
  Roanoke, 128, 129, 130, 131, 132
  Rose, 83
  Slate, 151, 155
  Smith, 136, 137, 138
  South, 81, 83
  South Fork of the Shenandoah, 7

Scout Pond, 181, 182, 183, 184, 185
Seashore State Park, 90
Seaside Road, 93
Shad, 147
Shark, 95
Shenandoah National Park, 1, 7, 81, 82, 83,
    84, 85
Skeet field, 111, 117
Skyline Drive, 7, 31
Sky Meadows State Park, 55
Snowshoe hares, 23, 29
South Bay, 95
South River tract, 81, 83
Spot, 169
Squirrel
  Delmarva fox, 96, 106
  fox, 28, 156, 203, 220
  gray, 13, 20, 21, 28, 38, 46, 57, 65, 72, 78,
    85, 109, 116, 124, 132, 148, 155, 156,
    162, 171, 178, 185, 186, 187, 192,
    193, 203, 204, 206, 212, 220, 228
  southern flying, 156, 172, 179
  talkative red, 156, 172

Stables, 117
Steel Bridge Launching Area, 131
Stewart tract, 144, 145
Stillhouse Branch, 199
Suckers, 64, 192
Summerall Road, 63
Sunfish, 12, 52, 71, 78, 192
  pumpkinseed, 154, 162
  redbreast, 37, 64, 71
  redear, 37, 57, 115, 122, 123, 154, 162, 192
Sunfish Pond, 161
Swamp, Mount, 76
Swan
  tundra, 77, 95, 101, 105, 145, 147
  mute, 95, 105

Tarpon, 95
Ticks, 47, 86, 95, 105, 146
Trails
  Appalachian, 53, 55, 56, 58
  Arrowhead, 159, 160, 163
  Banister River, 189
  Bolar Ridge, 11
  CCC, 157, 159, 163
  Coles Mountain, 13
  Conway, 81
  Dogwood, 159, 160, 163
  Fescue, 157
  Foot Hill, 55
  High Top Fire, 13
  Holly, 159, 163
  Marsh Point, 113
  Pine, 159
  Power-Line, 157, 159
  Sweet Acorn, 11, 13
  Ted Lake, 55, 56, 58
  Top Fire, 11
  Verlin Smith, 55, 58
  Winding, 23, 27, 29
  Woodcock, 113
Trimbles Mill Hunter Access, 17
Trojan tract, 97, 99, 101

Index

Trout
  brook, 20, 28, 81, 85, 177, 179, 201, 203, 211, 212
  brown, 12, 85, 138, 211
  gray, 95, 105, 169
  rainbow, 12, 57, 59, 81, 138, 139, 203, 209, 210, 211, 225
  speckled, 105
Tunnels Island, 103
Turkey, wild, 3, 9, 12, 20, 21, 28, 39, 46, 57, 58, 65, 72, 78, 85, 109, 116, 119, 124, 132, 136, 139, 148, 155, 162, 163, 183, 184, 186, 193, 195, 203, 204, 205, 206, 212, 220, 221, 228
  hen, 72
Turkey Island, 139

U.S. Army Corps of Engineers, 38, 109, 135, 138, 139

Virginia Power Company, 144, 147

Walleye, 64, 71, 115, 116, 139, 228
Walnut Point, 143
Warner Branch, 151
Waterfowl, 13, 46, 52, 63, 69, 72, 97, 99, 101, 102, 105, 106, 123, 130, 136, 139, 147, 168, 170, 192, 212, 228
Weasel, 172
  long-tailed, 179
Whitehurst tract, 97, 99, 101
Wolftown, 82
Woodchuck, 172
Woodcock, 38, 57, 65, 78, 85, 116, 139, 155, 163, 185, 193